HORSE-RACING

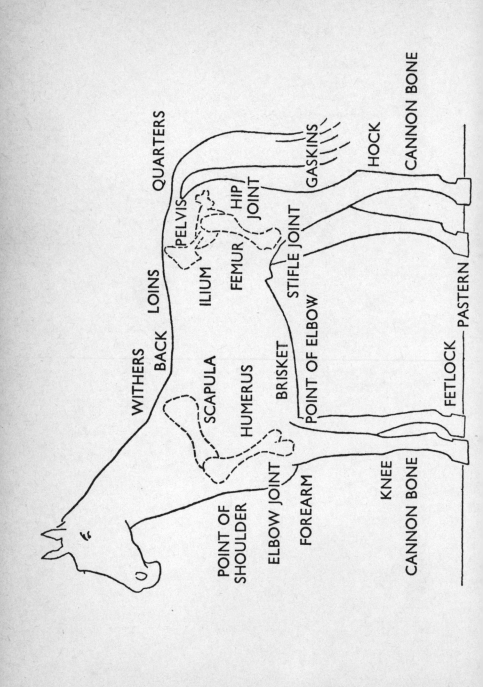

THE BREEDING OF THOROUGHBREDS
AND A SHORT HISTORY OF
THE ENGLISH TURF

Horse-Racing

by

DENNIS CRAIG

Revised by Miles Napier

"Horse races and wild goose chases,
which are disports of greater men, and good in themselves,
though many a gentleman by such means
gallop themselves out of their fortunes."

ROBERT BURTON

'*The Anatomy of Melancholy*'

J. A. Allen & Co. Ltd.
London

First published in 1949 by
Penguin Books Ltd.
Second Edition 1953

Third enlarged and
revised edition
published by

©J. A. Allen & Co. Ltd. 1963

Fourth edition revised
published in 1982 by
J. A. Allen & Co. Ltd.
1 Lower Grosvenor Place
London SW1W oEL

British Library Cataloguing in Publication Data
Craig, Dennis
Horse-racing.—4th ed., rev.
1. Horse-racing—Great Britain
I. Title   II. Napier, Miles
798.4'3'0941   SF335.G7

ISBN 0-85131-357-4

Photoset in 11/12 Baskerville by
Rowland Phototypesetting Limited, Bury St Edmunds, Suffolk
Printed by St Edmundsbury Press, Bury St Edmunds, Suffolk
Bound by Weatherby Woolnough Limited, Northants

Preface

ALTHOUGH many excellent books have been written on the history of the English Turf; the origin, development, and organization of horse-racing; the breed and conformation of the thoroughbred; the famous races in the calendar; and the owners, breeders, trainers, jockeys, and horses who have become celebrated in the annals of the sport; and although memoirs and reminiscences of the Turf, yearly form books and racing manuals, continue to roll off the printing presses, there is still no complete, popular guide to horse-racing, which can serve both as a general reference book for the expert and as a simple textbook for the novice.

It has been the endeavour of the author to meet this demand in the present volume on the English Turf, which covers both the racing and the breeding of thoroughbreds. A proper appreciation of breeding is essential to a fuller enjoyment of racing, and, indeed, the fascination of the Turf largely lies in its continuity of interest, as to-day we see the progeny of rival champions of yesterday battling on the race-course, as did their sires and dams before them and as will their sons and daughters after them, emulating the deeds of their ancestors and so maintaining the supremacy of the breed of the thoroughbred racehorse.

I desire to express my grateful thanks to my brother, the Viscount Craigavon, for many helpful suggestions; to the late Lieutenant-Commander Count Serge Orloff-Davidoff, R.N.V.R., for his assistance in the preparation of this book; and to Mr J. A. Allen, for his courtesy and kindness in allowing me to make extensive use of his unique collection of books on horse-racing.

DENNIS CRAIG

Contents

DRAWING

TABLES

NOTE

Due to unforeseen circumstances a long period of time has elapsed since the completion of this work. Since work had already commenced on the setting up of the type, it was clearly not practicable to incorporate the additional information within the main body of the book.

I have therefore completed an *Addenda* to the present volume, which takes into account the major developments to the end of the 1981 flat racing season.

The Addenda follows the Index.

MILES NAPIER

DEDICATED

to the memory of

Two Brilliant Racing Journalists

ARTHUR FITZHARDINGE BERKELEY PORTMAN

'Audax'

OF

Horse and Hound

AND

'Professor'

JAMES BELL ROBERTSON

M.R.C.V.S.

'Mankato'

The Sporting Chronicle

AND

The Sunday Times

For Joy

CHAPTER I

The Thoroughbred Racehorse

Full many a daintie horse had he in stable.
Chaucer, *Canterbury Tales.*

Origin of the Thoroughbred

THE thoroughbred racehorse, whose remote ancestor, *Eohippus*, was a small, hoofed quadruped about the size of a fox, is the most beautiful animal bred by man. By a careful process of selection through the race-course test over a period of two hundred and fifty years, a noble and courageous beast has been fashioned in the hands of skilled breeders, from an original blend of the imported, pure-bred Arabian, and so-called Turkish or Barbary sires, and the 'English' hybrid mares existing in this country at the end of the seventeenth century.

Sir Theodore Cook, in his monumental *History of the English Turf*, correctly pointed out that unless the improvement in the home-bred animal had gone on steadily from the time of Richard I until the reign of Charles II, there would not have been any chance whatever for the imported Eastern blood to do what it did, which was to put the finishing touch to the native 'English' racing galloway, hobby horse, or running horse, 'as beautiful as can be anywhere, for he is bred out of all the horses of all nations'. As this great authority on the subject aptly put it: 'What they already had in endurance they improved in speed and what was fast was made to last as well'.

Cross between Eastern Stallions and English brood-mares

The late Lady Wentworth, whose researches into the origins of thoroughbred racing stock from 'Equus Agilis' onwards must command the respect of all students of breeding, even if they cannot agree with every conclusion she reached, has claimed that almost the entire credit for the racehorse of the twentieth century must go to its Arabian ancestors, but, if this were so, one might expect the pure-bred Arab of to-day to be superior to the modern English thoroughbred, and this is certainly not the case.

For long distances and hard work, involving stamina alone, the pure-bred Arab may still be perfect, but as a racer he is not so successful, because his stride is not long enough for high speed.

The modern thoroughbred is clearly not descended only from pure-bred Arab stock, but is the result of many years of progressive development from an original blend of the high qualities of the Arabian horse crossed with the sterling attributes of the mixed English breed at one particular and important stage of its evolution. Owing to skilful breeding and to the excellent effect of our climate and soil on the development of the racehorse, a good English thoroughbred would hopelessly outmatch the best horse to be found in the East to-day.

'By a process of selection and by careful training, the whole body of English racehorses have come to surpass in fleetness and size the parent stock.' So wrote Charles Darwin, and, to quote again from *On the Origin of Species*, he also stated that 'our English racehorses differ slightly from the horses of every other breed; but they do not owe their difference and superiority to descent from any single pair, but to continued care in selecting and training many individuals during many generations'.

Attributes of a Good Horse

Dame Julyana Berners, in the first sporting publication ever issued in England, which was printed in 1481, insisted that a horse should have fifteen properties, to wit:

'Of a man, bolde, prowde, and hardy;
'Of a woman, fayrbrested, fayr of heere, and easy to leape upon;
'Of a fox, a fayr taylle, short eeres, with a good trotte;
'Of a haare, a grete eye, a dry hede, and well runnynge;
'Of an asse, a bygge chyn, a flatte legge and a good hoof.'

In *Venus and Adonis* Shakespeare described the nobleman's horse as:

'Round-hoofed, short-jointed, fetlocks shag and long,
 Broad-breast, full eye, small head, and nostril wide,
 High crest, short ears, straight legs, and passing strong,
 Thin mane, thick tail, broad button, tender hide.'
The attributes required of the racehorse of to-day might be summarized as good breeding, correct conformation, soundness of wind and limb, an easy action, a sweet disposition, the will to exert physical abilities and the courage to go on exerting them at hight speed over a distance of ground; all of which, when blended together, may be said to stamp a racehorse with 'quality'.

Conformation of the Racehorse

Lieutenant-Colonel P. E. Ricketts wrote in the Lonsdale Library volume on Flat Racing: 'Exactly what proportion of a horse's merit is due to his conformation is impossible to determine; all that can be said with certainty is that although much should rightly be attributed to nervous energy, the rate of power of nerve stimulus and response, courage and temperament, nevertheless, be the amount great or small, conformation must at least have some value, and that this is the very general view is apparent at every sale ring, where there is no doubt whatever make and shape command a price.'

Points of a Thoroughbred

The most important factors in the 'make and shape' of a thoroughbred were formerly considered to be the perpendicularity of the slope from the point of the shoulder to the point of the elbow and the proportionate length of the humerus to the scapula. The other fundamental characteristics in the appearance of a good racehorse are now generally agreed to be an intelligent and handsome head; a long, strong, light, and muscular neck, bringing the centre of gravity well forward; low, free elbows and well-placed, sloping shoulders; high withers running well back; good depth at the brisket; body well ribbed up; a short back, powerful loins and quarters; a long pelvis behind the hipjoint; a long femur sloping to a well-developed stifle joint; broad gaskins and strong, straight hocks; plenty of bone in the leg below the knee; good fetlocks and pasterns; and well-balanced general proportions (*See Diagram: Points of a Horse, facing title page.*)

Height alone cannot be accepted as a sure indication of merit, although there is doubtless much truth in the old maxim 'a good big 'n is better than a good little 'un'. Eclipse, from whom nearly all thoroughbreds are descended, was over 15 hands 2 inches in height in 1764, the year he was foaled, and this was well above the average of racehorses at that time.[1]

Giving evidence before the Committee of the House of Lords on Horse Breeding in 1873, Admiral Rous testified that in 1700 the average size of the thoroughbred was 13 hands 3 inches and that it had increased an inch every 25 years since: the average size when he spoke being 15 hands 3 inches.

The heights of some famous racehorses of recent times for comparison are: Hyperion 15.1½, Bahram 16.2, Alycidon, and Aureole, 16.0½, Ballymoss 15.3, Alcide 16.0½, St. Paddy 16.1, Psidium 16.0¼, Relko 16.1½, Santa Claus 16.1¾, Sea Bird II, 16.0½, Brigadier Gerard 16.2, Mill Reef 15.3, and The Minstrel 15.2½. But, as one writer has commented, 'the value of a blood-horse cannot be calculated at so much a yard.'

If racehorses in general have increased in size and substance over the years, it is by no means so certain that they have developed in speed and stamina to the same extent. In fact the Earl of Stradbroke declared to the 1873 Committee, already referred to, that 'there are not four horses in England now that could run over the Beacon Course (4 miles 388 yards at Newmarket) in eight minutes', a feat which was not uncommon in bygone days.

Speed and Stamina

Sir Theodore Cook dedicated 'with profound respect and admiration' the first volume of *A History of the English Turf* 'To the Memory of His Grace the first Duke of Westminster, owner of the finest stud of thoroughbreds ever seen in England, who won the Triple Crown of Guineas, Derby and St Leger twice and has now, to the lasting regret of all who valued honesty, courage, and the truest sportsmanship, joined the great company of his predecessors, those noble patrons of the English

[1] 1 Hand = 4 inches.

Turf now settling in the Elysian Fields the problem we must still debate whether Eclipse or Ormonde was the faster horse'.

This 'problem' of whether the crack racehorse of to-day is faster than the champion of yesterday is always interesting to 'debate' but not by any means so easy to resolve. A comparison of times taken by the different horses concerned to win classic races like the Derby or the St Leger does not suffice to settle the question, as the state of the weather, direction and force of the wind, state of going, condition of the course, pace at which the race is run, and changes in the methods of riding, serve to render such a comparison unreliable. Moreover accurate records do not exist, and in any case in England horses do not race against the clock, as is the practice in the United States, so that if a horse is not hard pressed to win it may not be ridden full out at the finish.

There can, however, be little doubt that the general tendency of bloodstock breeders in recent times has been to develop the speed of the thoroughbred at the expense of its stamina. The huge financial outlay of the stud farm and the training stable, the high cost of breeding and racing thoroughbreds, and the fantastic prices which have to be paid to acquire the best bloodstock, have compelled owners to demand a quick return on the money they have invested.

This means that owners will race and in some cases even over-race, thoroughbreds as two-year-olds, in the hope of picking up one or more big-money prizes over short distances as soon as possible. Again a Derby winner can immediately command huge fees as a stallion and this is obviously a strong inducement to his owner to retire his classic winner to stud at the end of his three-year-old career, and not keep the horse in training to run the risk of subsequently depreciating his stud value, by possibly being defeated as a four-year-old in races over distances of two miles or more.

This places a premium on sprinting over staying, and a further inducement to breeders to develop speed rather than stamina in the racehorse is the fact that the shorter races are on the whole more numerous and worth more money in stakes than the longer ones, although enormous efforts have been made in recent years to correct this state of affairs by the increase in prize money added to long-distance races like the

Ascot Gold Cup, to which event the sum of £30,000 is now added.

Nomenclature of the Racehorse

Before proceeding to a consideration of the principal events in the racing year, it should perhaps be explained that although the normal period of gestation in the horse is eleven months and foaling takes place at any time during the first six months of the year, the age of a thoroughbred racehorse is always calculated as being on the 1st January in the year in which it is foaled.

It must also be made clear, for the benefit of those who do not already know these facts, that until they are a year old thoroughbreds are called foals; they are then known as yearlings until they become two-year-olds. The male racehorse is called a colt and the female a filly up to the age of five. From then onwards they are known as a horse and a mare respectively. When they go to the stud for breeding purposes they become known as a stallion and a brood-mre, and subsequently, as the parents of the next generation of thoroughbreds, they are referred to as a sire and a dam. Finally, a gelding is a horse which has been cut or castrated, as opposed to an 'entire' colt or horse, and it cannot therefore be used for breeding purposes.

CHAPTER II

The Racing Year

This day there is a great throng to Banstead Downs
upon a great horse-race.

Samuel Pepys, *Diary.*

RACES FOR TWO-YEAR-OLDS

THE flat-racing season begins during the third week in March and ends during the second week in November.

Foals and yearlings are not allowed to run in any races on the race-course and two-year-olds are not permitted to run more than five furlongs before the Derby meeting at Epsom or more than six furlongs before September 1.

Although some of the leading owners in the country do not start their more promising two-year-olds until the Ascot Meeting in June, or even later in the year, most of the young colts and fillies competing in the valuable two-year-old events at the Royal Meeting have usually made at least one previous public appearance earlier in the season.

There are races for two-year-olds at all the principal meetings in the spring, in which owners can try out their youngsters for the first time on the race-course. However, it is by winning one of the big races for two-year-olds at Ascot that a young colt or filly can first establish a reputation and come to be regarded as a potential winner of one of the classics in the following year.

The most important events for two-year-olds in the racing calendar are as follows:

Woodcote Stakes
Great Surrey Stakes
Acorn Stakes

Founded in 1807 and included in the programme of the Epsom Summer meeting at the end of May or the beginning of June, the Woodcote Stakes is the first race of the year for two-year-olds (colts and fillies) run over six furlongs. The Great Surrey Stakes for colts, fillies and geldings is run over five furlongs on Derby day and the Acorn Stakes for fillies is run over the same distance on Oaks day.

Coventry Stakes
Queen Mary Stakes
Norfolk Stales (formerly run as the New Stakes)
Chesham Stakes
Windsor Castle Stakes
    The Coventry Stakes and Chesham Stakes are now run over six furlongs and the other three races over the straight five furlongs at Ascot in June. Only fillies can compete for the Queen Mary Stakes, but the other races are open to colts and fillies and geldings.

July Stakes
Cherry Hinton Stakes
    The July Stakes was instituted in 1786 and is the oldest two-year-old race in the calendar. It is now run over six furlongs at the summer course at the First July meeting at Newmarket. It is open to colts and geldings only. The Cherry Hinton Stakes, open to fillies only, is run over the same course at the same meeting.

National Stakes
    Run at Sandown Park in July over the straight five furlongs course, this race, to which £11,000 is now added, is one of the most valuable races of the year for two-year-old colts, fillies and geldings and was first competed for in 1889.

Richmond Stakes
Molecomb Stakes
    These races are run at Goodwood at the end of July. The Richmond Stakes, to which £17,000 is added, is run over six furlongs, and is open to colts, fillies and geldings. The Molecomb Stakes, which is run over five furlongs, is open to fillies only.

Seaton Delaval Stakes
    This race, which is run over seven furlongs at the Newcastle First August meeting, and to which £11,000 is added, is open to colts, fillies and geldings.

Gimcrack Stakes
Lowther Stakes
The former is a six furlong event at York for colts, and fillies and geldings, with £20,000 added to the stakes money, which was founded in 1846 and named after the 'sweetest little horse that ever was', a grey called Gimcrack (1760). The owner of the two-year-old that wins this race at the end of August is the guest of honour at the annual dinner of the Gimcrack Club and is expected to make an after-dinner speech on matters of moment concerning the Turf. The Lowther Stakes, also run at York, is open to fillies only and is run over six furlongs.

Champagne Stakes
Flying Childers Stakes
The former race, which is now run over seven furlongs at the Doncaster St. Leger meeting early in September, for an added value of £18,000, and is open to colts, fillies and geldings. The latter race, to which £25,000 is added, is run over five furlongs at the same meeting and is open to colts and fillies.

Mill Reef Stakes
This is a relatively new race and is run over six furlongs at the Newbury September meeting. It is open to colts, fillies and geldings.

Royal Lodge Stakes
Hoover Fillies Stakes (formerly Argos Star Fillies' Stakes).
Both these races are run over a mile at the Ascot September meeting. The former is open to colts and fillies, the latter is open to fillies only.

Middle Park Stakes
Cheveley Park Stakes
These two races, both run over the straight six furlongs course at Newmarket, are generally regarded as the most important events for two-year-olds during the racing season. Both races carry added money of £25,000; the former founded in 1866, is for colts and fillies, the latter for fillies only. The Middle Park Stakes is the last big event of the season for two-year-olds of both sexes run over six furlongs and the

winners of other valuable two-year-old races, decided earlier in the year, often meet in this race for the first time at level weights; colts carry 9 stone, and fillies, in receipt of 3 lbs sex allowance, 8 stone 11 lbs to decide which is to be regarded as the champion two-year-old of the season.

Cornwallis Stakes
This race is contested over five furlongs at the Ascot October meeting and is open to colts, geldings and fillies.

Dewhurst Stakes
This race is run over seven furlongs at the Newmarket Houghton Meeting and is open to colts and fillies. It is frequently won by a horse who later develops into a good stayer.

Horris Hill Stakes
Run over an extended seven furlongs at the Newbury October meeting, this event is open to colts, fillies and geldings.

William Hill Futurity
This race, which was first run as the Timeform Gold Cup and later as the Observer Gold Cup, carries £25,000 in added money and is run over a mile on the round course at the Doncaster October meeting. It is open to colts and fillies.

OTHER TWO-YEAR-OLD RACES

In addition to these twenty seven important events there are other big races for two-year-olds which must be mentioned in passing, like the Princess Margaret Stakes at Ascot in July; the New Ham Stakes at Goodwood in July; the Star Stakes at Sandown in July; the Solario Stakes at Sandown in September; and the Hyperion Stakes at Ascot in September.

THE FREE HANDICAP FOR TWO-YEAR-OLDS

At the end of the flat racing season the official handicapper to the Jockey Club compiles what is known as the Free Handicap for Two-Year-Olds, in which he places in order of merit the leading two-year-olds colts and fillies who have run during the year, giving top weight to the one he considers to be the best horse of it's age and allotting lesser weights to the others in a gradually descending scale.

Among famous two-year-olds placed at the top of the Free Handicap in recent years were The Tetrarch (1913), Tetratema (1919), Town Guard (1922), Mumtaz Mahal (1923), Tiffin (1928), Orwell (1931), Myrobella (1932), Colombo (1933), Bahram (1934), Sun Chariot (1941), Dante (1944), Tudor Minstrel (1946), Abernant (1948), Nearula (1953), Our Babu (1954), Sing Sing (1959), Crocket (1962), Talahasse (1963), Double Jump (1964), Young Emperor (1965), Bold Lad (Ireland) (1966), Petingo (1967), Nijinsky (1969), My Swallow (1970), Crowned Prince (1971), Jacinth (1972), Apalachee (1973), Grundy (1974), Wollow (1975), J. O. Tobin (1976) and Try My Best (1977).

My Swallow was rated at the head of both the English and French Two-Year-Old Free Handicaps in 1970. Unbeaten at two years, he succeeded in accomplishing the unprecedented feat of winning four of France's top two-year-old races; the Prix Robert Papin, Prix Morny, Prix de la Salamandre and Grand Criterium.

Try My Best, who won the Larkspur Stakes and the Dewhurst Stakes, amassed the total of £44,816 as a two-year-old. Other horses who have won large totals include Grundy, who was the unbeaten winner of four races as a two-year-old, including the Champagne Stakes and Dewhurst Stakes, and amassed a total of £37,947. Wollow, who was also unbeaten as a two-year-old, was the winner that year of £33,401. Apalachee was the winner of three races value £31,374, which included the Observer Gold Cup. J. O. Tobin won £26,292, Double Jump, the equivalent of £25,699 in England and France, and Bold Lad the total of £21,106.

The two-year-olds retire to their winter quarters at the end of the racing season in November until they re-appear on the racecourse in the following spring as three-year-olds.

RACES FOR THREE-YEAR-OLDS

The most important events for three-year-olds in the racing calendar are as follows:

Two Thousand Guineas
One Thousand Guineas

Both these valuable races, the former worth more than
£40,000 to the winner, the latter worth more than £35,000 to the
winner, are run over the famous Rowley Mile at Newmarket at
the end of April or beginning of May; the former, founded in
1809, is for colts and fillies, and the latter founded in 1814, for
fillies only.

Derby Stakes
Oaks Stakes

Both these celebrated races are run over the stiff course of 1
mile 4 furlongs and 5 yards on Epsom Downs at the end of May
or beginning of June. The first race for the Derby, the most
famous horse-race in the world, took place at Epsom on May
4th, 1780. It was founded by Edward Smith Stanley, 12th Earl
of Derby who lived at 'The Oaks', a shooting-box near Epsom
Downs, after which the Oaks, first run in 1779, had already
been named. Both colts and fillies can run in the Derby, which
is now worth over £85,000 to the winner, but only fillies are
eligible to compete in the Oaks, which is worth over £45,000.

THE DERBY 1978

The 199th renewal of the Derby Stakes of £200 each, £50
extra unless forfeit be declared by April 25th 1978, £200 in
addition unless forfeit be declared by May 16th, 1978, a
further £50 if declared to run. With £85,000 added to
stakes, distributed in accordance with Rule 194 (11)
(which includes a fourth prize) for three-year-olds, entire
colts and fillies; colts, 9 stone, fillies 8 stone 9 lbs. The race
was run on Wednesday, June 7th, 1978 and was worth
£98,410 to the winner.

It was won by Shirley Heights, bred by Lord Halifax
and Lord Irwin and owned by Lord Halifax, trained by
John Dunlop and ridden by Greville Starkey, who finished
a head in front of Hawaiian Sound, with Remainder Man
third in 2 minutes 36.30 seconds. Shirley Heights, who is
by Mill Reef out of Hardiemma by Hardicanute, is descended from Paraffin (No. 1 Family).

St. James's Palace Stakes
Coronation Stakes
King Edward VII Stakes
Ribblesdale Stakes
These four valuable races for three-year-olds are run at Ascot in the middle of June, the first and second over 1 mile, the third and fourth over 1 mile 4 furlongs; the Coronation Stakes and the Ribblesdale Stakes being for fillies only.

Gordon Stakes
This race, worth more than £15,000, is now run over 1 mile and 4 furlongs at Goodwood at the end of July.

Great Voltigeur Sweepstakes
Yorkshire Oaks
The former is a comparatively new event included in the August meeting at York. It is a mile and a half race worth £25,000 added money. The latter race for fillies over the same distance has £30,000 added to the stakes.

St Leger Stakes
This famous race, now worth over £65,750 to the winner, is run at Doncaster early in September over a distance of 1 mile 6 furlongs and 127 yards. It was founded in 1778 and is therefore older than the Derby and the Oaks.

Park Hill Stakes
This is a race for fillies run at the Doncaster St Leger meeting over the same course as the St Leger.

THE CLASSIC RACES

The five 'classic' races are the 2,000 Guineas, the 1,000 Guineas, the Derby, the Oaks and the St Leger. As colts are not eligible to run in the 1,000 Guineas and Oaks, it follows that only a filly can win all five of these events. In point of fact this feat has never yet been accomplished, although two fillies have won four classic races, namely Sceptre, who won the 2,000 Guineas, the 1,000 Guineas, the Oaks, and the St Leger in 1902, finishing fourth in the Derby; and Formosa, who won the same four classics in 1868, her victory in the 2,000 Guineas being a dead-heat.

THE TRIPLE CROWN

Only twelve colts in the whole history of the English Turf have succeeded in winning the three classic races for which they can compete, namely the 2,000 Guineas, the Derby and the St Leger, known as the 'Triple Crown'. These celebrated horses were West Australian in 1853, Gladiateur in 1865, Lord Lyon in 1866, Ormonde in 1886, Common in 1891, Isinglass in 1893, Galtee More in 1897, Flying Fox in 1899, Diamond Jubilee in 1900, Rock Sand in 1903, Bahram in 1935 and Nijinsky in 1970.

Seven fillies have succeeded in winning the 1,000 Guineas, the Oaks and the St Leger. These were Formosa in 1868, Hannah in 1871, Apology in 1874, La Fleche in 1892, Sceptre in 1902, Pretty Polly in 1904 and Meld in 1955.

In the 2,000 Guineas both colts and fillies carry 9 stone. In the Derby all colts carry 9 stone and the fillies, in receipt of 5 pounds sex allowance, 8 stone 9 pounds; in the St Leger the colts carry 9 stone and the fillies, in receipt of 3 pounds sex allowance, carry 8 stone 11 pounds. In the 1,000 Guineas and the Oaks all the fillies carry 9 stone as they are not competing against horses of the other sex.

OTHER THREE-YEAR-OLD RACES

There are of course a number of races early in the season in which owners can give their classic entries a preliminary gallop in public, before the 2,000 and the 1,000 Guineas are run at the Spring meeting at Newmarket. The most important of these events are the Craven Stakes and Nell Gwyn Stakes for fillies at Newmarket; the Greenham Stakes and Fred Darling Stakes for fillies at Newbury; the 2,000 Guineas and 1,000 Guineas Trial Stakes at Salisbury; the Blue Riband Trial Stakes and Princess Elizabeth Stakes at Epsom; the White Rose Stakes at Ascot and the Ladbroke Classic Trial Stakes at Sandown.

After the running of the Guineas and up to the advent of the Derby and Oaks we have the Cheshire Oaks, Chester Vase and Dee Stakes at Chester; the Dante Stakes and Musidora Stakes for fillies at York; the Derby and Oaks Trial Stakes at Lingfield; and the 'Lupe' Stakes at Goodwood.

Amongst other races for three-year-olds later in the year which must be mentioned in passing are the Jersey Stakes at Ascot in June and the Lancashire Oaks for fillies at Haydock Park in July.

THE FREE HANDICAP FOR THREE-YEAR-OLDS

At the end of the flat-racing season the official handicapper to the Jockey Club also compiles a Free Handicap for Three-Year-Olds placing them in what he considers to be their order of merit, judged by their performance on the Turf.

Among famous three-year-olds placed at the top of the Free Handcap in recent years were Fairway (1928), Cameronian (1931), Hyperion (1933), Windsor Lad (1934), unbeaten Bahram (1935), Blue Peter (1939), Owen Tudor (1941), Sun Chariot and Big Game bracketed together (1942), Dante (1945), Airborne (1946), Nimbus (1949), Tulyar (1952), Pinza (1953), Meld (1955), Crepello (1957), Alcide (1958), Petite Etoile (1959), St Paddy (1960), Relko (1963), Santa Claus (1964), Sea-Bird II (1965), Royal Palace (1967), Sir Ivor (1968), Nijinsky (1970), Mill Reef (1971), Deep Diver (1972), Dahlia (1973), Bustino (1974), Grundy (1975), Pawneese (1976) and Alleged (1977).

The three-year-olds may then either retire to the stud or remain in training during the winter to re-appear as four-year-olds in the following season.

WEIGHT-FOR-AGE RACES

There are a number of races in which three-year-olds and four-year-olds or older horses can compete against each other on weight-for-age terms, the younger, and therefore less fully developed, thoroughbreds carrying less weight than the older and more mature animals according to an accepted scale (see table on page oo), and indeed those are among the most interesting events of the racing season, as winners of the classic races in any current year can meet those who won them in the previous or earlier years.

The most important of these races are as follows:

Jockey Club Stakes

Founded in 1873, this event is competed for at the Newmarket Spring meeting at the beginning of May over a mile and a half. It was for a time run at the Newmarket October meeting, but has now reverted to being run at the beginning of the season.

Coronation Cup

This race is worth over £50,000 to the winner and is run over the Derby course of 1½ miles at Epsom after the Derby and before the Oaks. The present name was given to this event in 1902 to celebrate the coronation of King Edward VII; prior to that year it was known as the Epsom Cup.

Gold Cup

This famous race, also worth over £30,000 to the winner, was founded in 1807 and is run over a course of 2½ miles at the Royal Ascot meeting in June. It is regarded as the most important event in the racing calendar after the King George and Queen Elizabeth Stakes and the classic races and if the winner of the Derby, Oaks, or St Leger can also win the Gold Cup before retiring to stud, it stamps that colt or filly as a really outstanding thoroughbred.

Only three of the eleven winners of the Triple Crown already referred to also succeeded in winning the Ascot Gold Cup. These were West Australian, who won it in what was then the record time for the race; Gladiateur, who won it by 40 lengths; and Isinglass, who was perhaps the greatest of all racehorses. Other famous winners of the Trophy were Sagaro, the only horse in the history of the Turf to win the race three times; Touchstone and Prince Palatine, who both won the Gold Cup twice as well as the St Leger; The Flying Dutchman and Persimmon, who had already won the Derby and the St Leger; and Apology and La Fleche, both winners of the 1,000 Guineas, Oaks and St Leger. Other horses who have won the Gold Cup twice are Anticipation, Bizarre, The Emperor, The Hero, Fisherman, Isonomy, The White Knight, Inveshin, Trimdon and Fighting Charlie. Among other celebrated winners of the Gold Cup to be mentioned are, Memnon, Glencoe, Lanercost, Beeswing, Van Tromp, Teddington, Thormanby, Blue Gown,

Cremorne, Doncaster, Petrarch, Robert the Devil, Foxhall, Tristan, St Simon, St Gatien, Cyllene, Bachelor's Button, Bayardo, Golden Myth, Massine, Precipitation, Caracalla 11, Alycidon, Botticelli and Levmoss.

The only winners of the Derby, Oaks or St Leger in recent years who went on to win the Ascot Gold Cup were the St Leger winner Solario, the Oaks winner Quashed, and the war-time substitute Derby winner Ocean Swell.

Hardwicke Stakes
This event is run over 1½ miles at Ascot on the day of the Gold Cup. The race was first competed for in 1879. It was won by Tristan three years in succession in 1882, 1883, and 1884.

Princess of Wales's Stakes
Founded in 1894 this race is included in the programme of the Newmarket First July Meeting and is competed for over a distance of 1½ miles.

Eclipse Stakes
This is one of the most valuable races of the year. In fact the prize of £13,306 won by Fairway, when he secured the Eclipse Stakes in 1928 was the largest sum in stake money ever won in a single race on the English Turf prior to 1948.

This important sweepstakes for three-year-olds and four-year-olds is run over 1¼ miles at Sandown Park in mid-July. Among famous winners of the race have been Bendigo, Ayrshire, Orme (twice), Isinglass, St Frusquin, Persimmon, Velasquez, Flying Fox, Diamond Jubilee, Ard Patrick (beating Sceptre by a neck), Your Majesty, Bayardo, Lemberg and Neil Gow (who ran a dead-heat), Swynford, Prince Palatine, Tracery, Buchan (twice), Craig-an-Eran, Polyphontes (twice), Coronach, Colorado, Fairway, Windsor Lad, Blue Peter, Migoli, Tulyar, Darius, Ballymoss, Saint Crespin 111, St Paddy, Ragusa, Busted, Royal Palace, Mill Reef, Brigadier Gerard and Artaius.

King George VI and Queen Elizabeth Stakes
The King George VI Stakes was a new event added to the calendar in 1946. A race open to three-year-olds only it was run

over a distance of 2 miles at Ascot in October, being worth about £7,000 to the winner. During the first three years of its existence it was won by Souverain, Arbar, and Alycidon, all of whom won the Ascot Gold Cup subsequently as four-year-olds.

The Queen Elizabeth Stakes was another new post-war event, being a weight for age race run over a mile and a half at Ascot in July. It was won in 1948 by the Italian Derby and St Leger winner Tenerani, who defeated Black Tarquin by a short head and who subsequently went on to win the Goodwood Cup.

In 1951, the Festival of Britain year, the two races were merged into the King George VI and Queen Elizabeth Stakes for three-year-olds and upwards, run in July over 1 mile and 4 furlongs at Ascot. Three-year-olds now carry 8 stone 8 pounds and older horses 9 stone 7 pounds, fillies and mares being allowed 3 pounds sex allowance.

This is now the most valuable race on the English Turf, as the huge sum of £123,000 is added to the sweepstakes. In the year of its inception the race was won by Supreme Court, whose winnings amounted to £25,322, and in 1952 Tulyar won by a neck from Gay Time.

Subsequent winners of this race have included such famous horses as Pinza, Aureole, Ribot, Ballymoss, Alcide, Aggressor (who defeated Petite Etoile by half a length), Right Royal V (who beat St Paddy by three lengths), Match 111, Ragusa, Aunt Edith, Busted, Royal Palace, Park Top, Nijinksy (who won by two lengths from Blakeney), Mill Reef and Brigadier Gerard. Dahlia won the race in 1973, defeating Rheingold by five lengths, and in 1974, defeating Highclere by two lengths. But probably the most exciting race for the King George VI and Queen Elizabeth Stakes was in 1975, when, after a most exciting long-drawn out struggle, Grundy triumphed by half a length from Bustino in the record time of 2 minutes 26.9 seconds. Subsequent winners of the race have been Pawneese, The Minstrel and Ile de Bourbon.

Sussex Stakes

This is a mile race for colts and fillies aged three years old and upwards at the Goodwood July meeting, to which the sum of £50,000 is added.

Goodwood Cup
Doncaster Cup

The former race was founded in 1812 and is run over a course of about 2 miles 5 furlongs in July; the latter in 1766, over 2 miles 2 furlongs in September. Fleur de Lis, Prima, Harkaway, Charles XII, Canezou, Count Schomberg and Proverb all won the Goodwood Cup twice, and Touchstone, Alice Hawthorn, Vedette, Velocity and Agreement the Doncaster Cup twice. Beeswing, who won 52 out of the 63 races in which she ran during eight seasons on the Turf, won the Doncaster Cup no less than four times as well as the Ascot Gold Cup. King William IV actually owned the first three horses to finish in the Goodwood Cup in 1830.

Geoffrey Freer Stakes

This is a comparatively new race, contested over a mile, five furlongs and 60 yards at the Newbury August meeting, for horses of three years old and upwards, to which £23,000 is now added.

Benson and Hedges Gold Cup

This is a relatively new race, to which the sum of £75,000 is added to the stakes. Open to colts and fillies aged three years old and upwards, it is run over 1 mile 2 furlongs and 110 yards at the York August meeting.

Jockey Club Cup

Founded in 1873 this event is competed for at the Newmarket October meeting over 2 miles. Formerly a two and a quarter mile race, it was for a time run in the Spring, but has now reverted to being run in the Autumn. St Gatien won the Cup three years in succession in 1884, 1885 and 1886 and High Line performed the same feat during the years 1969, 1970 and 1971, and Radium, Aleppo, Son-in-Law and Quashed all won it twice.

Champion Stakes

This event is run over 1 1/4 miles at the Houghton meeting at Newmarket. It was first run in 1877, and Triston won the race twice in 1882 and 1883 and dead-heated for the stakes in 1884.

In recent years the Jockey Club has scheduled the race to receive additional prize money (in 1978 £45,000, was added to the stakes). Since the decision was made to increase the prize money the race has been won by ten fillies, Rose Royale 11, Bella Paola, Petite Etoile, Marguerite Vernaut, Hula Dancer, Flossy, Hurry Harriet, Rose Bowl, Flying Water and Swiss Maid.

It will be seen that these races vary in distance from the 1 mile of the Queen Elizabeth II Stakes to the 2 miles 5 furlongs of the Goodwood Cup. However, the longest race in the calendar is the Queen Alexandra Stakes at Ascot founded in 1865, which is run over a course of 2 miles 6 furlongs and 34 yards. It is inseparably linked with the name of Brown Jack, the gallant old gelding who won the race six years in succession from 1929 to 1934 inclusive, in addition to the Ascot Stakes, Ebor Handicap, Chester, Goodwood and Doncaster Cups and other races, including the Champion Hurdle Challenge Cup at Cheltenham, and £21,646 in stakes.

OTHER WEIGHT-FOR-AGE RACES

Other important weight for age races are the *John Porter Stakes* at Newbury; the *Earl of Sefton Stakes* at Newmarket, the *Westbury Stakes* at Sandown; the *Ormonde Stakes* at Chester; the *Yorkshire Cup* at York; the *Lockinge Stakes* at Newbury; the *Brigadier Gerard Stakes* and *Henry II Stakes* at Sandown; the *Diomed Stakes* at Epsom; the *Prince of Wales's Stakes*, *Queen Anne Stakes* and *Queen's Vase* (formerly the Gold Vase) at Ascot; the *Child Stakes*, for fillies and mares at Newmarket; the *Nassau Stakes* for fillies and mares at Goodwood; the *Hungerford Stakes* at Newbury; the *Waterford Crystal Mile* at Goodwood; the *Cumberland Lodge Stakes* at Ascot; the *Sun Chariot Stakes* for fillies and mares at Newmarket; the *Princess Royal Stakes* for fillies and mares at Ascot and the *St Simon Stakes* at Newbury.

SPRINT RACES

There are, of course, many brilliant horses who lack the stamina to win races over distances even up to a mile in length, let alone the two miles or more of the big Cup races; and special events are therefore provided in the Calendar for those sprinters, who are often among the fastest horses in training.

The most important of the sprint races are the *Palace House Stakes* run over five furlongs at the Newmarket Spring meeting; the *Duke of York Stakes* run over six furlongs at the York May meeting; the *Temple Stakes*, run over five furlongs at the Sandown Park Spring Bank Holiday meeting; the *Cork and Orrery Stakes* and the *King's Stand Stakes*, both run at the Royal meeting at Ascot, over six furlongs and five furlongs respectively; the *July Cup* run over six furlongs at the Newmarket First July meeting; the *King George Stakes* run over five furlongs at the Goodwood July meeting; the *William Hill Sprint Championship* (formerly the Nunthorpe Stakes), run over five furlongs at the York August meeting; the *Diadem Stakes* run over six furlongs at the Ascot September meeting and the *Vernon's Sprint Cup*, run over six furlongs at the Haydock Park First November meeting. In 1978 it was announced that the last-named race would in future be run in September.

Among famous sprinters in recent years were Diomedes, Tag End, Tiffin, Sir Cosmo, Xandover, Concerto, Myrobella, Bellacose, Shalfleet, Honeyway, The Bug, Abernant, Royal Serenade, Set Fair, Pappa Fourway, Right Boy, Bleep-Bleep, Be Friendly, Balidar, Abergwaun, Bay Express, Deep Diver, Gentilhombre, Godswalk, Lochnager and Solinus.

PENALTIES AND ALLOWANCES

It should perhaps be pointed out that in many of these weight-for-age races, both for sprinters and for stayers, penalties in the form of extra weight are imposed on horses who have previously won races, usually above a certain value in stake money, and sometimes allowances in the form of less weight are given to animals who have not yet won a race and who, irrespective of their sex, are known as 'maidens'. In addition fillies and mares always receive sex allowance of weight when racing against animals of the other sex.

PATTERN RACES

In 1965 a Committee was sent up, under the chairmanship of
the late Duke of Norfolk to examine the pattern of racing. As a
result of its examinations the Committee recommended that
'over the correct distance and at the correct time of the years,
races should be available to test the best class horses of all ages.'
The committee added that in their opinion, the race-course was
the ultimate test of a horse's stud value.

In 1967 the Race Fixtures Committee was set up under
Lord Porchester. This committee designated 130 races to
receive added money. These races became known as Pattern
races. They comprised the five classic races, the major events
confined to three-year-olds, the principal weight for age races,
and the major sprint races as well as the most important events
confined to two-year-olds.

Pattern races are also run in France, Germany, Ireland and
Italy and are framed on an internationally agreed format.

The Pattern races are divided into Group 1, 2 or 3 according
to the amount of added money allotted to them.

RACES IN IRELAND

Although racing in the Republic of Ireland is conducted under
different rules to those in force in Great Britain, the following
races are included because they have been accorded Group 1
status by the International Pattern Race Committee (see
above), and because they have been contested in recent years
by an increasing number of horses trained in Great Britain.

Irish 2,000 Guineas
Irish 1,000 Guineas
Irish Sweeps Derby
Irish Guinness Oaks
Irish St Leger

These races, which are confined to horses of three years of
age, are all contested at the Curragh, which is situated outside
the town of Newbridge, some 30 miles south west of Dublin.
The Irish 1,000 Guineas and Irish Guiness Oaks to which the
sums of £13,000 and £20,000 respectively are added, are open to
fillies only. The races are run over 1 mile and 1½ miles

THE BYERLEY TURK (*From a painting by John Wooton*)

ECLIPSE (*From a painting by George Stubbs*)

respectively, and all carry 9 stone. The remaining three races are open to both colts and fillies; colts carry 9 stone and fillies, in recept of 3lbs sex allowance, 8st. 11lbs. The Irish 2,000 Guineas, contested over 1 mile, carries £15,000 in added money; the Irish Sweeps Derby, which is run over 1½ miles in June, has £30,000 added to the stake money; the Irish St Leger, which is run over 1¾ miles, has £10,000 added to the stakes.

HANDICAPS

Many horses in training are, of course, not capable of competing with any hope of success in the classic races or on weight-for-age terms in the other valuable events which have been described, because they are not up to what is known as classic standard. Primarily for these horses special races called handicaps are provided, in which the chances of the competing animals are equalized by the allotment of different weights, calculated by the handicapper mainly on the form already shown in public by the horses concerned, so that those animals who have previously won races or run well are made to carry more weight than those who have never even been placed. After 1 September, Nursery Handicaps, in which only two-year-olds can compete, are included in the programme at some race-meetings.

The most important handicaps are as follows:

Lincolnshire Handicap

This is the first big race of the season. Formerly run at Lincoln, it is now contested over a mile on the round course at Doncaster in late March or early April. In 1948 there were 58 runners for 'The Lincolnshire', a record for any race under Jockey Club Rules. Babur won the race twice in 1957 and 1958.

City and Suburban Handicap

Run over 1 mile 2 furlongs and 15 yards at the Epsom Spring Meeting in April. Coronation Year won the race twice, in 1955 and 1957.

Victoria Cup

This is a sprint handicap over 7 furlongs. It was formerly run at Hurst Park, but is now run at Ascot in late April or early

SCALE OF WEIGHT FOR AGE FOR FLAT RACES

Allowance, assessed in lbs, which 3 yrs old will receive from 4 yrs old, and 2 yrs old will receive from 3 yrs old.

	&	MARCH/APRIL		MAY		JUNE		JULY		AUG		SEPT		OCT		NOV
		1 15	16 30	1 15	16 31	1 15	16 30	1 15	16 31	1 15	16 31	1 15	16 30	1 15	16 31	
5 Furlongs	2	32	31	29	27	26	25	25	23	21	20	19	18	17	16	15
	3	13	12	11	10	9	8	7	6	5	4	3	2	1	—	—
6 Furlongs	2	—	—	30	29	29	28	27	26	26	24	22	21	21	20	18
	3	15	14	13	12	11	10	9	8	7	6	5	4	3	2	1
7 Furlongs	2	—	—	—	—	—	—	—	—	—	—	24	23	23	22	21
	3	16	15	14	13	12	11	10	9	8	7	6	5	4	3	2
1 Mile	2	—	—	—	—	—	—	—	—	—	—	27	27	26	25	24
	3	18	17	16	15	14	13	12	11	10	9	8	7	6	5	4

SCALE OF WEIGHT FOR AGE FOR FLAT RACES
Allowance, assessed in lbs, which 3 yrs old will receive from 4 yrs old.

		MARCH/APRIL		MAY		JUNE		JULY		AUG		SEPT		OCT		NOV
	&	1 15	16 30	1 15	16 31	1 15	16 30	1 15	16 31	1 15	16 31	1 15	16 30	1–15	16–31	
9 Furlongs	3	18	17	16	15	14	13	12	11	10	9	8	7	6	5	4
1¼ Miles	3	19	18	17	16	15	14	13	12	11	10	9	8	7	6	5
11 Furlongs	3	20	19	18	17	16	15	14	13	12	11	10	9	8	7	6
1½ Miles	3	20	19	18	17	16	15	14	13	12	11	10	9	8	7	6
13 Furlongs	3	21	20	19	18	17	16	15	14	13	12	11	10	9	8	7
1¾ Miles	3	21	20	19	18	17	16	15	14	13	12	11	10	9	8	7
15 Furlongs	3	22	21	20	19	18	17	16	15	14	13	12	11	10	9	8
2 Miles	3	22	21	20	19	18	17	16	15	14	13	12	11	10	9	8
2¼ Miles	3	23	22	21	20	19	18	17	16	15	14	13	12	11	10	9
2½ Miles	3	25	24	23	22	21	20	19	18	17	16	15	14	13	12	11

For calculating weight one length equals 3lb, a neck equals 1lb and a head equals 1lb, which also equals 1/15th of a second.

The scale of weight for age is published by authority of the Stewards of the Jockey Club as a guide to Clerks of Courses in the framing of races. It is founded on the scale published by Admiral Rous and revised by him in 1873. It was modified in 1973 by Major David Swannell, MBE, the Jockey Club Handicapper, and has been further revised since and republished in 1976 in its present form.

May. In 1946 the trophy was won by Honeyway, who carried the top weight of 9 stone 7 pounds to victory, a feat also accomplished by My Babu in 1948. Alf's Caprice won the race in 1955 and dead-heated for the race in 1959. Enrico, who won in 1966, carried 9 stone 10 pounds.

Chester Cup

Founded in 1824, this handicap of 2 miles 2 furlongs and 97 yards is also run in May. Brown Jack won the race in 1931 when seven years old, carrying 9 stone 6 pounds, and Heron Bridge in 1950, carrying 9 stone 7 pounds. Sea Pigeon won the race in 1977 and 1978.

Jubilee Stakes (Handicap)

Formerly run as the Great Jubilee Handicap, the race is contested over 1¼ miles at Kempton in May. The race was first competed for in 1887, when Bendigo was carrying 9 stone 7 pounds, Minting being the winner the following year, with the crushing weight of 10 stone on his back. Victor Wild, Ypsilanti, Abbot's Speed, Royal Tara, Durante, Alcimedes, Water Skier, Antiquarian and Jumpabout each won the Jubilee two years in succession.

Ascot Stakes

A race of 2½ miles run in mid-June, this was the longest handicap run on the English Turf prior to 1946. Brown Jack won the race in 1928 and Reynard Volant carried 9 stone 4 pounds to victory in 1947, having also won the same event in the previous year. Trelawny won with 9 stone 8 pounds in 1962, and again with 10 stone in 1963, also winning the Queen Alexandra Stakes at the same meeting in the same two years, an amazing quadruple event to bring off successfully.

Royal Hunt Cup

This famous race is now run over the new straight mile course at the Royal meeting at Ascot. It was founded in 1843 and is one of most valuable handicaps in the calendar. Irish Elegance won the event in 1919 under the big weight of 9 stone 11 pounds, and Master Vote was the winner both in 1947 and 1948.

Stewards' Cup

This is a sprint handicap over 6 furlongs at Goodwood, run at the end of July.

Goodwood Stakes

Founded in 1823, this race of about 2 miles 3 furlongs is the oldest handicap still in the calendar. It is also the only race still started by a flag. Auralia won the event in 1948, carrying 9 stone 6 pounds, Osborne in 1954 with 9 stone 7 pounds, Predominate three years in succession 1958, 1959 and 1960, and Golden Fire twice, in 1962 and 1963, in addition to the Cesarewitch and Chester Cup.

Ebor Handicap

This race is now one of the most valuable handicaps of the year, as £20,000 is added to the stakes. It is run over 1¾ miles at York during August.

The most notable winners in recent years were Brown Jack in 1931 with 9 stone 5 pounds on his back, and that gallant mare Gladness, winner also of the Ascot Gold Cup and Goodwood Cup, who carried no less than 9 stone 7 pounds to victory in the Ebor in 1958.

Portland Handicap

Run at the St Leger meeting at Doncaster in September, this is a race over 5 furlongs 140 yards. Irish Elegance, then a four-year-old, followed up his win of the Royal Hunt Cup under 9 stone 11 pounds by also winning the Portland Handicap in the same year, 1919, carrying no less than 10 stone 2 pounds, a wonderful performance.

Cesarewitch
Cambridgeshire

These are two of the best known and most valuable handicaps of the racing year and both were inaugurated in 1839. The former is run over 2 miles 2 furlongs and the latter over 1 mile 1 furlong at Newmarket in late Autumn. Perhaps the heaviest betting of the year takes place on these two races, which are known as the 'Autumn Double' as opposed to the Lincolnshire Handicap and the Grand National, which are known as the 'Spring Double'.

Famous winners of the Cesarewitch have been Rosebery 7.5 (1876), Robert the Devil 8.6 (1880), Foxhall 7.12
(1881), St Gatien 8.10 (1884), Plaisanterie 7.8 (1885), Willonyx
9.5 (1911), Son-in-Law 8.4 (1915), in record time, Noble Star
8.12 (1931), Grey of Falloden 9.6 (1964) and John Cherry 9.13
(1976).

Famous winners of the Cambridgeshire have been Rosebery 8.5 (1876), Isonomy 7.1 (1878), Foxhall 9.0 (1881),
Bendigo 6.10 (1883), Plaisanterie 8.12 (1885), La Fleche 8.10
(1892), Polymelus 8.10 (1906), Wychwood Abbot 8.6 (1934),
Sayani 9.4 (1946), Tarqogan 9.3 (1965) and Negus 9.0 (1972).

It will be seen that Rosebery, then a four-year-old, and the
American horse Foxhall and Plaisanterie, then three-year-olds,
won both events in the same season. Noble Star won the Ascot
Stakes, Goodwood Stakes and Jockey Club Cup as well as the
Cesarewitch in 1931. Sterope won the Cambridgeshire two
years in succession in 1948, as a three-year-old with 7.4 and
again by a head in 1949 as a four-year-old with 9.4 on his back,
having won the Royal Hunt Cup. Prince de Galles also won the
race twice, in 1969 as a three-year-old with 7.12 and again in
1970 as a four-year-old with 9.7.

OTHER HANDICAPS

Among many other handicaps, of which space precludes more
than a brief mention in passing may be noted the Zetland Gold
Cup at Redcar, the David Dixon Gold Cup and Yellow Pages
Sprint at York, the Canada Dry Shield Handicap at Ayr; the
Wokingham Handicap at Ascot; the Northumberland Plate,
run at Newcastle and known as the 'Pitman's Derby'; the
Magnet Cup at York; the Vaux Gold Tankard at Redcar, run
over 1 mile 6 furlongs and 132 yards and worth over £10,000 to
the winner and the Extel Stakes at Goodwood, worth over
£15,000.

In the second half of the racing season we have the William
Hill Gold Cup at Redcar, worth over £12,000; the Ayr Gold
Cup; the Newbury Autumn Cup, the Ladbrokes Ayrshire
Handicap and the Chesterfield Cup at Goodwood. And to wind
up the year the William Hill November Handicap, run over 1½
miles at Doncaster in the last week of the flat racing season.

This race replaces the Manchester November Handicap, which was founded in 1876 and was run, as its name suggests at the now defunct Manchester, on the final day of the flat racing season.

SELLING RACES

In an event of this kind the conditions require that the winner should be offered for sale by auction, immediately after the race. The winner may, however, be bought in by his owner at the auction. All other runners can be claimed by anyone except their owners for the advertised selling price, plus the value of stakes or plate.

AUCTION, CLAIMING AND OPPORTUNITY RACES

An *Auction* race is one confined to horses purchased as yearlings at public auction for below the price specified by the conditions of the race. A *Claiming* race is one in which all horses starting may be claimed for not less than their published claiming price. An *Opportunity* race is one in which the winner does not incur a penalty.

SWEEPSTAKES

Any race in which the entrance fees, forfeits, subscriptions, or other contributions of three or more owners go to the winner or placed horses, and any such race, whether weight-for-age, handicap, or selling race, is still a sweepstakes when cup, money, or other prize is added. Added money is money actually contributed towards the stakes by race-fund or from other sources, as distinct from money contributed by the owners of the horses engaged.

PLATES

These are races for which a prize of definite value is guaranteed by the race-fund; the entrance fees, forfeits, subscriptions, or other contributions of the owners going to the race-fund.

MATCHES

A match is a race between two horses, the property of two different owners, on terms agreed by them. As will be seen later on in this book, both flat-racing and steeplechasing originated from the earlier practice of one owner pitting his favourite horse against that of another in a trial match over an agreed distance for sometimes as much as £1,000 or more a side. Two memorable matches of this kind were those between Hambletonian and Diamond in 1799 and between The Flying Dutchman and Voltigeur in 1851. The most notorious match in recent years was that between the English Derby winner Papyrus and the American horse Zev, which was run in the United States in 1923.

CHAPTER III

Race-Courses and Racing Officials

*We returned over Newmarket Heathe, the way being
mostly a sweet turfe and down, the jockies breathing their
fine barbs and racers, and giving them their heates.*

John Evelyn, *Diary*.

Newmarket

NEWMARKET has been the headquarters of the Turf since the
days of Charles II. There are twelve meetings held there during
the flat-racing season. The Craven meeting early in April and
the Spring Meeting, held two weeks later with the 1,000
Guineas on the Thursday and the 2,000 Guineas on the Saturday. The July meeting is held on the Summer Course and there
are five Saturday meetings throughout the summer. At the
October meeting the programme includes the Middle Park
Stakes, the Cheveley Park Stakes, the Jockey Club Cup, and the
Cambridgeshire. At the Houghton Meeting, a fortnight later,
the programme includes the Champion Stakes, the Dewhurst
Stakes and the Cesarewitch, the other 'leg' of the Autumn
double.

Ascot

The Royal meeting at Ascot in June was formerly the only
one held on the famous course, which was founded by Queen
Anne in 1711, but five extra flat-racing fixtures in April, July,
September and October are now included in the calendar. Six
races are run on each of the four days of the Royal Meeting and
every race is worth over £8,000. The Ascot Stakes is run on the
Tuesday, the Royal Hunt Cup on the Wednesday, the Gold
Cup on the Thursday, and the Hardwicke Stakes on the Friday.
There is now an extra day's racing on the Saturday, when the
Churchill Stakes is normally the main event on the card.

One of the most picturesque and colourful scenes of the English summer season is the royal procession down the course at Ascot, when Her Majesty the Queen and other members of the royal party drive in open landaus, drawn by the famous Windsor Greys, past the Stewards and the Royal Enclosure, round to the entrance of the Royal Box. Although the Royal meeting at Ascot is a great social occasion of top hats and pretty frocks, it also provides the finest programme of valuable and important races in the world.

The King George VI and Queen Elizabeth Stakes; the Cumberland Lodge Stakes, Diadem Stakes, Queen Elizabeth II Stakes and Royal Lodge Stakes, and the Cornwallis Stakes and Princess Royal Stakes are the most valuable events run at the July, September and October meetings respectively.

Goodwood

The present race-course, which is one of the most beautiful in the world, was laid out by Lord George Bentinck in the Duke of Richmond's spacious park 700 feet up on the Sussex downs with distant views of the English Channel.

Formerly there was only one meeting held each year at Goodwood. Now there are five meetings, held in May, July, August, September and October. The main meeting is held in July on five consecutive days. Six races are run each day, with the exception of Friday, on which day seven races are contested. The principal races at the meeting are the Gordon Stakes and the Stewards Cup on the Tuesday, the Sussex Stakes, the Richmond Stakes, and the Goodwood Stakes on the Wednesday, the Goodwood Cup on the Thursday, the Extel Stakes on the Friday, and the Nassau Stakes on the Saturday. The main event at the late August meeting is the Waterford Crystal Mile, to which £22,000 is added.

Epsom

There were formerly two meetings a year held on the famous Epsom Downs in Surrey, a three-day fixture in the spring and a four-day one in the early summer. These have been held every year since 1730 except during the two world wars.

At the Spring Meeting the Derby is normally run on the

Wednesday, the Coronation Cup on the Thursday, and the Oaks on the Saturday. The stiff Derby course of 1 mile 4 furlongs and 5 yards, over which these three famous races are run, is a severe test of a thoroughbred, as it is uphill and bends to the right for the first half-mile, and then sweeps in a wide curve to the left downhill to Tattenham Corner, where there is a sharp turn into the last straight four furlongs, which end uphill to the winning-post.

A new August Bank Holday two-day meeting at Epsom has also been added to the fixture list in recent years.

Doncaster and York

The two most celebrated race-courses in the north country are at Doncaster and York; eight meetings are held on the former track and seven on the latter.

The meetings on the Town Moor at Doncaster are run by a Race Committee appointed by the Corporation which has a proprietary interest in them. The first big meeting, at which the principal event is the Lincolnshire Handicap, held in April. The others are held in May, June, July, September, October and November; but most of the big prizes are competed for at the meeting in September. The Champagne Stakes is normally run on the Wednesday, the Park Hill Stakes and the Doncaster Cup on the Thursday, the Portland Handicap on the Friday, and the St Leger and the Flying Childers Stakes on the Saturday. The Doncaster yearling sales are held annually in the mornings and evenings of several days of the St Leger meeting.

The first fixture on the Knavesmere at York is held in May, with the Yorkshire Cup as the chief item on the card. The other meetings are held in June, July, August, September and October. The principal meeting, however, is that held in August, on three consecutive days. The Benson and Hedges Gold Cup and Yorkshire Oaks predominate on the Tuesday, the Great Voltigeur Stakes and Ebor Handicap are run on the Wednesday and the Gimcrack Stakes and William Hill Sprint Championship on the Thursday.

Sandown and Kempton Park

These racing tracks are known as 'park courses and during the flat racing season seven fixtures are held at Sandown and five at Kempton. The former, founded in 1875, is laid out in an attractive setting at Esher in Surrey. The most important events run at Sandown Park are the Westbury Stakes, and Classic Trial Stakes run in April, the Brigadier Gerard Stakes, Temple Stakes and Henry II Stakes run in May and the Eclipse Stakes and National Stakes both run in July, while at Kempton Park, founded in 1878, the principal prize is the Jubilee Stakes (Handicap) run in May.

Other Race-courses

The Roodee at Chester is the oldest race-course in England, since horse-racing is recorded as having taken place there as long ago as 1540; and Newbury race-course is the most recent track to be added to the fixture list, as it was opened only in 1905, largely owing to the energy and influence of the famous trainer John Porter of Kingsclere.

Space does not permit more than a passing reference to the many other race-courses where flat-racing fixtures are held under Jockey Club rules during the season from March to November. These are Bath; Beverley; Brighton; Carlisle; Catterick Bridge; Chepstow; Folkestone; Haydock Park; Leicester; 'Lovely' Lingfield; Newcastle at High Gosforth Park; Nottingham at Colwick Park; Pontefract; Redcar; Ripon, Salisbury; Teesside Park; Thirsk; Warwick; Windsor; Wolverhampton; Worcester; and Yarmouth.

In Scotland race-meetings are held at Ayr, Edinburgh and Hamilton Park; while in Northern Ireland the Ulster Derby is run at Down Royal.

A detailed description of the different race-courses, explaining if they are right-handed or left-handed; straight, oval or circular; uphill, flat or downhill; and the effect of the draw for positions at the start on the chances of the competing horses; is given in these two publications, one or other of which is indispensable to all students of the Turf, namely *Raceform* and *Racing Up-to-Date*.

In recent years some of the smaller racecourses have been closed down and more fixtures have been allotted to the more important tracks. In the past the Jockey Club have been reluctant unduly to tamper with the established fixture list, presumably on the grounds that local race-meetings scattered throughout the country, constituted the backbone of the sport in England and were an improtant fact in maintaining the traditions of the Turf. Nevertheless further centralization seems desirable, and force of circumstances mainly economic, may eventually bring it about.

Racing Officials

The Stewards of the Jockey Club are the three men who control flat-racing in this country, acting on behalf of the Jockey Club, under whose rules the sport is conducted. They grant the necessary licences to race-courses to hold meetings, and draw up the fixture list for the season. They also issue licences to racing officials, trainers, and jockeys, and can suspend or withdraw a licence in the event of the licence holder being proved guilty of any serious breach of the rules of racing. Finally they have power to warn any undesirable character off Newmarket Heath and hence virtually banish him from the Turf.

Stewards

Stewards are the Officials at each meeting, usually three in number, whose duty is to see that the rules of racing are observed during the meeting over which they preside. They have power to hear objections to the winner on any grounds and to fine or suspend a jockey for crossing, jostling, bumping, boring or other forms of foul riding. They can also order saliva and other dope tests to be taken and report their findings to the Stewards of the Jockey Club.

Handicapper

This official adjusts the weights to be carried by the horses in any Handicap races, for the purpose of equalizing their chances of winning. It was formerly the practice to make individual officials responsible for the handicapping duties at individual meetings. Nowadays handicappers work in teams, each team concentrating on the horses of a specific age or distance group. When a horse has raced three times, he is allotted a rating, which is stored on a computer maintained at the offices of Messrs Weatherby at Wellingborough in North-amptonshire, and is brought up-to-date to take into account each day's racing. In a handicap the horse placed at the top of the list must be awarded not less than 10 stone (except in handicaps confined to horses of two years of age, when the maximum weight must not be less than 9 stone 7 pounds) and the horse placed at the bottom of the handicap must be allotted not less than 7 stone, except in apprentice races.

Clerk of the Course

This official is, in the majority of cases, the Managing Director of the race-meeting. He is responsible for the maintenance of the track and for the general arrangments on the course and for such things as the issue of official race-cards, the numbering of the horses to assist in their identification, and the parade of the runners in the paddock before each race. The most out-standing Clerk of the Course, in recent years was the late Sir John Crocker Bulteel, K.C.V.O., D.S.O., M.C., who held this appointment from 1946 until his death ten years later. It was under his able administration that the new straight course at Ascot was constructed and the new King George VI and Queen Elizabeth Stakes inaugurated.

Clerk of the Scales

This official is responsible for seeing the full and correct details of all horses and riders, weights to be carried, and results of the draw, are hoisted on the number board for the information of the general public. He then weighs out on the scales each jockey in turn, to see that all are carrying the correct weights specified for each horse in the particular race. The clerk of the Scales also weighs in the jockeys after the race as a final check that the winner and placed horses ran under the actual burdens imposed by the conditions of the race.

Starter

The starter of horse races is the official who has the responsibility of lining up the competitors in the correct order in their starting stalls according to the draw, A with No. 1 on the left of the course and releasing the starting 'gate' when all the horses are in position. In older times races were started by dropping a flag, a starting contraption was first used in the Derby of 1901, and starting stalls were introduced at Newmarket in 1965 and for starting the Derby in 1967.

Judge

The function of this official is to place the first three horses in the correct order and give the distances which separated them. The result of the race is then hoisted on the number board. The Judge's box is placed directly opposite the winning post, but on a wide course in a close finish it is not by any means always an easy task to determine the result. In order to assist the Judge to reach a correct decision in difficult cases the Jockey Club has approved the installation of an automatic dual camera system on all race-courses in the country.

The Judge actually called for a copy of the photograph of the finish of the 1949 Derby before announcing that Nimbus had won by a short head, and this was made compulsory when in 1952 the Stewards of the Jockey Club directed that if a Judge estimates that the distance between the winner and the second or the second and the third or the third and the remainder of the field is a neck or less he shall consult the photograph before announcing his decision.

Veterinary Surgeon

A skilled 'vet' is always available in the event of an accident to any of the horses competing at the meeting, and an ambulance is also provided in case a jockey or one of the spectators is injured.

Of all people connected with the Turf in a professional capacity, the veterinary surgeon perhaps receives the least public recognition for his services, and it may not be out of place to mention at this stage the remarkable work that is now being done at the Equine Research Station of the Animal Health Trust, established at Balaton Lodge, Newmarket, in 1947, under the directorship of Professor W. C. Miller, M.R.C.V.S. Professor Miller retired in 1966, when he was succeeded by Dr. R. K. Archer. The last named was in his turn succeeded in 1978 by Mr. W. B. Singleton, C.B.E., F.R.C.V.S. Investigations are carried out into such subjects as sterility, parasitism, redworm, diseases of foals, uterine, and other bacterial infections in mares, equine rhinopneumonitis, equine metritis and other matters of the utmost importance to breeders and owners of thoroughbreds.

HORSERACE BETTING LEVY BOARD

The Horserace Betting Levy Board was established by Act of Parliament on 1st September 1961 and its function is to assess and collect a monetary contribution from the Horserace Totalisator Board (see page 206) and also a levy from bookmakers under the Betting, Gaming and Lotteries Act 1963, and to apply these revenues to the improvement of breeds of horses, the advancement of veterinary science and education and the improvement of horseracing.

The Board provides the finance required to give effect to the recommendations of the late Duke of Norfolk's committee on doping, as well as meeting the cost of the late forfeit and overnight declaration schemes; the cost of the race photo finish and patrol cameras; allocations from the racecourse fund for capital expenditure and modernising racecourses and for increasing prize-money added to prestige and feature races; and grants to the Equine Research Station and to other charitable organisations (see page 206).

In 1962 the Board acquired a majority holding in the stallion Counsel and allotted its nominations to British breeders by ballot; and in 1963 it also took over from the Ministry of Agriculture responsibility for the National Stud (see page 000).

Field Marshal Lord Harding was appointed the first Chairman and Sir Rupert Brazier-Creagh the first Secretary of the Horserace Betting Levy Board.

In 1967 Racecourse Technical Services Ltd became a wholly owned subsidiary of the Horserace Betting Levy Board. This organisation is concerned with photo-finish cameras, starting stalls and race-course commentaries.

In 1972, on the instigation of Lord Wigg of Lambeth, the then chairman of the Horserace Betting Levy Board, Racecourse Security Services Ltd was formed to co-ordinate the activities of the forensic laboratory which carries out dope tests and the activities of the old Jockey Club security services.

In 1974, Sir Desmond Plummer, the Chairman of the Levy Board, introduced a scheme for the training both of apprentices and lady jockeys at the National Equestrian Centre at Stoneleigh Abbey in Warwickshire.

The Horserace Betting Levy Board has also acquired control of the Epsom Grand Stand Association and also of Sandown Park and Kempton Park racecourses, via its wholly owned subsidiary Metropolitan and County Racecourse Management and Holdings Ltd.

CONFLICT BETWEEN JOCKEY CLUB AND LEVY BOARD

At the time that the Levy Board was formed, the Jockey Club (see page 000) laid down that while it was the task of the Board to collect the revenue, the decision as to how it should be allocated was solely the responsibility of the Jockey Club. However, Lord Wigg who was chairman of the Levy Board between 1967 and 1972 insisted upon deciding how the money was to be spent. Since then the Horserace Betting Levy Board has always striven to influence decisions on matters concerning the conduct of horse-racing.

JOINT RACING BOARD

The Joint Racing Board is composed of three members of the Jockey Club and three members of the Horserace Betting Levy Board. The function of the Board is to formulate the policies concerning the organisation of horse-racing.

BLOODSTOCK AND RACING INDUSTRIES CONFEDERATION LIMITED

The Bloodstock and Racing Industries Confederation is an organisation which seeks to be truly representative of all groups and individual interests in the British racing and breeding industry. As the united voice of the industry, its main objective is to halt the financial decline by seeking to achieve,

(a) the injection of more money into racing, particularly through substantially increased prize money.

(b) a better understanding of the industry among the general public and in Parliament.

(c) closer liaison between the industry and Government without duplication of effort, or conflict between the various bodies.

Negotiations between the Jockey Club and Bloodstock and Racing Industries Confederation are conducted through the *Racing Industry Liaison Committee.*

CHAPTER IV

Famous Thoroughbreds: The Sire Lines and Leading Stallions

Eclipse first, and the rest nowhere.
Colonel Dennis O'Kelly.

ALL thoroughbred racehorses throughout the world are descended in direct male line from one or other of only three out of nearly two hundred Arabian, Turkish, or Barbary steeds imported into England during the seventeenth and eighteenth centuries, viz: The Darley Arabian, The Byerley Turk, and the Godolphin Arabian or Barb.

The Darley Arabian to Eclipse
The Darley Arabian was bought for Mr James Darley in 1704 by his son, who was a merchant in Aleppo. He became the paternal great-great-grandsire of the famous, unbeaten Eclipse, who was bred by the Duke of Cumberland, third son of King George II, and foaled in 1764, the year of the great eclipse of the sun.

Eclipse did not race until he was five years old. After a secret trial, one old woman asserted that she had seen 'a horse with a white leg running away at a monstrous rate and another horse a great way behind trying to race after him'. She was sure that 'no horse would ever catch the white-legged one if he ran to the world's end'. She was to prove quite correct because Eclipse won all the 26 races and matches in which he took part, including 18 King's Plates. Sir Theodore Cook wrote of Eclipse: 'His excellence was not only owing to the races he won, but even more clearly to the astonishing ease with which he won them, and to the fact that in addition to his undoubted speed and stride, he possessed sound wind, an ability to carry heavy weight, and an endurance over long distances which could never be thoroughly tested, for its limit was never reached.'

At the stud his fee rose from 25 to 50 guineas a mare and altogether he sired 344 winners of over £158,000 in stakes before he died from inflammation of the bowels in 1789.

The Byerley Turk to Herod

The Byerley Turk (probably an Arabian) is believed to have been obtained by Captain Robert Byerley when fighting against the Turks in Hungary in 1687 and was subsequently used by him as a charger during the Battle of the Boyne, on July 12th, 1690, when, as Colonel Byerley, he commanded the Sixth Dragoon Guards under King William of Orange. He became the paternal great-great-grandsire of Herod, or King Herod as he was at first called, who, like Eclipse, was also bred by the Duke of Cumberland and foaled in 1758.

Herod was a good racehorse, but he had weak fore-legs and developed a tendency to break blood-vessels. His stud fee was 10 guineas, later rising to 25 guineas, and his stock won over £200,000, 40 hogsheads of claret, 3 Cups, and the Whip. He died in 1780.

The Godolphin Arabian to Matchem

The Godolphin Arabian is believed to have been a present to the King of France from the Emperor of Morocco. He was eventually bought in Paris by Mr Edward Coke in 1729 and subsequently came into the possession of Lord Godolphin. He became the paternal grandsire of Matchem, who was foaled in 1748.

Matchem went to the stud at a fee of 25 guineas and his stock won over £150,000 before he died in 1781, at the great age of 33.

These are the only three male stirps which have lasted to the present day in direct descent from father to son. They are known as the Eclipse, Herod, and Matchem sire lines.

THE MALE LINES OF ECLIPSE

The principal lines which trace from Eclipse are those through four celebrated stallions, namely Touchstone, Stockwell, Isonomy, and Vedette.

Eclipse to Touchstone, Stockwell, and Isonomy (Chart 1)

One of the sons of Eclipse, bred by the Earl of Abingdon, was Pot8os, so called because a stable lad, instead of writing Potato on his box, wrote Potoooooooo. He raced in the ownership of Lord Grosvenor until he was ten years old and won 34 out of the 46 races in which he ran. One of his sons, Champion, was the first winner of both the Derby and the St Leger in 1800, and another of his sons, Waxy, won the Derby on his first appearance on the race-course, together with 10 other races.

From Waxy out of a mare called Penelope, herself a winner of 18 races, the 3rd Duke of Grafton and his son bred the full brothers Whalebone and Whisker, who, like their sire, both won the Derby. A son of Whisker, named Memnon, was the first horse to win the St Leger and the Ascot Gold Cup, and the male line of Whisker was carried on for a few more generations through Economist, Harkaway, winner of two Goodwood Cups, and King Tom to Hannah, winner of the 1,000 Guineas, Oaks, and St Leger for Baron Rothschild in 1871.

It was, however, through Whalebone and his sons Camel and Sir Hercules that the Eclipse-Pot8os-Waxy line survived. Another son of Whalebone, named Defence, sired The Emperor, who won the Gold Cup twice and was sold to France, where he produced Monarque, winner of the French Derby and the Goodwood Cup, who in turn got Gladiateur.

Gladiateur won 12 races, including the Triple Crown of Derby, St Leger, and 2,000 Guineas, together with the Grand Prix de Paris in 1865, and the Ascot Gold Cup by 40 lengths in 1866. When his racing days were over, he was sold by his owner, Count F. de Lagrange, to Mr Blenkiron, founder of the Middle Park Stud, but this splendid racehorse died young, before he had had time to make a name for himself as a sire, and his line did not survive. The achievements of Gladiateur on the race-course were all the more remarkable when it is realized that he suffered from almost chronic lameness through swellings on his fetlock joints, a disability that he no doubt inherited from his dam, who was so crippled that she could never race.

The male line of Monarque survived in France through Consul, Fripon, Le Pompon, Prestige, and Sardanapale, winner of the Grand Prix de Paris and the French Derby in 1914.

Camel, 'quartered like a cart-horse', was the sire of the

redoubtable Touchstone, and Sir Hercules, 'jet-black with a bunch of grey hairs at the root of his tail', was the great-grandsire of the might Stockwell and the great-great-grandsire of Isonomy; the lines coming down through Birdcatcher and The Baron, 'slim, neat, and savage', winner of the St Leger and the Cesarewitch, to Stockwell and his full brother, the Doncaster Cup winner Rataplan, who also won 21 Queen's Plates; and through Birdcatcher, Oxford and Sterling to Isonomy. Sir Hercules was also the sire of Faugh-a-Ballagh, another winner of the St Leger and the Cesarewitch and full brother to Birdcatcher, who got Leamington, the sire of the American horse Iroquois, winner of the Derby and the St Leger in 1881 with Fred Archer in the saddle.

The descendants of Touchstone, Stockwell, and Isonomy will be considered later, as the other surviving male line from Eclipse, through King Fergus to Vedette, must first be noted, together with offshoots through Joe Andrews, Saltram, and Mercury, which have died out.

Eclipse to Vedette (Chart 2)
King Fergus, another son of Eclipse, was 'a horse of great size, remarkably full of bone, well shaped and free of blemishes', and he became the sire of two St Leger winners, Beningbrough and Hambletonian.

Beningbrough sired Orville, like his sire winner of the St Leger, who got Emilius, winner of the Derby and sire of Priam, 'a beautiful dark bay horse with black legs and slight tips of white', who won the Derby and two Goodwood Cups and, before being exported to America, got Crucifix. This splendid filly was bought by Lord George Bentinck from Lord Chesterfield for £60 and trained by John Kent and ridden by J. B. Day was an unbeaten winner of 12 races, including the 2,000 Guineas, the 1,000 Guineas, and the Oaks in 1840, the latter race, which was run in the presence of Queen Victoria and the Prince Consort, after no less than 16 false starts.

The Hero, by Chesterfield a son of Priam, won the Ascot Gold Cup twice, the Goodwood and Doncaster Cups, the Ascot Gold Vase, Ebor Handicap, and 16 Queen's Plates.

Two other sons of Orville were Andrew, sire of Cadland, winner of the 2,000 Guineas and the Derby, after running off a dead-heat with The Colonel, and Muley, sire of Muley Moloch, who got Alice Hawthorn. This wonderful mare ran in 71 races during seven seasons on the Turf, winning 52 of them including the Chester Cup, the Ascot Gold Vase, the Goodwood Cup, two Doncaster Cups, 12 other cups and 18 Queen's Plates. Later at the stud she became the dam of Thormanby, winner of the Derby and the Ascot Gold Cup.

However, the male line of Beningbrough, through Orville and his sons, died out, and present-day descendants of the Eclipse-King-Fergus stirp come down through Hambletonian, Whitelock, Blacklock, Voltaire, Voltigeur, and Vedette.

Hambletonian won 20 races and matches, including the St Leger, being only once beaten, when he bolted and jumped the cords at York. Ridden by Frank Buckle, he won a famous match by a head for Sir Henry Vane-Tempest against Mr Cookson's Diamond for 3,000 guineas over the Beacon Course at the Newmarket Craven Meeting in 1799. His grandson, the ugly Blacklock, was the sire of Velocipede, who got Queen of Trumps, the first filly to win the Oaks and the St Leger, and of Voltaire, winner of the Doncaster Cup, who got Charles XII, winner of the St Leger, after running off a dead-heat with Euclid, two Goodwood Cups, and the Doncaster Cup. But it was another son of Voltaire, namely, Lord Zetland's Voltigeur, winner of the Derby, the St Leger, after running off a dead-heat with Russborough, and the Doncaster Cup, beating The Flying Dutchman by a neck, who passed on the Eclipse-King Fergus blood to posterity through Vedette, the grandsire of St Simon.

Extinct Lines of Eclipe (Chart 2)

The Joe Andrews male line of Eclipse died out in the middle of the last century, after surviving for a time through Dick Andrews, Tramp, a winner of the Doncaster Cup, Lottery, who also won the Doncaster Cup, Sheet Anchor, Weatherbit, and Beadsman, winner of the Derby and sire of Blue Gown, who, trained by John Porter and ridden by 'Tiny' Wells, won the Derby in 1868 and the Ascot Gold Cup in the same year, as a three-year-old, for Sir Joseph Hawley, later being exported to America and dying on the voyage over. The Palmer, a son of Beadsman, sired Pilgrimage, who won the 2,000 and 1,000 Guineas and ran second in the Oaks, later becoming the

maternal grandam of Chaucer and Swynford. Another son of
Tramp called Liverpool got Lanercost, the winner of the first
race for the Cambridgeshire, who also won the Gold Cup and
who in turn out of Barbelle got Van Tromp, a winner of the St
Leger, Goodwood Cup, and Ascot Gold Cup.

The only other son of Eclipse that need be mentioned in
passing was Saltram, who won the Derby and before being sent
to the United States sired Whiskey, who got Sir Charles
Bunbury's Eleanor, the first winner in 1801 of the Derby and
the Oaks, and dam of Muley.

Another extinct line of Eclipse descended through Mercury,
Gohanna, Golumpus, Catton, and Sandbeck to Barbelle, the
dam of Van Tromp and The Flying Dutchman.

Consideration will now be given to the continuation of the
male lines of Eclipse, through stirps which sprang from the four
famous sires who were descended from him, Touchstone and
Stockwell, Isonomy and Vedette.

Touchstone to Carbine and Bay Ronald (Chart 1A)

Touchstone was bred by Lord Westminster and foaled in
1831. He was trained by John Scott of Whitewall, 'The Wizard
of the North', and won the St Leger at odds of 40 to 1 against,
the Doncaster Cup twice, and the Ascot Gold Cup twice. His
stud fee was 30 guineas rising to 60 guineas, and before he died
in 1861 he got Cotherstone, Ithuriel, Orlando, Surplice, Newminster, the Lord of the Isles, among many of his offspring.

Cotherstone won the 2,000 Guineas and the Derby; Orlando won the Derby and sired Trumpeter, whose son Plutus got
the Goodwood Cup winner Flageolet; Teddington, winner of
the Derby, Doncaster Cup, and Ascot Gold Cup for Sir Joseph
Hawley (beating Stockwell by a head in the latter race); and
Imperieuse, winner of the 1,000 Guineas and the St Leger.
Surplice won the Derby and the St Leger, and Lord of the Isles
won the 2,000 Guineas and sired Scottish Chief, winner of the
Ascot Gold Cup, whose daughter Marie Stuart won the Oaks
and the St Leger.

Ithuriel carried on one branch of the Touchstone line
through Longbow, winner of the Stewards Cup, Toxophilite,
beaten a length by Beadsman in the Derby, and Musket, who
won the Ascot Stakes as a three-year-old and was exported to

New Zealand in 1878 where he got Carbine. This fine specimen of a thoroughbred, who won 33 races, including the Melbourne Cup in record time with 10 stone 5 pounds on his back, was bought by the late Duke of Portland for £13,000 and imported into England in 1895 to stand at the Welbeck Abbey stud.

But the main line of Touchstone was passed down through Newminster, winner of the St Leger, whose dam was the celebrated mare, Beeswing. He sired Cambuscan and Adventurer, Hermit, and Lord Clifden.

Cambuscan got Kinscem, a mare who was brought to England from Hungary and who was an unbeaten winner of 54 races, including the Goodwood Cup, a truly phenomenal performance; and Adventurer got Pretender, winner of the 2,000 Guineas and the Derby, and Apology, winner of the 1,000 Guineas, Oaks, St Leger, Coronation Stakes, and Ascot Gold Cup.

Orlando was exported to the United States where his male line is extant to-day. The line's most successful representative in Europe is Youth, winner of the French Derby as well as winning the Washington International Stakes, who descends through American Eclipse, Alarm, Himyar, Domino, Commando, Colin, Neddie, Good Goods, Alsab, Armageddon, Battle Joined and Ack Ack.

Hermit

Hermit was bought for 1,000 guineas at the sale of the Middle Park yearlings in 1865 by Mr Henry Chaplin, later Lord Chaplin, when he was only 25 years of age. Trained under the management of Captain Machell, Hermit broke a bloodvessel in his nostril a week before the Derby in 1867. Snow fell up to the time the starter dropped his flag and Hermit won a sensational race by a neck, at odds of 100 to 1, after ten false starts. The Marquis of Hastings, who had eloped with Lady Florence Paget, to whom Mr Chaplin was engaged, lost £120,000 over the result of the race and a year later, beset by creditors, took his own life.

At stud Hermit was an outstanding success, as he headed the list of winning sires, from 1880 to 1886 inclusive. He sired Tristan, who won the Hardwicke Stakes three times, the Champion stakes three times including a dead-heat, the Gold

Vase and the Gold Cup; Thebais, who won the 1,000 Guineas, Oaks and Doncaster Cup; and Shotover, a filly who won the 2,000 Guineas and Derby for the Duke of Westminster. The male line of Hermit died out in England but continued in France through Heaume, Le Roi Soleil, Sans Souci II, winner of the Grand Prix de Paris, La Farina and Bubbles. The line has recently been revived in England through Precipice Wood, winner of the Ascot Gold Cup, a great-grandson of Bubbles through Ocarina and Lauso, winner of the Italian Derby.

Lord Clifden, beaten by a head by Macaroni in the Derby and winner of the St Leger, sired Hampton, who began his racing career as a selling plater but won 20 races including the Goodwood, Doncaster, and Epsom Cups; Petrarch, winner of the 2,000 Guineas, St Leger, and Ascot Cup; and Jannette, winner of the Oaks, St Leger, Champion Stakes, and Jockey Club Cup.

Hampton sired Reve d'Or, winner of the 1,000 Guineas, Oaks, City and Suburban Handicap, and Jockey Club Cup for the Duke of Beaufort; Ayrshire, winner of 11 races, including the 2,000 Guineas, Derby, Eclipse Stakes, and £35,915 for the Duke of Portland; Ladas, winner of the 2,000 Guineas, Newmarket Stakes, and Derby, for which he started as the hottest favourite ever to win the premier classic at odds of 9 to 2 on in 1894 wearing the colours of Lord Rosebery, who was acting Prime Minister at the time; and Bay Ronald, winner of the Hardwicke Stakes, City and Suburban Handicap, and Epsom Cup, who, apart from Carbine, alone carried on the male line of Touchstone to the present day and became the great-grandsire of Hyperion.

Stockwell to Rock Sand, Flying Fox, Orby, and Cyllene (Chart 1B)

Stockwell, by The Baron out of Pocahontas, dam also of the Doncaster Cup winner Rataplan and of King Tom the sire of Hannah, was bred by Mr Theobald and foaled in 1849 at the Stockwell Stud within three miles of St Paul's Cathedral. He was bought by Lord Exeter as a foal for £180 and later sold to Lord Londesborough. He won the 2,000 Guineas, St Leger, and 9 other races, being only beaten by a head by Teddington in the Gold Cup. His stud fee was 30 guineas and before his death in 1870 he sired 209 winners of 1,147 races to the value of

£362,451, being head of the list of winning sires from 1860 to 1862 and from 1864 to 1867 inclusive, and being second on the list in 1863, 1868, 1872, and 1873. Three of his sons, Blair Athol, Lord Lyon, and Doncaster, won the Derby; one of his daughters, the Oaks; six of his offspring, St Albans, Caller Ou, The Marquis, Blair Athol, Lord Lyon, and Achievement, the St Leger; four of his sons including The Marquis and Lord Lyon, the 2,000 Guineas; and three of his daughters, including Achievement, the 1,000 Guineas.

St Albans, whose disposition was vile and whose perpetual fits of temper made it dangerous for strangers to approach him, carried on one branch of the Stockwell line that exists to-day, as he got Springfield, winner of the first race for the Champion Stakes, who was bred by Queen Victoria at the Hampton Court Stud and who in turn sired Sainfoin winner of the Derby, who got Rock Sand. This horse, ridden by Danny Maher, was the winner of the Triple Crown of Derby, St Leger, and 2,000 Guineas in 1903, as well as the Princess of Wales's Stakes, Jockey Club Stakes, Hardwicke Stakes, and £45,618 for his owner, Sir James Miller, on whose death the colt was sold to Mr August Belmont, President of the New York Jockey Club, for £25,000, later being sent to France where he died in 1914.

Caller Ou was a most remarkable mare. She ran 86 times in six seasons and won 44 races, including the St Leger and 29 Queen's Plates.

Blair Athol, who was by Stockwell out of Blink Bonny, by Melbourne out of Queen Mary, won the Derby in record time when making his first appearance in public on a race-course, and at the dispersal of the Middle Park Stud in 1872 was bought for 12,500 guineas, then the highest price ever paid for a thoroughbred. He was the leading sire in 1872, 1873, 1875, and 1877, and got The Rover, who sired St Gatien, winner of 16 races, who ran a dead-heat with Harvester for the Derby and scored victories in the Cesarewitch, Alexandra Stakes, three Jockey Club Cups, Gold Vase, and Gold Cup, and who went first to Germany and then to America in 1898. Blair Athol also got Silvio, who, trained by Matthew Dawson and ridden by Fred Archer, won the Derby, St Leger, and Jockey Club Cup for Lord Falmouth, who later sold the horse to a French breeder for 7,000 guineas.

Melton, also ridden by Archer, was another winner of the Derby (by a head from Paradox), and of the St Leger. He was a descendant of Stockwell, through Lord Ronald and Master Kildare, while through The Duke and Bertram came Robert the Devil, a high class racehorse, who won the Grand Prix de Paris, St Leger, Champion Stakes, Cesarewitch, Alexandra Stakes, and Ascot Gold Cup and was only beaten a head in the Derby by Bend Or.

Lord Lyon, by Stockwell out of Paradigm, who was leased by Colonel Pearson to Mr Sutton, won the Triple Crown in 1866. The 2,000 Guineas was his first race, as he did not run as a two-year-old. He started favourite for the Derby, but only won by a head in the last stride. All the first three horses in the 1866 Derby were sons of Stockwell.

It was, however, left to Doncaster, got by Stockwell at the age of twenty, to carry on the main sire line. He was bred out of a daughter of Teddington called Marigold by Sir Tatton Sykes at Sledmere, and as a yearling, then named 'All Heart and No Peel', was bought by Mr James Merry for 950 guineas. Winner of the Derby at the long odds of 45 to 1, Doncaster was only beaten a head in the St Leger by Marie Stuart, winner of the Oaks, also owned by Mr Merry. Doncaster, who subsequently won the Alexandra Stakes, Goodwood Cup, and Ascot Gold Cup, was then sold to his trainer, Robert Peck, for £10,000 and resold by him a few days later for £14,000 to the Duke of Westminster.

Bend Or and Ormonde

From Doncaster out of Rouge Rose by Thormanby, son of Windhound and Alice Hawthorn, the Duke bred Bend Or to win him the Derby of 1880. Fred Archer, with the muscles of one arm badly torn as a result of being savaged by a vicious animal called Muley Edris, and with his left leg on the favourite's neck rounding Tattenham Corner, rode the race of his life to beat Robert the Devil by a head in what was probably the most desperate finish ever seen in the famous classic. Archer received £500 and Peck £1,000 as present from the Duke for winning him his first Derby. Bend Or also won the Champion Stakes, St James's Palace Stakes, City and Suburban Handicap, and Epsom Cup, but it was at the stud that he was to achieve lasting fame.

Ormonde, by Bend Or out of Lily Agnes by Macaroni, was his most brilliant son. Bred and owned by the Duke of Westminster, trained by John Porter of Kingsclere, and ridden in most of his races by Fred Archer, Ormonde was never beaten. He won the Triple Crown of Derby, St Leger, and 2,000 Guineas, in 1886, as well as the Champion Stakes, for which he started at the fantastic price of 100 to 1 on, and the Hardwicke Stakes twice, altogether 16 races and £28,465 in stakes. Unfortunately he was a roarer, unsound in wind, and the Duke eventually sold him to an Argentine breeder in 1889, and later, in 1893, he was resold to an American breeder for £30,000. Almost sterile, he had to be destroyed in 1904, after getting only 16 foals during the 11 years he stood at stud in the United States.

Orme, winner of 14 races, including the Eclipse Stakes twice, the Champion Stakes, and £32,484 in stakes, was a son of Ormonde out of Angelica, full sister to St Simon by Galopin out of St Angela by King Tom, and he produced two sons, Flying Fox and Orby, to carry on the male line of Ormonde, the former through Ajax and Teddy, and the latter through The Boss.

Trained by John Porter and ridden by Mornington Cannon, Flying Fox, a magnificent specimen of a thoroughbred, won 9 races and £40,096 in stakes for the Duke of Westminster, including the Triple Crown, Princess of Wales's Stakes, Eclipse Stakes, and Jockey Club Stakes, all in the same year, 1899. On the death of the Duke he was sold to Monsieur Edmond Blanc for 37,500 guineas, thus creating a new world record price for a thoroughbred.

Orby won the Derby and became progenitor of a line notable for its sprinters. He was, however, nothing like as good a horse as his sire Orme or grandsire Ormonde.

Kendal, another son of Bend Or, sired Galtee More out of Morganette. Owned by Mr J. Gubbins and trained by Sam Darling, Galtee More won the Triple Crown and the Newmarket Stakes in 1897 and was successful in 11 races altogether. He was subsequently purchased by the Russian Government and later bought by Count Lehndorff on behalf of the German Government. In England the male line of Kendal was handed

down through Tredennis to Golden Myth, winner in 1922 of the
Gold Vase, the Gold Cup easily in the record time for the race of
4 minutes 17 seconds, and the Eclipse Stakes by a head.
Another son of Tredennis, Bachelor's Double, won the Irish
Derby, Royal Hunt Cup, Great Jubilee Handicap, and City
and Suburban Handicap, later becoming the sire of Comrade,
winner of the Grand Prix de Paris and the Prix de l'Arc de
Triomphe.

Radium, also by Bend Or, won the Goodwood and Doncaster Cups and two Jockey Club Cups, and got Clarissimus, who
won the 2,000 Guineas and the Champion Stakes, and Night
Raid, who became the sire of the famous Australian racehorse
Phar Lap; but it was Bona Vista, winner of the 2,000 Guineas,
by Bend Or out of a mare called Vista, dam also of Sir Visto and
Velasquez, who passed on the Stockwell-Doncaster-Bend Or
blood to that great sire Cyllene, winner of 9 races, including the
Newmarket Stakes, Jockey Club Stakes, and Ascot Gold Cup,
whose descendants through Pharos and Fairway will be considered later.

Isonomy to Swynford (Chart 1)

Isonomy was bred by Miss Graham, foaled in 1875, and
bought as a yearling by John Porter on behalf of Mr Gretton for
360 guineas. He won the Cambridgeshire, Ebor Handicap,
Epsom, Goodwood, and Doncaster Cups, Ascot Gold Vase,
and two Ascot Gold Cups. His owner won £40,000 in bets when
his small, dark bay horse won the Cambridgeshire. He was
subsequently bought by Mr W. S. Crawfurd for 9,000 guineas
and went to the stud at a fee of 50 guineas.

One of his sons was Gallinule, a famous sire of thoroughbred mares, who got 'peerless' Pretty Polly, a billiant filly who
was trained by Peter Gilpin and won for her owner-breeder,
Major Eustace Loder, 22 out of the 24 races in which she ran,
including the 1,000 Guineas, the Oaks, the Coronation Stakes,
the St Leger in record time, the Champion Stakes, two Coronation Cups, and the Jockey Club Cup. Her stake total was
£37,297 and she only failed by a length to win the Ascot Gold
Cup.

Seabreeze, a daughter of Isonomy, who was bred by Caro-
line, Duchess of Montrose, known to the ribald as 'Six Mile

Bottom', won the Oaks, Coronation Stakes, and St Leger, having finished second in the 1,000 Guineas; and Common, a son of Isonomy and Thistle, who was owned jointly by Lord Alington and Sir Frederick Johnstone, trained by John Porter and ridden by G. Barrett, won the Triple Crown in 1891, the 2,000 Guineas on his first appearance on a race-course. He was eventually sold for stud purposes to Sir Blundell Maple for £15,000.

Isinglass

But the greatest of the sons of Isonomy and the connecting link in the male line chain was the famous racehorse Isinglass, who was foaled in 1890, bred and owned by Colonel Harry McCalmont, trained by Captain J. O. Machell, and ridden by T. Loates. Machell had bought his dam Deadlock for nineteen sovereigns from Lord Alington, resold her, and then luckily got her back again out of a farmer's cart.

Islinglass was very lazy by temperament but a superb racehorse, winning 11 out of the 12 races in which he ran, including the Triple Crown of Derby, St Leger, and 2,000 Guineas, in 1893, the Newmarket Stakes, Princess of Wales's Stakes, Eclipse Stakes, Jockey Club Stakes, and Ascot Gold Cup. Lord Howard de Walden subsequently bought him on the death of his previous owner. Isinglass won more money in stakes than any other thoroughbred on the English Turf prior to 1952, namely £57,455, and is the only horse who has ever gained the Triple Crown, Eclipse Stakes, and Ascot Gold Cup. His only defeat was when asked to give 10 pounds in the weights to Raeburn in the Lancashire Plate.

At the stud Sir Tatton Sykes of Sledmere mated Isinglass and La Fleche, perhaps the best colt and the best filly in the long history of the English Turf, and the offspring of this mighty union was John O' Gaunt. Bought as a yearling by Sir John Thursby for 3,000 guineas and ridden by Mr George Thursby into second place in the 2,000 Guineas and the Derby of 1904, John O' Gaunt was in turn mated with Canterbury Pilgrim, winner of the Oaks and the Jockey Club Cup, who was by Tristan, son of Hermit and Thrift, out of Pilgrimage. The result of this cross was Swynford, who was bred and owned by Lord Derby, foaled in 1907, and won the St Leger by a head, the

Princess of Wales's Stakes, the Eclipse Stakes, the Hardwicke Stakes twice, and the Coronation Cup. Swynford, as will be seen later, is the male ancestor of many notable horses of modern times, including Bahram and his sons Big Game and Persial Gulf; and Blenheim and his son Donatello II (the sire of Crepello).

A curious throwback to Isinglass occurred when Bella Paola won the Oaks, 1,000 Guineas, and Champion Stakes in 1958, together with £35,000 in stakes, as her pedigree comes down in direct male line from Isinglass through Louviers, Landgraf, Ferro, and Athanasius to her sire Ticino, after an interesting experiment in breeding by her French owner, Monsieur François Dupre.

Vedette to Sunstar and the Sons of St Simon (Chart 2—*continued*)

Vedette was bred by Mr Chilton, foaled in 1854, sold to Lord Zetland as a yearling, and won the 2,000 Guineas, the Ebor Handicap, and two Doncaster Cups. One of the existing lines comes down from Vedette through Speculum, bred by Mr Greville, Clerk of the Privy Council, a winner of the Goodwood Cup; Rosebery, who won both the Cesarewitch and the Cambridgeshire in the same season; Amphion, a winner of the Hardwicke Stakes and the Champion Stakes; and Sundridge, winner of sixteen sprinting events, to Sunstar, who was bred and raced by Mr J. B. Joel and won the 2,000 Guineas, Newmarket Stakes, and Derby.

Galopin, son of Vedette out of Flying Duchess by The Flying Dutchman, son of Bay Middleton and Barbelle, was bought as a foal with his dam for 100 guineas by Mr Blenkiron of the Middle Park Stud and sold as a yearling for 520 guineas to Prince Batthyany, for whom he won the Derby.

Donovan, a son of Galopin and Mowerina, was bred and owned by the Duke of Portland, trained by George Dawson and ridden by T. Loates and F. Barrett. He won 18 out of the 21 races for which he ran during his two seasons on the Turf, including the Derby and St Leger in 1889 and £55,154 in stakes, being only beaten by a head in the 2,000 Guineas. At the stud Donovan out of Vista sired Valesquez, who ran second to Galtee More in the 2,000 Guineas and the Derby and won the

DIOMED (*From a painting by George Stubbs*)

THE GODOLPHIN BARB (*From a painting by George Stubbs*)

THE DARLEY ARABIAN (*From a painting by John Wooton*)

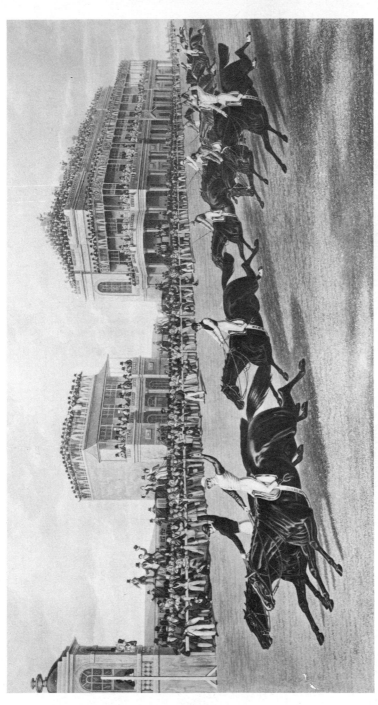

DONCASTER GREAT ST LEGER 1839. The dead heat between Charles XII and Euclid. *From an engraving of the painting by J. F. Herring senr.*

THE DERBY 1844 (Orlando)—The Start. *From the painting by J. F. Herring senr.*

Princess of Wales's Stakes, Eclipse Stakes, and Champion Stakes twice.

Galliard, another son of Galopin, carried on his male line in France through War Dance, Perth II, Alcantara II, and Pinceau, to Verso II, who won the French Derby, French St Leger and Prix de l'Arc de Triomphe, and in turn got Lavandin, winner of the English Derby.

St Simon

But the King Fergus line of Eclipse, in spite of the 'accursed Blacklock blood', produced its most outstanding scion in the mighty St Simon, son of Galopin and St Angela by King Tom, who was bred by Prince Batthyany, foaled in 1881, and bought by the Duke of Portland as a two-year-old for 1,600 guineas, after the Prince fell down dead in the luncheon room of the Jockey Club Stand at Newmarket just before the race for the 2,000 Guineas.

St Simon could not run in the 2,000 Guineas in the following year, as his nomination had become void on the death of his owner, but in the Duke of Portland's colours he won the Epsom Cup, Goodwood Cup, and Ascot Gold Cup by 20 lengths, and was never beaten. In a rough gallop before the St Leger, he easily defeated the eventual winner of that race, giving him 20 pounds, and St Simon was certainly one of the best racehorses of all time.

He went to the stud in 1886 at a fee of 50 guineas, which, as a result of his phenomenal success as a stallion, rose to 500 guineas during his last nine years and even reached 600 guineas in 1901. He died in 1908 after being head of the list of winning sires for seven consecutive years, 1890 to 1896 inclusive, and again in 1900 and 1901, and head of the list of winning sires of brood-mares for five consecutive years, 1903 to 1907 inclusive.

During 22 years at the stud St Simon was mated with 775 mares of which 554 were proved in foal and 423 delivered live foals, who between them won 571 races to the value of £553,158.

In 1900 St Simon was the sire of the winners of all the five classic races. Altogether two of his sons won the Derby, Persimmon and Diamond Jubilee; five of his daughters the Oaks, including Memoir and La Fleche; four of his offspring the St Leger, Memoir, La Fleche, Persimmon, and Diamond Jubilee;

two sons the 2,000 Guineas, St Frusquin and Diamond Jubilee; three daughters the 1,000 Guineas, including La Fleche; and three offspring, La Fleche, Persimmon, and William the Third, won the Ascot Gold Cup.

Memoir and La Fleche were full sisters by St Simon out of Quiver.

The former, owned by the Duke of Portland, won the Oaks in record time and the St Leger, finishing second in the 1,000 Guineas, in which race she was pulled back to allow Semolina to win, the Duke having declared to win with the latter filly, who was his other runner in the race.

La Fleche was one of the most famous racing mares of all time. She finished second in the Derby in 1892, and won 16 races, including the 1,000 Guineas, Oaks, St Leger, Champion Stakes, Cambridgeshire, and Ascot Gold Cup, together with £34,703 in stakes for her owner Baron de Hirsch, who had bought her as a yearling for the then record price of 5,500 guineas. La Fleche was bred by Queen Victoria at the Hampton Court Stud and, as noted earlier, when she had finished with racing, was mated with Isinglass, the produce being John O' Gaunt, the sire of Swynford.

St Florian, a son of St Simon and Palmflower, when mated with Morganette, dam of Galtee More, got Ard Patrick, winner of the Derby, Princess of Wales's Stakes, and Eclipse Stakes, in which memorable race he defeated Sceptre by a neck with Rock Sand third three lengths behind. Another son of St Simon named Florizel II, a winner of the Goodwood Cup and Jockey Club Cup, founded a sire line which has been a conspicuous success in France. And St Frusquin, yet another son of St Simon, won 9 races to the value of £32,960, including the 2,000 Guineas, Princess of Wales's Stakes, and Eclipse Stakes, only losing the Derby by a neck to Persimmon in a desperate finish. St Frusquin, who was owned by Mr Leopold de Rothschild, got St Amant, who won the 2,000 Guineas, Derby, and Jockey Club Stakes, for the same owner.

But the greatest of the sons of St Simon was Persimmon, bred and owned by the Prince of Wales, afterwards King Edward VII, trained by Richard Marsh and ridden by John Watts. This splendid specimen of a thoroughbred won 7 races to the value of £34,706, including the Derby of 1896 by a neck in the record time of 2 minutes 42 seconds, the St Leger, Eclipse Stakes, Jockey Club Stakes, and Ascot Gold Cup, Persimmon was four times head of the list of winning sires and while at the stud got Sceptre out of Ornament, full sister to Ormonde by Bend Or out of Lily Agnes by Macaroni.

Sceptre was a wonderful filly. She was bought by Mr R. S. Sievier as a yearling for the then record price of 10,000 guineas, and, trained by her owner, won four of the five classic races in 1902, the 2,000 and the 1,000 Guineas, both in record time, the Oaks, and the St Leger, together with the Jockey Club Stakes, in which she defeated Rock Sand by four lengths, the Champion Stakes and the Hardwicke Stakes, finishing third in the Ascot Gold Cup and fourth in the Derby and Grand Prix de Paris, and only being beaten by a neck by Ard Patrick in the Eclipse Stakes. She was bought by Sir William Bass as a four-year-old for 25,000 guineas. Her total winnings were 13 races value £38,225.

Persimmon also got Zinfandel, winner of the Gold Vase, Alexandra Stakes, Coronation Cup, Jockey Club Cup, and Ascot Gold Cup, for Lord Howard de Walden, his classic engagements having become void on the death of his former owner, Colonel Harry McCalmont. Other sons of Persimmon were Your Majesty, a winner of the St Leger and Eclipse Stakes for Mr J. B. Joel, and Prince Palatine, a winner of the St Leger, Eclipse Stakes, Jockey Club Stakes, Coronation Cup, Doncaster Cup, and two Ascot Gold Cups, together with £36,354 in stakes. Prince Palatine, beautifully bred by Persimmon out of Lady Lightfoot by Isinglass out of Glare by Ayrshire out of Footlight by Cremorne out of Paraffin by Blair Athol out of Paradigm, was bred by Lord Wavertree, raced in the colours of Mr T. Pilkington, who had bought him as a yearling for 2,000 guineas, was purchased by Mr J. B. Joel for £40,000 for breeding purposes, went to France in 1919, to the United States in 1920, and was burned to death in his stable in America in 1924.

Diamond Jubilee was a full brother to Florizel II and Persimmon, by St Simon out of Perdita II (by Hampton) one of the most famous of all brood-mares, and like them he was bred at the Sandringham Stud and owned by the Prince of Wales. Trained by Richard Marsh, and ridden by his stable attendant,

Herbert Jones, Diamond Jubilee won 6 races and £29,185, including the Triple Crown of 1900, for the heir to the throne. He won both the Derby and the St Leger in record time, the 2,000 Guineas, Newmarket Stakes, and Eclipse Stakes. After his racing days were over this splendid racehorse was sold for 35,000 guineas to an Argentine breeder. His temper was not as sweet as it might have been: he once bit off a stable boy's thumb!

Other sons of St Simon worthy of note were Desmond, who got The White Knight, winner of the Coronation Cup twice, the Goodwood Cup, the Gold Vase, and the Gold Cup twice; and William the Third, winner of the Doncaster Cup and Ascot Gold Cup, who got Willonyx, winner in 1911 of the Chester Cup, Ascot Stakes, Ascot Gold Cup, Jockey Club Cup, and Cesarewitch, carrying to victory the record weight of 9 stone 5 pounds.

However Chaucer, by St Simon out of Canterbury Pilgrim, dam also of Swynford, alone of all the brilliant sons and grandsons of St Simon earned any lasting reputation at the stud, and that was a sire of brood-mares. In fact the virtual extinction in England of the male line of St Simon still remains one of the most discussed topics among experts in bloodstock breeding, and the subject will be referred to again in a later chapter.

THE MALE LINES OF HEROD

(Chart 3)

During the first half of the last century Herod was the great rival of Eclipse at the stud. Two of his sons, Woodpecker and Highflyer, passed on his blood to famous horses like Thormanby and Glencoe, Bay Middleton and his son The Flying Dutchman, Cremorne and Macaroni, and good racing mares like Galata and Virago, Formosa and Brigantine, but by about 1875 the male lines of Herod, although they continued to flourish in France, had become almost extinct in England. In 1909, however, a successful attempt was made to revive the Herod blood in this country by the importation of Roi Herode from the continent.

Woodpecker Line (Chart 3)

Woodpecker, a large, coarse animal with wide lop ears, winner of 11 races and 3 matches, sired Buzzard, who won 22 races and matches and got the full brothers, Castrel, Selim, and Rubens, out of a mare by Alexander, son of Eclipse.

Castrel, a roarer, was the sire of Pantaloon, a big chestnut covered with dark spots, who got Windhound, who, mated with Alice Hawthorn, produced Thormanby. This horse, trained by Matthew Dawson and ridden by Harry Custance, won 14 races, including the Derby and the Ascot Gold Cup, for his owner, Mr James Merry, subsequently referred to by Disraeli in the House of Commons as 'The Member for Thormanby'. The stirp continued in France through Atlantic, a winner of the English 2,000 Guineas; Le Sancy, a winner of 14 races; Le Samaritain and Roi Herode.

When Roi Herode was brought over from France to compete in the Doncaster Cup in 1909, Mr E. Kennedy bought him for 2,000 guineas, for the express purpose of trying to revive 'the long lost line of Herod' in England, and in this worthy object he was successful, because one of the sons of Roi Herode bred by him was an unbeaten colt, The Tetrarch, of whom more hereafter.

Another son of Castrel called Bustard got Heron sire of the remarkable Fisherman, winner of 2 Ascot Gold Cups, 7 other cups, 2 Queen's Vases, 26 Queen's Plates, and 30 other events, a total of 67 races.

Selim was the sire of Sultan, a splendid bay with a blaze and four white feet, who got Galata, winner of the 1,000 Guineas, Oaks, and Ascot Gold Cup; Glencoe, winner of the 2,000 Guineas and Ascot and Goodwood Cups, who was exported to America; and unbeaten Bay Middleton, winner of the 2,000 Guineas and the Derby, who was bought for stud purposes by Lord George Bentinck from Lord Jersey for 4,000 guineas and out of Barbelle, dam also of Van Tromp, got The Flying Dutchman.

This famous racehorse, foaled in 1846, won 15 out of the 16 races in which he ran, including the Derby (in that year, 1849, worth the then record sum of £6,325 to the winner), the St Leger, and the Ascot Gold Cup, being the first thoroughbred ever to win these three great races. His only defeat was in the

Doncaster Cup in 1850, when Voltigeur, winner of that year's Derby and St Leger, as a three-year-old carrying 7 stone 7 pounds, beat the Dutchman by a neck, the latter as a four-year-old carrying 8 stone 12 pounds. One writer recorded at the time that the backers of The Flying Dutchman wandered about after his defeat, 'pale and silent as marble statues'. A return race was then arranged between Lord Eglinton, the owner of The Flying Dutchman, and Lord Zetland, the owner of Voltigeur, and this historic match took place at York in the spring of 1851 over a course two miles in length for a stake of 1,000 guineas. The Dutchman, conceding 8½ pounds to his rival, beat him by a short length in 3 minutes 55 seconds, after a desperate struggle between the two equine champions.

The Flying Dutchman was eventually exported to France, where he founded two branches of the Herod male line which descend through Dollar, Androcles, Cambyse, Gardefeu, and Chouberski to Bruleur, winner of the Grand Prix de Paris and the French St Leger; and through Dollar, Upas, Elf II, Nimbus, and Le Capucin to Pearl Cap, winner of the French 1,000 Guineas, French Oaks, and Prix de l'Arc de Triomphe.

Another line from Selim, now extinct, came down through Langar, Epirus, and the Derby winner Pyrrhus the First, to Virago, who won the 1,000 Guineas, Goodwood, and Doncaster Cups, and, on the same afternoon in 1854, the City and Suburban Handicap and Great Metropolitan Stakes at Epsom.

Rubens was the sire of Pastille, winner of the 2,000 Guineas and the Oaks.

Highflyer Line (Chart 3)

Highflyer, the other son of Herod to found a sire line, was bred by Sir Charles Bunbury, foaled in 1774, sold to Lord Bolingbroke and later bought from him by Mr Richard Tattersall, the founder of the famous firm of thoroughbred auctioneers. Highflyer was an unbeaten winner of 12 races and when he went to the stud his fee was fixed at 50 guineas. His stock won over £170,000 in stakes, and when he died in 1793 these lines were inscribed on his tombstone, referring to Eclipse and Flying Childers, as well as to Highflyer himself, all three of them winners of all their races:

> *To these three Patriarchs the Turf shall owe*
> *The long existence of superior breed;*
> *That blood in endless progeny shall flow,*
> *To give the Lion's strength, the Roebuck's speed.*

His epitaph opened with the words: 'Here lieth the perfect and beautiful symmetry of the much lamented Highflyer' and when Mr Tattersall gave his annual dinner to the jockeys the toast was always 'The Hammer and Highflyer'.

One of the sons of Highflyer was Sir Peter Teazle, who won 17 races, including the Derby, for the 12th Earl of Derby, the founder of the race, and who sired Walton and Sir Paul.

The line of Walton went down through Partisan, Gladiator, and the Doncaster Cup winner, Sweetmeat, to Parmesan, sire of Cremorne, and to Macaroni. Cremorne was only beaten a neck in the 2,000 Guineas and won the Derby and Grand Prix de Paris, the Alexandra Stakes and Ascot Gold Cup, while Macaroni won the 2,000 Guineas, Derby, and Doncaster Cup.

The line of Sir Paul went down through Paulowitz, Cain, Ion, and the Derby winner Wild Dayrell to Buccaneer, the sire of Formosa, who dead-heated for first place in the 2,000 Guineas and won three other classic races, the 1,000 Guineas, Oaks, and St Leger; of Brigantine, who won the Oaks and the Ascot Gold Cup; and of Kisber, who won the Derby and the Grand Prix de Paris.

But in spite of the bold prophecy on his tombstone, the Highflyer sire lines of Herod have been extinct in this country for over fifty years.

THE MALE LINES OF MATCHEM

(Chart 4)

Matchem was the third of the great sires to found a male line stirp which has lasted to the present day.

His son Conductor got Trumpator who sired Paynator and Sorcerer.

Paynator got Dr Syntax, a winner of 32 races, including the Preston Gold Cup seven years in succession and the Lancaster

Gold Cup five times, who sired Beeswing and Ralph, the latter a winner of the 2,000 Guineas and the Ascot Gold Cup. Beeswing, during eight seasons on the Turf, won 52 out of the 63 races in which she ran, including the Newcastle Gold Cup six times, the Chester Cup, the Doncaster Cup four times, and the Ascot Gold Cup. She was then hacked in the Park for a year before going to stud, where, mated with Touchstone, she produced Newminster.

Sorcerer got Comus, a winner of 10 races; Smolensko, the first horse to win the 2,000 Guineas and the Derby; and Bourbon, the sire of Fleur de Lis, winner of two Goodwood Cups and the Doncaster Cup, who was deliberately knocked down by another horse when she was seen to be winning the St Leger.

From Comus came Humphrey Clinker and Grey Momus, the latter a winner of the 2,000 Guineas and the Ascot Gold Cup. Humphrey Clinker was the sire of Rockingham, who won the St Leger and Goodwood and Doncaster Cups, and of Melbourne.

Melbourne to Hurry On (Chart 4)

Melbourne, who first covered at 'The Rose and Crown', Beverley, at 10 guineas a mare, got Sir Tatton Sykes, Canezou, West Australian, and Blink Bonny. Sir Tatton Sykes won the 2,000 Guineas and the St Leger; Canezou won the 1,000 Guineas, two Goodwood Cups, and the Doncaster Cup, running second to Surplice in the St Leger; and Blink Bonny, by Melbourne out of Queen Mary by Gladiator, won the Derby and the Oaks, later a stud becoming the dam of Blair Athol by Stockwell.

West Australian, foaled in 1850, by Melbourne out of Mowerina by Touchstone, bred and owned by Mr John Bowes, trained by John Scott, and ridden by Frank Butler, was the first horse ever to win the Triple Crown of Derby, St Leger, and 2,000 Guineas, and, after being sold to Lord Londesborough as a four-year-old, he also won the Ascot Gold Cup in what was then the fastest time for the race. West Australian had very bad distemper as a foal and was rather an ordinary horse to look at, although he had a beautiful head and was a very fine racehorse. He went to the stud at a fee of 30 guineas and in 1860 'the pick of

England' was sold to the French Government for 4,000 guineas.

His son Solon carried on the line to unbeaten Barcaldine, who got Sir Visto, winner of the Derby and the St Leger for Lord Rosebery, and Marco, winner of the Cambridgeshire. Marco sired Beppo, who won the Jockey Club Stakes and the Hardwicke Stakes and got Aleppo, winner of the Chester Cup, two Jockey Club Cups, and the Ascot Gold Cup; Marcovil, who like his sire won the Cambridgeshire; and Neil Gow, who won the 2,000 Guineas and ran Lemberg to a dead-heat in the Eclipse Stakes.

Other sons of Barcaldine were Winkfield and Goodfellow. Winkfield was the sire of Bachelor's Button, winner of the Champion Stakes, Hardwicke Stakes, Doncaster Cup, Jockey Club Cup, two Ascot Gold Vases, and the Ascot Gold Cup for Mr S. B. Joel; while Goodfellow was the sire of the Cesarewitch winner Chaleureux, whose daughter Signorinetta won the Derby and the Oaks in 1908. But it was through unbeaten Hurry On, a son of Marcovil, that the male line of Matchem survives to the present day, through Precipitation.

THE SIRE LINES IN RECENT YEARS

It will be seen from the foregoing analysis of the main sire lines that by 1914 there were virtually only 12 male stirps that were destined to survive in England through two World Wars to the present day; namely, the Eclipse lines through Touchstone to Carbine and Bay Ronald, through Stockwell to Rock Sand, Flying Fox, Orby, and Cyllene, through Isonomy to Swynford, and through Vedette to Sunstar and St Simon; the Herod lines through Thormanby to The Tetrarch and through The Flying Dutchman to Bruleur; and the Matchem line through West Australian to Hurry On.

Carbine to Felstead (Chart 1A)

Carbine, as already mentioned, was imported from the Antipodes by the late Duke of Portland in 1895. He died in 1914, having got Spearmint, who was bred by Sir Tatton Sykes at Sledmere, sold as a yearling for 300 guineas to Major Eustace Loder, and won the Derby in record time and the Grand Prix de Paris. At the stud Spearmint sired Spion Kop, who also won the

Derby in record time, and Royal Lancer, who won the St Leger.

The best of the sons of Spion Kop was Felstead, who won the Derby for the late Sir Hugo Cuncliffe-Owen in 1928, and who sired the filly Rockfel, also owned by Sir Hugo, winner in 1938 of the 1,000 Guineas, Oaks, and Champion Stakes and Steady Aim, winner of the Oaks. However Felstead did not produce any outstanding son to carry on the male line of Carbine and it does not seem that it can now survive in this country.

Bay Ronald to Son-in-Law and Gainsborough, Solario and Hyperion (Chart 1A)

Bay Ronald by Hampton out of Black Duchess, sired Dark Ronald and Bayardo, thereby becoming the progenitor of two flourishing sire lines.

Dark Ronald, who won the Royal Hunt Cup and the Princess of Wales's Stakes, was the sire of the Vaucluse, winner of the 1,000 Guineas, and Son-in-Law. The last-named horse was the winner of the Cesarewitch in record time and of two Jockey Club Cups for his owner Sir Abe Bailey. Son-in-Law was responsible for Straitlace, winner of the Oaks and for Rustom Pasha, winner of the Eclipse Stakes. It was however as a sire of stayers that he was to establish himself and he has no equal in this sphere.

Three of his sons won the Ascot Gold Cup. Trimdon won the race twice; Foxlaw won the race once and was the sire of two further Ascot Gold Cup winners in Tiberius, out of Glenabatrick, and Foxhunter, who was out of Trimestral, the dam of Trimdon; and Bosworth, who was out of Serenissima by Minoru, dam of Tranquil, winner of the 1,000 Guineas and St Leger. The 1940 Derby winner Pont l'Eveque, who was later exported to the Argentine, was descended from Son-in-Law through The Winter King and Barneveldt, winner of the Grand Prix de Paris.

The stamina tradition of the Son-in-Law male line has continued to this day. Souepi, who won the Ascot, Goodwood and Doncaster Cups of 1953, was a son of Epigram, by Son-in-Law, himself the winner of the Goodwood and Doncaster Cups. Trimdon was the sire of Marsyas II, bred in France by Monsieur Boussac from the famous mare Astronomie.

Besides winning the Queen Alexandra Stakes, the Goodwood Cup and the Doncaster Cup, Marsyas II was successful no less than four times in the Prix du Cadran, France's equivalent of the Ascot Gold Cup (on the fourth occasion defeating Souverain). At stud he was the sire of Macip, who won the French St Leger and Ascot Gold Cup.

It was however Bosworth who was ultimately responsible for the survival of the Son-in-Law male line. Bosworth sired Boswell, who won the St Leger and Eclipse Stakes for the late Mr William Woodward and became a successful sire in America, and Plassy, who won the Jockey Club Stakes and Coronation Cup for Lord Derby and was exported to France.

Plassy became the sire of Nepenthe (Prix du Cadran) and of Vandale (Prix du Conseil Municipal). Vandale's son Taine won the Prix du Cadran twice, and Fric won the Coronation Cup. But Vandale's most successful son both on the racecourse and at stud was undoubtedly Herbager, who win six races value 66,850,510 francs, including the French Derby (in which he defeated Shantung) and the Grand Prix de Saint-Cloud. Herbager was the leading horse of his year in France.

Through the importation to Ireland of two sons of Herbager, namely Sea-Hawk II and Appiani II, successful attempts have been made to revive the Son-in-Law male line in England and Ireland. Appiani II, who was out of the Italian Oaks winner Angel Rucellai, was the winner of seven races value £31,165, including the Italian Derby. Appiani II, having proved a somewhat disappointing stallion, was exported to France in 1973. However, whilst at stud in Ireland he succeeded in becoming the progenitor of Star Appeal, who was out of Sterna, by Neckar. Star Appeal was the winner of eleven races value £240,876, for his owner Mr A. Zeitelhack, including the Prix de l'Arc de Triomphe, the Eclipse Stakes and the Gran Premio di Milano. He was retired to the National Stud at Newmarket.

Sea-Hawk II was the winner of three races, including the Grand Prix de Saint-Cloud (in which he defeated Diatome) and was unbeaten in his two races as a two-year-old, which included the Criterium de Saint-Cloud; in his remaining races he was second in the Prix Hocquart, fourth in the Prix Greffulhe and Prix Noailles and fifth in the French Derby. Sea Hawk was imported to Ireland in 1966 and prior to his exportation in 1973 to Japan had proved a most successful sire of top-class stayers, his progeny including Bruni, winner of the St Leger and Yorkshire Cup for Mr C. A. B. St George, Paulista, winner of the Prix Vermeille, Erimo Hawk, winner of the Ascot Gold Cup, and Irvine, winner of the Jockey Club Cup. Meadow Mint, a further son of Herbager, died after only one season at stud in Ireland, but was the sire, from his only crop, of Funny Hobby, winner of the Grand Prix de Paris.

Bayardo, whose dam was Galicia, dam also of Lemberg, bred and owned by Mr A. W. 'Fairie' Cox, trained by Alec Taylor at Manton, and ridden by Danny Maher, won the St Leger, Eclipse Stakes, Champion Stakes, Ascot Gold Cup, and 22 out of his 25 races. He got Gay Crusader and Gainsborough, who both won war-time Triple Crowns together with substitute Gold Cups competed for at Newmarket in 1917 and 1918. Gay Crusader was bred and owned by Mr Cox and ridden by Steve Donoghue; Gainsborough was bred and owned by Lady James Douglas and ridden by Joe Childs. Both horses were trained by Alec Taylor at Manton. Gay Crusader was not a success at the stud but Gainsborough, before he died in 1945, produced four splendid sons in Solario, Singapore, Orwell, and Hyperion.

Solario

Solario was bred by Lord Dunraven, foaled in 1922, and bought as a yearling for 3,500 guineas by Sir John Rutherford. Trained by R. Day and ridden by Joe Childs, Solario finished fourth in the 2,000 Guineas and the Derby, won the Ascot Derby, Princess of Wales's Stakes, St Leger, Coronation Cup, and Ascot Gold Cup, and was beaten by a neck by Foxlaw in the Jockey Club Stakes and disqualified.

On the death of his owner in 1932 Solario was bought at auction by a syndicate of British bloodstock breeders for 47,000 guineas. At a stud fee of 500 guineas a mare, this magnificent stallion sired Mid-day Sun, winner of the Derby; Straight Deal, winner of a substitute Derby at Newmarket during the war; and Exhibitionist, winner of the Oaks and the 1,000 Guineas. Dastur, son of Solario and Frair's Daughter, who finished second in the 2,000 Guineas, Derby, St Leger, and Champion Stakes and won the Coronation Cup, got Umiddad, winner of a war-time substitute Gold Cup, whose dam was the Oaks winner Udaipur. Solario died in 1945.

Straight Deal is the sire of Ark Royal, winner of the Yorkshire Oaks and Park Hill Stakes; Kerkeb, winner of the Park Hill Stakes; Sicilian Prince, winner of the French St Leger; and Above Board, who won the Yorkshire Oaks and the Cesarewitch in the colours of King George VI. But it is doubtful whether the line of Solario will survive in England.

Singapore won the St Leger and Doncaster Cup and sired Chulmleigh, also a winner of the St Leger; while Orwell won the record sum in stakes for a two-year-old, namely £18,613, and in the following year carried off the 2,000 Guineas.

There is a line of Gainsborough extant in France, which descends via Artist's Proof, Fine Art and Fine Top to Sanctus (French Derby and Grand Prix de Paris) and Topyo (Prix de l'Arc de Triomphe).

Hyperion

Hyperion, by Gainsborough out of Selene, by Chaucer out of Serenissima, by Minoru out of Gondolette, a glorious chestnut with four white socks, who stood only 15 hands 1½ inches on the day he won the Derby, proved himself to be one of the finest thoroughbreds of modern times both on the race-course and at the stud.

Bred and owned by the late Lord Derby, trained by the Hon. George Lambton, and ridden by Tommy Weston, Hyperion won the Chester Vase, the Derby very easily by 4 generous lengths in the record time of 2 minutes 34 seconds, the Prince of Wales's Stakes at Ascot, and the St Leger in 1933, finishing third in the Ascot Gold Cup in the following year. His stake total was £29,509.

Before Hyperion won the Derby many people viewed him with disfavour, because of his small stature and four white socks. One correspondent wrote to *The Times* quoting the old adage:

> *One white foot, ride him for your life.*
> *Two white feet, give him to your wife.*
> *Three white feet, give him to your man.*
> *Four white feet, sell him—if you can!*

However, after he had won the premier classic, another old adage was remembered:

> *One white foot, keep him not a day;*
> *Two white feet, send him soon away;*
> *Three white feet, sell him to a friend;*
> *Four white feet, keep him to the end.*

Anyway, Lord Derby did 'keep him to the end' and Hyperion headed the list of winning sires in 1940, 1941, 1942, 1945, 1946 and 1954; was second in 1939 (when his first crop of foals were three years of age), and again in 1944, 1950, and 1952; was third in 1943 and fourth in 1947.

Hyperion was 30 years of age when he died at the end of 1960. While at stud he sired, amonst many winners of both sexes, Owen Tudor, winner of war time substitute races for the Derby and Gold Cup for the Hon Lady Macdonald-Buchanan and Sun Chariot, who trained by Fred Darling at Beckhamtpon and ridden by Gordon Richards, won the war-time substitute 1,000 Guineas, Oaks and St Leger in 1942 in the Royal racing colours of His Majesty King George VI, who had leased her from the National Stud, and whose first foal, by Blue Peter, was Blue Train, winner of the Newmarket Stakes.

Hyperion also sired Sun Castle, winner of the St Leger for the late Lord Portal; Sun Stream, out of the famous mare Drift, winner of the 1,000 Guineas and Oaks; Godiva, also winner of the 1,000 Guineas and Oaks; Hycilla, winner of the Oaks for the late Mr William Woodward; Hypericum, winner of the 1,000 Guineas, who was bred and owned by King George VI; and Gulf Stream, out of the 1,000 Guineas winner Tide-way, who won the Eclipse Stakes and became a leading sire in the Argentine. Other sons of Hyperion were the very game little horse Hornbeam, winner of 11 races, including the Great Voltigeur Stakes and the sire of Intermezzo (St Leger) and Windmill Girl, winner of the Ribblesdale Stakes and dam of the Derby winners Blakeney and Morston; Rockefella, the sire of Rockavon, who won the 2,000 Guineas, and of Linacre, the winner of the Irish 2,000 Guineas; and High Hat, who raced in the colours of the late Sir Winston Churchill, winning the Oxfordshire Stakes and Aly Khan International Memorial

Stakes at Kempton Park (defeating Petite Etoile). High Hat
was the sire of Glad Rags, winner of the 1,000 Guineas,
Cloonagh, winner of the Irish 1,000 Guineas, and High Line,
one of only two horses in the history of the Turf to win the
Jockey Club Cup three times.

Owen Tudor was responsible for Tudor Minstrel, a brilliant winner of the 2,000 Guineas for the late Mr J. A. Dewar;
Abernant, owned by Lady MacDonald-Buchanan, who was
champion sprinter and the sire of Abermaid, winner of the
1,000 Guineas; Elpenor, winner of the Ascot Gold Cup and Prix
du Cadran; and Right Royal V. The last named horse won the
French 2,000 Guineas, French Derby and King George VI and
Queen Elizabeth Stakes (defeating St Paddy, winner of the
Derby and St Leger by three lengths) in the colours of his
breeder Madame Jean Couturie. Right Royal V, who died in
1973, is the sire of Prince Regent, winner of the Irish Sweeps
Derby, Salvo, winner of the Hardwicke Stakes and Grosser
Preis von Baden-Baden, Rex Magna, winner of the French St
Leger, and Ruysdael, winner of the Italian Derby.

Tudor Minstrel's most successful son was King of the
Tudors, the winner of the Eclipse Stakes and second on the sires
list in 1962. He was the sire of Henry the Seventh, winner of the
Eclipse Stakes and of Crocket, the champion two-year-old of
1962. Henry the Seventh was the sire of Luciano, the champion
of his year in Germany, and Crocket sired Frontier Goddess,
winner of the Yorkshire Oaks.

Tudor Melody, a further son of Tudor Minstrel, was the
leading two-year-old of 1958 and headed the list of sires of
two-year-olds in 1968 and 1970. His most successful progeny
were Kashmir II, the winner of the 2,000 Guineas of 1966, and
the sire in 1974 of Moulines and Dumka, winners respectively
of the French 2,000 Guineas and French 1,000 Guineas; Welsh
Pageant, winner of the Queen Elizabeth II Stakes and the sire
of Orchestration (Coronation Stakes, Ascot); and Magic Flute,
winner of the Cheveley Park Stakes and Coronation Stakes.
Tudor Minstrel's son Sing Sing proved an outstanding sire of
sprinters, including Song, winner of the King's Stand Stakes.
Balidar, a grandson of Tudor Minstrel, was champion sprinter
of Europe and became the sire of Bolkonski, winner of the 2,000
Guineas, St James's Palace Stakes, and Sussex Stakes for Carlo

d'Alessio. Welsh Pageant is the sire of Swiss Maid (Champion Stakes). Swiss Maid was sold for 325,000 guineas at the 1978 Newmarket December Sales, the price realised being a record for a horse sold at auction in Europe.

Aristophanes, a son of Hyperion, who was exported to the Argentine, became the sire of Forli, the winner of the Argentine Quadruple Crown. Forli was the sire of Forego, twice horse of the year in America, and of Thatch, the champion two-year-old of 1972 and the winner at three years of the St James's Palace Stakes and Sussex Stakes. Alibhai, Heliopolis and Khaled are three sons of Hyperion who founded successful sire lines in the United States. The first named horse sired Your Host, the sire of Kelso, the winner of 31 races, including the Washington International, in the world record time for 1½ miles of 2 mins. 23.8 seconds, when carrying 9 stone as a three-year-old and five Jockey Club Gold Cups. Kelso won the world record total prize money of $1,977,896, which is the equivalent of approximately £852,500 in sterling.

Aureole

But the best of the sons of Hyperion was undoubtedly Aureole, who won a memorable race for the King George VI and Queen Elizabeth Stakes at Ascot in the royal racing colours in 1954, as well as the Coronation Cup and the Hardwicke Stakes, having finished second in the Derby and third in the St Leger the year before.

Aureole, a beautiful chestnut horse, by Hyperion out of Angelola by Donatello II out of Feola by Friar Marcus, was bred by the late King George VI at the Sandingham Stud and won £36,225 for his owner, Her Majesty the Queen, for whom he was trained by Captain Cecil Boyd-Rochfort, and ridden by E. Smith and W. Carr.

Aureole finished top of the winning sires' list in 1960 and 1961, and second in 1965. His most successful son was St Paddy, winner of the Derby, St Leger, Eclipse, Great Voltigeur and Hardwicke and Jockey Club Stakes, together with £97,192, for the late Sir Victor Sassoon, his trainer being Noel Murless, and his jockey Lester Piggott. St Paddy has sired Connaught, winner of the Eclipse Stakes and already a promising stallion; Parnell, the winner of 14 races and the equivalent of £111,755, including the Irish St Leger, and Prix Jean Prat, Longchamp, twice; and two further successful stallions in St Chad and Welsh Saint. He was second on the list of leading brood mare sires in 1977, being the maternal grandsire of Dunfermline, winner of the Oaks and the St Leger.

Further sons of Aureole were Aurelius, winner of the St Leger and Hardwicke Stakes; Provoke, winner of the St Leger and a successful sire in Russia; Hopeful Venture, winner of the Princess of Wales's Stakes and the Grand Prix de Saint-Cloud in the colours of the Queen, who was exported to Japan. Two other sons of Aureole who were exported to that country were Saint Crespin and Miralgo. Miralgo, who won the Hardwicke Stakes, was the sire in Europe of Mistigo, winner of the Irish 2,000 Guineas and of Roll of Honour, winner of the Grand Prix de Paris. Saint Crespin, by Aureole out of Tulyar's dam Neocracy by Nearco, won the Eclipse Stakes (by a neck) and the Prix de l'Arc de Triomphe (after a dead-heat with Midnight Sun, who was disqualified) and £54,760 for the late Prince Aly Khan. With his English crops Saint Crespin III sired Altesse Royale, the winner of the 1,000 Guineas, Oaks and Irish Guinness Oaks and a total of £76,934, at that time the highest sum ever to have been won by a filly in England or Ireland.

Vienna, a further son of Aureole, raced in the colours of the late Sir Winston Churchill, winning the Prix d'Harcourt, the Blue Riband Trial Stakes and the Lyons Maid Stakes, Sandown Park, twice. Although he was on the whole a disappointment as a sire, Vienna, none the less, earned lasting fame as the sire of Vaguely Noble.

Vaguely Noble, Dahlia and Exceller

Vaguely Noble is without question the outstanding member of the Hyperion male line. Bred by the late Major Lionel Holliday, he is by Vienna out of Noble Lassie by Nearco out of Belle Sauvage by Big Game out of Tropical Sun by Hyperion out of Brulette, the winner of the Oaks and Goodwood Cup. Trained as a two-year-old by Walter Wharton and owned by Mr. L. Brook Holliday, the son of his breeder, he was the winner of the Sandwich Stakes at Ascot by twelve lengths, and the Observer Gold Cup. Owing to the death of his breeder, he was submitted at the Newmarket December Sales of 1967, where he realised 136,000 guineas to the bid of Mr and Mrs Robert Franklyn. The sale price was, at the time, the highest realised by any horse at public auction in Europe. Mr Nelson Bunker Hunt, who was the underbidder at the auction, later purchased a half-share in Vaguely Noble. As a three-year-old Vaguely Noble brought his total winnings to the equivalent of £148,673. He was successful in the Prix de Guiche, Prix du Lys and Prix de Chantilly before finally establishing himself with a fine victory in the Prix de l'Arc de Triomphe. Ridden by W. Williamson, he defeated Sir Ivor, ridden by Lester Piggott, by three lengths. Vaguely Noble was syndicated for $5,000,000 and commenced stud duties at Mr. John Gaines' Gainesway Stud at Lexington in Kentucky in 1969. He has proved a most successful stallion and headed the list of sires in Great Britain and Ireland in 1973 and 1974.

Dahlia, who was bred in the United States by Mr. Nelson Bunker Hunt, by Vaguely Noble out of Charming Alibi by Honey's Alibi out of Adorada II by Hierocles out of Gilded Wave by Gallant Fox, was largely responsible for her sire's position at the top of the list of stallions.

Dahlia was the winner of 13 races in England, Ireland, France, America and Canada worth the equivalent of £497,136. Her winnings in England and Ireland alone amounted to £277,739.50, a figure far in excess of that won by any other filly racing in England or Ireland. Dahlia won the Irish Guinness Oaks by three lengths; the King George VI and Queen Elizabeth Stakes, twice (on the first occasion defeating Rheingold by six lengths, and on the second defeating Highclere, winner of the 1,000 Guineas, by 2½ lengths) and the Benson and Hedges Gold Cup, twice. In France she was the winner of the Prix Saint-Alary, Grand Prix de Saint-Cloud and Prix de la Grotte; in the United States, she was the winner of the Washington International Stakes and the Man O'War Stakes; and in Canada she won the Canadian Championship at Woodbine Park. She finished second in the French Oaks, and third in the French 1,000 Guineas, the King George VI and Queen Elizabeth Stakes and Washington International Stakes.

Vaguely Noble is also the sire of Exceller, the winner of the equivalent of over £423,451 in France, England, Canada and the U.S.A., including the Grand Prix de Paris, French St Leger,

Grand Prix de Saint-Cloud, Coronation Cup, Canadian International Championship and Hollywood Invitational Handicap. He also won the Jockey Club Gold Cup defeating Seattle Slew and Affirmed. Other sons of Vaguely Noble include Empery, winner of the Epsom Derby; Ace of Aces, winner of the Sussex Stakes; Duke of Marmalade, winner of the Premio Roma; and Noble Decree, winner of the Observer Gold Cup. All these horses with the exception of the Duke of Marmalade, were owned by Mr Nelson Bunker Hunt.

Rock Sand to Flyon (Chart 1B)

Rock Sand, the Triple Crown winner of 1903, got Tracery, out of Topiary by Orme out of Plaisanterie, who was bred in the United States and raced in England by Mr August Belmont. He won the St Leger, Eclipse Stakes, and Champion Stakes, finished third in the Derby and was brought down by a lunatic when running in the Gold Cup. He was sold to an Argentine breeder for 53,000 guineas in 1920, returned to England in 1923, and died in 1924.

Tracery sired Flamboyant, winner of the Goodwood and Doncaster Cups; Papyrus, winner of the Derby; and Obliterate, sire of that remarkable half-bred mare Quashed, winner of the Oaks, Jockey Club Cup twice, and Ascot Gold Cup by a short head.

Flamboyant got Flamingo, winner of the 2,000 Guineas, who sired Flyon, winner of the Ascot Gold Cup, and both were owned by the late Lord Milford.

The male line of Rock Sand seems unlikely to survive.

Flying Fox to Tantieme (Chart 1B continued)

Flying Fox, who won the Triple Crown in 1899, as related earlier, was bought by Monsieur Edmond Blanc on the death of the Duke of Westminster and went to France. His son Ajax, who won the French Derby and Grand Prix de Paris, became the sire of Teddy, who is primarily responsible for the survival of the Flying Fox male line to-day.

Teddy was the sire of Asterus, who raced in the colours of Monsieur Marcel Boussac, winning the French, 2,000 Guineas, the Champion Stakes (defeating the 2,000 Guineas winner Colorado) and the Royal Hunt Cup; Sir Gallahad III, out of the good brood mare Plucky Liege, winner of the French 2,000 Guineas and the Lincolnshire Handicap; Aethelstan; Bull Dog, a full brother to Sir Galahad III; Ortello, winner of the Prix de l'Arc de Triomphe; and Brumeux, winner of the Jockey Club Cup. The last named horse sired Borealis, winner of the Coronation Cup, who was out of Aurora, the dam of the Ascot Gold Cup winner Alycidon. Borealis sired many winners in England and Ireland, including Northern Gleam (Irish 1,000 Guineas). But his best son was probably Herero, winner of the German Derby.

Ortello was responsible for the Italian Derby winner Torbido, who although disappointing as a stallion in England, sired Antonio Canale. The last named horse in his turn sired the unbeaten champion Braque (who was out of Buonamica, the dam of the Ascot Gold Cup winner Botticelli) and Marco Visconti, winner of the Italian St Leger. Sir Gallahad III went to the United States where he produced Gallant Fox. This crack American racehorse won the Kentucky Derby, Preakness Stakes, Belmont Stakes, Classic Stakes, Jockey Club Gold Cup and $328,165, equivalent to over £65,000 in stakes, at that time a world record. At the stud Gallant Fox sired the full brothers Omaha (winner of the American Triple Crown – the Preakness Stakes, Kentucky Derby and Belmont Stakes – and second in the Ascot Gold Cup), and Flares, winner of the Newmarket Stakes, Princess of Wales's Stakes, Champion Stakes and Ascot Gold Cup by a neck, for his breeder and owner Mr. William Woodward. The male line of Sir Gallahad III has on the whole enjoyed more success in North America than it has in Europe. However, there are two branches of this line that have figured prominently in European racing. The first traces through Roman and Hasty Road to Berkeley Springs, winner of the Cheveley Park Stakes for Mr. Paul Mellon; the second traces through Fighting Fox, (an own brother to Gallant Fox) Crafty Admiral and Neptune to Neptunus, winner of the French 2,000 Guineas.

From Bull Dog's son Bull Lea came the Kentucky Derby winner Hill Gail, whose son Martial won the 2,000 Guineas in 1960; and Citation. The latter horse, who was bred at the Calumet Stud Farm, Lexington, Kentucky, was out of Hydroplane by Hyperion out of Toboggan by Hurry On, and won the

American Triple Crown of Kentucky Derby, Preakness Stakes and Belmont Stakes, together with the American Derby, Jockey Club Gold Cup, Empire City Gold Cup and Hollywood Gold Cup as well as $1,085,760 in stakes money, thus in 1951 becoming the first equine 'millionaire' with a new world record in prize money. Citation was bred and owned by Mr and Mrs. Warren Wright, trained by H. A. Jones, and ridden by crack American jockey, Eddie Arcaro. Out of 45 races, Citation won 32, finished second in 10, third in 2, and fifth in his only other start.

Asterus was responsible for Atys, sire of Pan II, winner of the French St Leger and Ascot Gold Cup; Merry Boy, sire of Thunderhead II, winner of the 2,000 Guineas; and Astrophel, sire of Bagheera, winner of the French Oaks and Grand Prix de Paris; the most influential of his descendants was, however, his grandson Sunny Boy III (by Jock II), who was out of Fille de Soleil by Solario out of Fille de Salut by Sansovino out of Friar's Daughter. Sunny Boy was champion sire in France in 1954. His most successful progeny were Sun Cap, winner of the Oaks; Sica Boy, winner of the French St Leger and Prix de l'Arc de Triomphe; and Tamanar, winner of the French Derby.

It is however, the line descending from Aethelstan that has done most to propagate the male stirp of Flying Fox. Aethelstan was the sire of Maurepas, winner of the Grand Prix de Paris and the sire in his turn of Camaree, winner of the 1,000 Guineas; and of Deiri, the sire of the Grand Prix de Paris winner Deux Pour Cent.

The last-named horse was responsible for a really outstanding performer in Tantième, who was bred by the late M. Francois Dupré and trained by Francois Mathet. Tantième raced from two to four years, winning the French 2,000 Guineas, the Queen Elizabeth Stakes, the Coronation Cup and the Prix de l'Arc de Triomphe, twice. He was the winner of 12 races, and 68,381,018 francs and £12,005 in stakes money. Tantième, the leading French sire in 1962 and 1965, was the sire of La Sega, winner of the French 1,000 Guineas and French Oaks and of Danseur, winner of the Grand Prix de Paris. The most prominent members of this line however were Match III, Reliance II, and Relko.

Match III, Reliance II and Relko

These three horses were bred by Monsieur Francois Dupré from that excellent broodmare Relance III, by Relic out of Polaire by Le Volcan out of Stella Polaris, the dam of the French Derby and Grand Prix de Paris winner Northern Light II. Relance III traced in tail female line to Sceptre. All these three horses were trained by Francois Mathet and ridden in the majority of their races by Yves Saint-Martin.

Match III and Reliance II were own-brothers, being both sons of Tantième. Match III, who was voted 'Horse of the Year' in 1962 was the winner of seven races in England, France and the USA value 854,698 francs, £23,515 and $70,000. His victories included the French St Leger, the Grand Prix de Saint-Cloud, the King George VI and Queen Elizabeth Stakes (in which he defeated the St Leger winner Aurelius) and the Washington D. C. International. He finished second to Right Royal V in the French Derby.

Match III was imported to England in 1963 to stand at the stud of Mr Herbert Blagrave. It was a great blow to breeders when he died only two years later, for his progeny showed plenty of ability. Probably the most successful of his get were Palatch, who dead-heated for the Yorkshire Oaks and Ovaltine, winner of the Goodwood Cup.

Reliance II, Match III's own-brother, was an even more successful performer on the racecourse. He was the winner of five races value £152,435, including the French Derby (in which he defeated Diatome), the Grand Prix de Paris, the French St Leger and the Prix Hocquart. In his only other race, the Prix de l'Arc de Triomphe, he finished second to Sea-Bird II. Reliance II was also imported by Mr. Blagrave in 1966 and he sired a large number of pattern race winners. Probably his most successfull progeny are Recupere, winner of the Prix du Cadran, and Proverb, who besides winning the Chester Vase and Doncaster Cup, is the only horse to have won the Goodwood Cup twice during the course of the twentieth century.

Relko was three-parts a brother to Match III and Reliance II being by Tanerko, a son of Tantieme. Relko was the winner of nine races worth the equivalent of £149,136, including the French 2,000 Guineas, the Epsom Derby (which he won by six lengths from Merchant Venturer), the French St Leger, the

Coronation Cup and the Grand Prix de Saint-Cloud. Relko was also imported in 1965 to stand in England. He has proved a most successful sire, his winners including Relkino, winner of the Benson and Hedges Gold Cup, Olwyn, winner of the Irish Guinness Oaks, Relay Race, winner of the Jockey Club Stakes and Hardwicke Stakes, and Tierceron, the winner in Italy of the Italian St Leger, Gran Premio d'Italia and Gran Premio del Jockey Club. Tanerko, the sire of Relko, was also responsible for White Label (Grand Prix de Paris) and for Djakao, winner of the Grand Prix de Deauville and the sire of Mariacci (Grand Criterium).

It certainly seems that the attempts to revive the Teddy male line in England have been successful.

Orby to Whistler

Orby, winner of the Derby, sired Grand Parade, who also won the Derby for Lord Glanely and who got Diophon, winner of the 2,000 Guineas and sire of Diolite, winner of the same classic, who later went to Japan. But the best son of Orby was probably Orpheus, who finished third in the Derby and won the Princess of Wales's Stakes and the Champion Stakes, twice. However, the line of Orby which survives in this country to-day, comes down through The Boss, Sir Cosmo, Panorama and Whistler, and through The Boss, Golden Boss, Gold Bridge and Golden Cloud. Although it is predominantly a male line of high-class sprinting stock, it is a line that has yielded horses of top class ability at a mile, such as Quorum, winner of the Sussex Stakes, and Track Spare, winner of the St James's Palace Stakes.

Cyllene to Pharos, Fairway, and Pinza (Chart 1B)

Cyllene sired Polymelus out of Maid Marian, by Hampton out of Quiver, dam also of Memoir and La Fleche, and produced four winners of the Derby, Cicero, Minoru, Lemberg, and Tagalie. Cicero, by Cyllene out of Gas by Ayrshire out of Illuminata a daughter of Paraffin, won the Derby in record time for Lord Rosebery and got Frair Marcus, a good sire of brood-mares, whose offspring are notable for speed rather than stamina, the male line coming down through Beresford and Portlaw. Minoru won the 2,000 Guineas and the Derby, by a head, when leased for racing by King Edward VII from his breeder Lord Wavertree, and was subsequently exported to Russia. Lemberg, bred and owned by Mr 'Fairie' Cox, trained by Alec Taylor and ridden by Bernard Dillon, was a very good racehorse by Cyllene out of Galicia, dam also of Bayardo. He was only beaten by a short head by Neil Gow in the 2,000 Guineas, finished third to Swynford in the St Leger, and won the Derby in record time, Eclipse Stakes, Jockey Club Stakes, Chamption Stakes twice, Coronation Cup, Doncaster Cup, and £41,594 in stakes. Tagalie won the 1,000 Guineas as well as the Derby.

Another son of Cyllene was Captivation, from whom descended, through Kircubbin and the French Derby winner, Chateau Bouscaut, that good staying horse, Chanteur II, winner of the Coronation Cup and Winston Churchill Stakes, who, in recent years, has got Pinza and Cantelo and Only For Life and headed the winning sires list in 1953.

Pinza, a bay colt bred by the late Mr Fred Darling, the famous Beckhampton trainer, by Chanteur II out of Pasqua by Donatello II, owned by Sir Victor Sassoon and trained by N. Bertie, won the Derby by 4 lengths from Aureole in Coronation Year and at last gave Sir Gordon Richards his first and only victory ride in the premier classic. Pinza also won the King George VI and Queen Elizabeth Stakes and total prize money amounting to £47,401.

Cantelo, a bay filly bred and owned by Mr William Hill, the well-known commission agent, by Chanteur II out of Rustic Bridge by Bois Roussel, trained by Captain Charles Elsey and ridden by E. Hide, won the St Leger and Ribblesdale Stakes, together with £40,265. Only For Life won the 2,000 Guineas and King Edmond VII Stakes.

But it was Polymelus, winner of the Princess of Wales's Stakes, Champion Stakes, and Cambridgeshire, five times head of the list of winning sires, who carried on the line of Phalaris, the leading progenitor of modern times. Other offspring of Polymelus were Pommern, who, ridden by Steve Donoghue, won a war-time Triple Crown in 1915 for Mr 'Solly' Joel and got Adam's Apple, winner of the 2,000 Guineas; Fifinella, who, ridden by Joe Childs, won the substitute Derby and Oaks at Newmarket in 1916 for Sir Edward Hulton; Invincible, who got Invershin, winner of the Jockey Club Cup and two Ascot Gold

Cups; and Humorist, who won the Derby by a neck from Craig-en-Eran in the colours of Mr 'Jack' Joel with Steve Donoghue up, and who less than a month later bled to death in his box from internal hæmorrhage.

Phalaris, winner of sixteen races at Newmarket in the 1914–18 war, during his outstanding career sired the winners of over 400 races to the total value of close on £335,000, before he died in 1931. His best sons were Pharos, Manna, Colorado, Fairway, and Caerleon. In addition Phalaris had two sons who were exported to the United States, but whose lines have been successfully revived in Great Britain. These were the full-brothers Sickle and Pharamond, who were both out of Selene, the mother of Hyperion.

Colorado, bred by Lord Derby out of Canyon, the winner of the 1,000 Guineas, won the 2,000 Guineas, Eclipse Stakes and Princess of Wales's Stakes. It was a tragedy that he died after only two seasons at stud, for his progeny included Felicitation, winner of the Jockey Club Cup and Ascot Gold Cup, who was exported to Brazil in 1943, and Loaningdale, winner of the Eclipse Stakes who went to Uruguay in 1941. Caerleon, a full-brother to Colorado, also won the Eclipse Stakes and died in 1939.

Manna, who died in 1939, won the 2,000 Guineas and the Derby and got Miracle, winner of the Eclipse Stakes, who went to Uruguay in 1942, and Colombo, the winner of the 2,000 Guineas. The last named horse sired Happy Knight, also winner of the 2,000 Guineas, Dancing Time, winner of the war-time substitute 1,000 Guineas and British Empire, out of the Oaks winner Rose of England, who won the July Stakes and was exported to the Argentine in 1940.

Although the male line of Manna did not survive in England, a throwback to it occurred in the 1978 Irish 2,000 Guineas. The winner Jaazeiro, descends in male line from Manna, through Colombo, British Empire, Endeavour II, Pretense and Sham. Jaazeiro also went on to win the St James's Palace Stakes at Ascot and the Sussex Stakes at Goodwood.

Pharos (Chart 1B—*continued*)

Pharos, who died in 1937, won the Champion Stakes, together with thirteen other races, and got Cameronian, Firdaussi, Rhodes Scholar, Fastnet, Phideas, Pharis II, and Nearco.

Cameronian won the 2,000 Guineas, Derby, Champion Stakes, and £31,286 for Mr John Dewar, who only the year before had been left all the bloodstock owned by his uncle, the late Lord Dewar, who died in April 1930. As the *Bloodstock Breeders' Review* put it: 'But for the fact that the old "void nominations" rule was swept into oblivion by the result of the friendly action at law which Mr Edgar Wallace persuaded the Jockey Club to take, Cameronian would have lost all his "book" engagements by reason of the death of Lord Dewar, his breeder and nominator'. So 'Lucky' Dewar won the Derby at the first opportunity with a horse bred by his uncle, who never won a classic during all the thirty years he owned racehorses. Cameronian was exported to Argentina in 1941, having already sired Scottish Union, winner of the St Leger and Coronation Cup, and Finis, winner of a war substitute Gold Cup, who went to New Zealand in 1943.

Firdaussi, winner of the St Leger and Jockey Club Stakes, was sent to France and then to Rumania; and Rhodes Scholar, winner of the Eclipse Stakes, went to the United States in 1940, where he sired Black Tarquin, winner of the St Leger.

Fastnet was the sire of Le Paillon, winner of the Prix de l'Arc de Triomphe; Flocon, winner of the Eclipse Stakes, and Fast Fox, who won the Doncaster Cup and became the sire of Wallaby II, winner of the French St Leger and Ascot Gold Cup, and of Javelot, winner of the Eclipse Stakes, Pharis II, bred by Monseiur Marcel Boussac out of Carissima, was unbeaten in the three races in which he ran, including the French Derby and Grand Prix de Paris. He was due to take on Blue Peter in the St Leger of 1939, but this never materialised owing to the outbreak of war and the cancellation of the Doncaster meeting. Pharis II, after one season at stud in France, was annexed by the Germans. He headed the sires' list with his initial French crop, returning after the war to resume his place of honour. He died in 1957.

Pharis II's most successful sons were Ardan, winner of the French Derby, Prix de l'Arc de Triomphe and Coronation Cup; the St Leger winners Scratch II and Talma II; Auriban and Philius, both winners of the French Derby; Priam II, winner of the Hardwicke Stakes; and Pardal, an own-brother to Ardan, out of the French Oaks winner Adargatis, winner of the Princess of Wales's Stakes and Jockey Club Stakes.

Ardan's son Hard Sauce was responsible for Hard Ridden, the winner of the Irish 2,000 Guineas and Epsom Derby for the late Sir Victor Sassoon; Gazpacho, the winner of the Irish 1,000 Guineas; and the good sprinter Hard Tack. Hard Ridden was the sire of Hardicanute, who won the Timeform Gold Cup and was the sire in his turn of Hard to Beat, the winner of the French Derby. Hard Tack was the sire of Right Tack, the only horse in history to win both the English and Irish 2,000 Guineas, and of Sparkler, the winner of thirteen races, including the Prix du Moulin du Longchamp, the Lockinge Stakes and the Prix Quincey, twice, and sire in his first crop of Enstone Spark, winner of the 1,000 Guineas. Right Tack was exported to Australia in 1977 having first sired Take A Reef, who, despite the fact that his most important success was registered in a handicap, was rated at the top of the 1974 Three-Year-Old Free Handicap, above the winners of all the English classics.

Pardal was imported into England in 1951, where he sired Psidium, winner of the Derby in the colours of the late Mrs Arpad Plesch (who was exported to the Argentine in 1970, having sired Sodium, winner of the Irish Sweeps Derby and Doncaster St Leger); Parbury and Pardallo, both winners of the Ascot Gold Cup; Pardao, winner of the Jockey Club Stakes, the Princess of Wales's Stakes and the San Juan Capistrano Handicap in the United States of America; and Firestreak, winner of the Rous Memorial Stakes at Ascot. Firestreak was the sire of Snow Knight, winner of the Derby and the Canadian International Championship for his Canadian owner Mrs N. Phillips; and of Hotfoot, the winner of the Coronation Stakes at Sandown Park and a very promising stallion. Pardao, who died in 1971, was responsible for Sovereign, the winner of the Coronation Stakes at Ascot; and for Moulton, the winner of the Benson and Hedges Gold Cup, the Premio Presidente Della Repubblica and the Prix Henry Delamarre, and the leading first crop sire in England and abroad in 1977.

Nearo

Nearco, who was an unbeaten winner of 14 races, including the Grand Prix de Paris, was bought by Mr Martin Benson for £60,000, then the world record price for a thoroughbred, and imported into England from Italy in 1938. The male line that he founded in the most powerful in the world to-day. He died in 1957, having twice been champion sire in Great Britain.

Nearco's most successful sons were Dante, Sayajirao, Nimbus, Nasrullah, Mossborough, Royal Charger, Narrator, Arctic Star and Nearctic. The most successful of his daughters were the brilliant but temperamental Masaka, the winner of the Oaks and Irish Oaks for the late Aga Khan, and Neasham Belle, out of the great broodmare Phase, who won the Oaks for the late Major Lionel Holliday.

Dante was the winner of the war-time substitute Derby at Newmarket in 1945 for his owner-breeder Sir Eric Ohlson. He became the sire of Darius, owned by the late Sir Percy Loraine, who won the 2,000 Guineas, Eclipse and St James's Palace Stakes and £38,105; and of Carrozza, winner of the Oaks and the Princess Elizabeth Stakes for the Queen. A further son of Dante, Toulouse Lautrec, was a top class horse in Italy, winning the Gran Premio d'Italia and becoming the sire of that good filly Marguerite Vernaut, the winner of the Champion Stakes. Toulouse Lautrec was also the great grandsire of Hawaiian Sound, the winner of the Benson and Hedges Gold Cup. Darius in his turn was responsible for Pia, who won the Oaks in the colours of Countess Margit Batthyany; Pola Bella, who was out of the famous mare Bella Paola, and who won the French 1,000 Guineas; and the top class miler Derring-Do, bred and trained by Arthur Budgett, a winner of the Queen Elizabeth II Stakes and Hungerford Stakes.

Derring-Do's death in 1978 was a great loss to the bloodstock breeding industry. For he had sired High Top, winner of the Observer Gold Cup and 2,000 Guineas and a promising sire of fillies; Roland Gardens, also winner of the 2,000 Guineas; Peleid, winner of the St Leger for his owner-breeder Colonel William Behrens, who was later exported to Hungary; Jan Ekels, winner of the Queen Elizabeth II Stakes; and of Huntercombe, who was champion sprinter of Europe and sired

Radetzky, winner of the St James's Palace Stakes and Queen Anne Stakes.

Sayajirao, an own-brother to Dante, out of the famous brood-mare Rosy Legend was bought for the Maharajah of Baroda for 28,000 guineas, then a world record price for a yearling. He was the winner of the St Leger and the Hardwicke Stakes. At stud he was the sire of the remarkable mare Gladness, winner of the Ascot Gold Cup, Goodwood Cup and Ebor Handicap, for her owner, Mr J. McShain. He was also the sire of Indiana, winner of the St Leger for the late Mr Charles Engelhard; I Say, winner of the Coronation Cup; and Lynchris, the leading middle distance filly of her year in Ireland, and the winner of the Yorkshire Oaks, the Irish Oaks and the Irish St Leger.

Nimbus won the 2,000 Guineas and the Derby in 1949 for the late Mrs M. Glenister (both victories were awarded to him only after the judge had examined photographs of the finish of the two classic races concerned), together with £33,076 in stakes. Nimbus was exported to Japan in 1962, having previously sired Nagami, the winner of the Coronation Cup, Gran Premio del Jockey Club in Italy and Grand Prix du Printemps in France, and later a successful sire in Italy.

Narrator, an own-brother to Neasham Belle, won the Champion Stakes and the Coronation Cup and became the sire of Night Off, the winner of the 1,000 Guineas. Both horses were owned by the late Major L. B. Holliday.

Mossborough became the leading sire in 1958 and was high on the list in 1963, due in the first instance to his fine son Ballymoss and in the second to his brilliant daughter Noblesse. Mossborough was also the sire of Cavan, winner of the Belmont Stakes in America; and of Yelapa, whose son Buckskin won the Prix du Cadran, twice and the Jockey Club Cup.

Royal Charger, who was the winner of the Challenge Stakes, was the first stallion to be purchased by the newly-formed Irish National Stud. Whilst in Ireland he was the sire of Happy Laughter, winner of the 1,000 Guineas and the Coronation Stakes for Mr H. D. H. Wills; Gilles de Retz, winner of the 2,000 Guineas for Mr A. G. Samuel, and Royal Serenade, the champion sprinter. Royal Charger was exported to the USA in 1953 where his line continues to flourish. His most successful son was Turn-To, the champion two-year-old in America, and the winner of $282,030, including the Garden State Stakes. Turn-To was the sire of First Landing, the sire of Riva Ridge, winner of the Kentucky Derby; Sir Gaylord; and Hail to Reason, winner of the Preakness Stakes. The last named horse was the sire of Personality, the Horse of the Year in the USA and winner of the Kentucky Derby, Preakness Stakes and $444,049; and Roberto. Roberto, bred by his owner, Mr Dan Galbreath, by Hail to Reason out of Bramalea, by Nashua out of Rarelea by Bull Lea, and trained in Ireland by Vincent O'Brien, was the champion two-year-old of his year and was the winner at three years of the Derby in which he defeated Rheingold by a short head, and the Benson and Hedges Gold Cup, which he won by three lengths from Brigadier Gerard, and the winner at four years of the Coronation Cup. Roberto is already the sire of some smart two-year-olds.

Sir Gaylord, who was second on the list of sires in Great Britain in 1968, has exerted a considerable influence in England and Ireland through the great horse Sir Ivor and through Habitat, the champion miler of Europe. He is also sire of Gaily, winner of the Irish 1,000 Guineas.

Gunner B, a grandson of Royal Charger, was the winner of the Eclipse Stakes.

Nearctic was foaled in Canada, his dam, Lady Angela, by Hyperion out of Sister Sarah by Abbot's Trace, having been exported to that country in 1955. Nearctic was the winner of 21 races in Canada and was voted Canadian horse of the year. At stud he was the sire of Nonoalco, the winner of the English 2,000 Guineas, and of Northern Dancer. The second of these horses was the winner of 14 races and $580,806, including the Preakness Stakes and the Kentucky Derby in record time. He headed the list of sires in Great Britain in 1970 and in 1977 due to his brilliant sons Nijinsky and The Minstrel. He also sired Lyphard, the winner in France of the Prix de la Foret and Prix Jacques Le Marois, who was a most successful stallion in France, his progeny including Dancing Maid, the winner of the French 1,000 Guineas, and Reine de Saba, winner of the French Oaks. Northfields, a further son of Northern Dancer, who was out of Little Hut, the dam of Habitat, was imported to Ireland, where he sired Northern Treasure, winner of the Irish 2,000

Guineas, and North Stoke, winner of the Joe McGrath Memorial Stakes and Furstenburg-Rennen in Germany.

A further son of Nearo, the unraced Arctic Star, became the sire of Arctic Storm, the winner of the Champion Stakes and the Irish 2,000 Guineas.

Ballymoss, Noblesse and Royal Palace

Ballymoss, a chesnut colt, was bred by Mr R. Ball and foaled in 1954 by Mossborough out of Indian Call by Singapore out of Flittemere by Buchan out of Keysoe by Swynford out of Keystone II by Persimmon. Wearing the colours of Mr J. McShain, trained by M. V. O'Brien in Ireland, and ridden in most of his major races by Scobie Breasley, Ballymoss won races to the value of over £60,000 in England and over £46,000 in France, his victories including the King George VI and Queen Elizabeth Stakes, St Leger, Eclipse Stakes, Coronation Cup, Irish Derby and Prix de l'Arc de Triomphe. He was second on the sires' list in 1967, due to the exploits of his son Royal Palace.

Bred by his owner, Mr H. J. Joel, by Ballymoss out of Crystal Palace by Solar Slipper out of Queen of Light, by Borealis out of Picture Play, the winner of a war-time 1,000 Guineas, Royal Palace was trained by Noel Murless and ridden by George Moore and Sandy Barclay. He was the winner of nine races to the value of £166,063, including the 2,000 Guineas (by a short head from Taj Dewan), the Derby by a length and a half from Ribocco (the winner of the St Leger and Irish Sweeps Derby), the Coronation Cup, the Eclipse Stakes in a very exciting finish, from Taj Dewan and Sir Ivor, and the King George VI and Queen Elizabeth Stakes. The last performance was particularly meritorious, since he was found to be lame after pulling up. Royal Palace was the sire of Dunfermline, who celebrated the Year of the Silver Jubilee of the Queen's accession by winning the Oaks and the St Leger and £106,977, carrying the colours of Her Majesty. Dumfermline, who was bred at the Royal Stud at Sandringham, was out of Strathcona, by St Paddy out of Stroma, the mother of Canisbay, who had won the Eclipse Stakes for the Queen.

Noblesse, who was foaled in 1960, was bred by Mrs M. P. Margetts, by Mossborough out of Duke's Delight by His Grace out of Early Light by Easton. She was owned by Mrs P. Olin, trained in Ireland by P. J. Prendergast and ridden by Garnet Bougoure. Noblesse was one of the outstanding fillies to race during this century, winning four races including Timeform Gold Cup, the Misidora Stakes at York and the Oaks by 10 lengths. Her only defeat came about in her last race, the Prix Vermeille at Longchamp, in which she was not at her best. At stud Noblesse bred a total of six foals, all of whom were winners. They included the filly Where You Lead, by Raise a Native, who won the Musidora Stakes and finished second in the Oaks.

Sir Ivor and Habitat

Bred in the United States of America by Mrs Reynolds W. Bell, Sir Ivor was a bay colt foaled in 1965 by Sir Gaylord out of Attica by Mr Trouble out of Athenia by Pharamond II out of Salaminia by Man O'War. He carried the colours of Mr Raymond Guest, was trained in Ireland by Vincent O'Brein and was ridden by Lester Piggott and by Liam Ward. He was the winner of eight races value over £220,000 including the 2,000 Guineas, the Derby, the Champion Stakes and the Washington International Stakes. He finished second in the Irish Sweeps Derby and the Prix de l'Arc de Triomphe and third in the Eclipse States. Sir Ivor, after standing for two seasons at Mr Guest's Ballygoran Stud in Country Kildare, was syndicated for $2,080,000 to stand at the Claiborne Stud in Kentucky. His most successful progeny to date have been Ivanjica, the winner of the French 1,000 Guineas and the Prix de l'Arc de Triomphe, and Lady Capulet, the winner of the Irish 1,000 Guineas.

Habitat is a chesnut colt, foaled in 1966, and was bred in the United States of America by Nuckols Bros, and is by Sir Gaylord out of Little Hut by Occupy out of Savage Beauty by Challenger II out of Khara. He was owned by the late Mr Charles Engelhard and trained by Fulke Johnson-Houghton and ridden by Lester Piggott. Habitat, who raced only at three years, was the winner of five races, including the Lockinge Stakes at Newbury, the Prix Quincey at Deauville, the Wills Mile at Goodwood, defeating Lucyrowe, and the Prix du Moulin de Longchamp, defeating Right Tack. Syndicated for £400,000 to stand at the Grangewilliam Stud in Ireland, Habi-

THE DERBY 1970 (Nijinsky)—Rounding Tattenham Corner

RABELAIS

Courtesy: British Racehorse.

THE TETRACH

Courtesy: British Racehorse.

PHALARIS

Courtesy: British Racehorse.

BLANDFORD

Courtesy: British Racehorse.

NEARCO

RIBOT

tat was the leading sire of Two-Year-Olds in 1973, 1974, and 1975. In each of these years he was responsible for the winner of the Middle Park Stakes, who were in chronological order, Habat, Steel Heart and Hittite Glory. The most successful of his progeny were, however, Flying Water, who won the 1,000 Guineas, Champion Stakes and Prix Jacques Le Marois for Mr Daniel Wildenstein; Rose Bowl, the winner of the Champion Stakes and the Queen Elizabeth Stakes, twice; and Roussalka, the winner of Royal Ascot's Coronation Stakes.

Nijinsky and The Minstrel

Bred in Canada by Mr E. P. Taylor, Nijinsky was a bay colt, foaled in 1967, by Northern Dancer out of Flaming Page by Bull Page out of Flaring Top by Menow out of Flaming Top by Omaha. Nijinsky was sold as a yearling for $86,000 dollars, carried the colours of the late Mr Charles Engelhard, was trained in Ireland by Vincent O'Brien and was ridden by Lestor Piggott. He is the first and only horse to have won the Triple Crown of 2,000 Guineas, Derby and St Leger since Bahram performed this feat in 1935. Nijinsky won eight other races including the Irish Sweeps Derby and the King George VI and Queen Elizabeth Stakes, defeating Blakeney, the winner of the 1969 Derby, by two lengths. Nijinsky's only defeats were when he was second in the Prix de l'Arc de Triomphe, beaten ¾ length by Sassafras, and in the Champion Stakes. He amassed the total of £238,716 in prize money, which was a new European record and surpassed the total previously gained by Sea-Bird II.

Nijinsky retired to the Claiborne Stud in Kentucky, being syndicated for the equivalent of £2¼m. His most successful progeny to-date have been Ile de Bourbon, winner of the King Edward VII Stakes, King George VI and Queen Elizabeth Stakes and Geoffrey Free Stakes; Green Dancer, winner of the Observer Gold Cup and French 2,000 Guineas, and Quiet Fling, the winner of the Coronation Cup.

The Minstrel, who was also bred in Canada by Mr E. P. Taylor, was three-parts a brother to Nijinsky, and was a chesnut colt, foaled in 1974, by Northern Dancer out of Fleur by Victoria Park out of Flaming Page, the dam of Nijinsky. He raced in the colours of Mr Robert Sangster, was trained in

Ireland by Vincent O'Brien and ridden by Lester Piggott. The Ministrel won seven races, including the Derby, the Irish Sweeps Derby and the King George VI and Queen Elizabeth Stakes. He finished second in the Irish 2,000 Guineas and third in the English 2,000 Guineas. His total winnings amounted to £333,197. The Minstrel was syndicated as a stallion for a record sum, 4½ million dollars having been paid for a 50% holding in him.

Nasrullah

It was, however, Nasrullah who proved the most powerful link in the chain of male descent from Nearco. A bay horse, foaled in 1940, he was bred by his owner, the late Aga Khan out of Mumtaz Begum, by Blenheim out of Mumtaz Mahal, by The Tetrarch. The winner of the Coventry Stakes and the Champion Stakes, Nasrullah stood in Ireland until 1951, in which year he headed the list of winning sires, being places second in 1953 and 1954. He was exported to the United States of America in 1950 and was five times champion sire in that country.

In England his most successful progeny were Never Say Die, the winner of the Derby and the St Leger; Nearula, the winner of the 2,000 Guineas and the Champion Stakes for Mr W. Humble; Belle of All, the winner of the 1,000 Guineas for Colonel the Hon. H. S. Tufton; Musidora, who won the 1,000 Guineas and the Oaks for Mr N. P. Donaldson; Nasram II, out of the famous mare La Mirambule, winner of the King George VI and Queen Elizabeth Stakes and the sire of Zug, winner of the French 2,000 Guineas; the brilliant but temperamental Zucchero, winner of the Coronation Cup and the Princess of Wales's Stakes; and three very successful stallions in Princely Gift, Grey Sovereign and Red God.

Nearula died in 1960, having sired Kythnos, the winner of the Irish 2,000 Guineas.

The owner of Never Say Die, the late Mr Robert Sterling Clark, very generously presented him to the English National Stud, where he stood until his death in 1975. Never Say Die was the champion sire in 1962 in which year his son Larkspur won the Derby in the colours of Mr Raymond Guest. Larkspur was exported to Japan in 1967. Never Say Die, was also the sire of that very good filly Never Too Late II who won the 1,000 Guineas and Oaks for Mrs Howell Jackson. Immortality, an unraced son of Never Say Die, was responsible for the 1,000 Guineas winner Fleet, who was out of the famous mare Review, also dam of the 1,000 Guineas winner Pourparler.

Red God, the winner of five races, including the Richmond Stakes at Goodwood, was imported into Ireland for stud duties in 1959, heading the list of sires of two-year-olds in 1969. His most successful son is Blushing Groom, bred by the Boyne Hill Stud out of Runaway Bride by Wild Risk out of Aimee by Tudor Minstrel. Blushing Groom, the champion two-year-old in France in 1976, was the winner of seven races including the Grand Critericum and the French 2,000 Guineas. He was undoubtedly a very brilliant horse over distances of up to a mile. Prior to the Epsom Derby, Blushing Groom was syndicated for $6,000,000 for stud in America, a price which came to look a little excessive when he failed to stay the distance and could finish only third. Red God is also the sire of Red Lord, winner of the French 2,000 Guineas; Jacinth, winner of the Coronation Stakes at the Royal Ascot meeting; Green God, the champion sprinter, who died in 1976; St Alphage, sire of the champion sprinter Sandford Lad; and Yellow God. The last named horse, who was exported to Japan in 1973 after only three seasons at stud in Ireland, won five races including the Gimcrack Stakes and the 2,000 Guineas Trial Stakes and finished second to Nijinsky in the 2,000 Guineas. It became clear during the 1977 season that it had been a mistake to let Yellow God go, for, during that season he sired Nebbiolo, who won the English 2,000 Guineas for Dr Nils Schibbye; Pampapaul, the winner of the Irish 2,000 Guineas; and Don (Ger); winner of the St James's Palace Stakes.

Grey Sovereign, who died in 1976, was responsible for Zeddaan, the winner of the French 2,000 Guineas and sire of a further winner of the race in Kalamoun; Don II, also a winner of the French 2,000 Guineas; Sovereign Path, winner of the Queen Elizabeth II Stakes; and Fortino II, winner of the Prix de Meautry. The last named horse was the sire of Caro, the winner of the French 2,000 Guineas and Pidget, winner of the Irish 1,000 Guineas and Irish St Leger. He was also the grandsire of Gentilhombre, twice successful in the Prix de l'Abbaye de

Longchamp, the most valuable race for sprinters in Europe. Caro became a leading sire in France, being responsible for Crystal Palace, winner of the French Derby and for that brilliant but ill-fated filly Madelia, the unbeaten winner of the French 1,000 Guineas and French Oaks.

Sovereign Path was second on the sires' list in 1970, during which year his daughter, Humble Duty, was the winner of the 1,000 Guineas, the Coronation Stakes, the Sussex Stakes and the Wills Mile in the colours of the late Jean, Lady Ashcombe. Supreme Sovereign, a further son of Sovereign Path, won the Lockinge Stakes and became the sire of Nocturnal Spree, the winner of the 1,000 Guineas in the colours of Mr John Mulcahy. But the most successful son of Sovereign Path was the Eclipse Stakes winner Wolver Hollow, who headed the sires' list in 1976. During that year his son Wollow, carrying the colours of Carlo d'Alessio, won the 2,000 Guineas, Sussex Stakes and Benson and Hedges Gold Cup, being awarded the Eclipse Stakes on the disqualification of Trepan II. Wollow's earnings amounted to £200,790. Wolver Hollow also sired Furry Glen, the winner of the Irish 2,000 Guineas.

Princely Gift was responsible for more good stallion sons than almost any other stallion of his generation. His most successful progeny were Sun Prince, the winner of the Prix Robert Papin, the Coventry Stakes at the Royal Ascot meeting and the St James's Palace Stakes; King's Troop, who sired King's Company, winner of the Irish 2,000 Guineas, and was exported to New Zealand in 1973; Tribal Chief; and Faberge II. Tribal Chief, a very fast sprinter, did not stay beyond 5 furlongs, but surprised all breeders by becoming the sire of Mrs McArdy, the winner of the 1,000 Guineas for Mrs L. Kettlewell, who owned a hotel in Yorkshire. Mrs McArdy was sold at the Newmarket December Sales of 1977 for 154,000 guineas, then a record price in England for a horse in training. Tribal Chief was sent to Japan in 1975, to which country Faberge II had preceded him in 1970.

Faberge II was the sire of Giacometti, the winner of the Champion Stakes for Mr C. A. B. St George; Gay Lussac, the champion of his year in Italy, and winner of the Italian Derby; and Rheingold.

A bay colt, foaled in 1969, Rheingold was bred in Ireland by the late Dr James Russell, out of Athene by Supreme Court out of Necelia by Nearco; his dam had once been the first prize in the raffle at a charity meeting at Sandown Park. Rheingold was bought as a yearling for 3,000 guineas by a syndicate of owners, headed by Mr Henry Zeisel, the owner of a London nightclub, and was trained by Barry Hills. He was the winner of 9 races in England and France, and the equivalent of £361,746 in stakes money, his principal successes being the Hardwicke Stakes, the Prix Ganay, the Grand Prix de Saint-Cloud, twice, and the Prix de l'Arc de Triomphe, in which he defeated the great mare Allez France by 2½ lengths. Rheingold was syndicated as a stallion in Ireland for a reputed £1,000,000.

Nasrullah was exported in 1951 to stand at the Claiborne Stud in Kentucky. He was to head the sires' list in America no less than five times. His most successful sons in America were Nashua, who won over $1,000,000 including the Belmont Stakes, the Preakness Stakes, Classic Stakes and the Jockey Club Gold Cup, twice; and Jaipur, a further winner of the Belmont Stakes. However, there is no doubt that the most influential of his American-bred sons were Bold Ruler and Never Bend. The last named horse, who set a new earnings record when the champion two-year-old of his year, and was second in the Preakness Stakes and Kentucky Derby, was the sire of Riverman, the winner of the French 2,000 Guineas, and of J. O. Tobin, the champion two-year-old in England in 1976. By far his greatest claim to fame, however, is the fact that he is the sire of the mighty Mill Reef, of whom more presently.

Bold Ruler and Secretariat

Bold Ruler was undoubtedly the most successful stallion to stand in the United States during the twentieth century. He headed the American sires' list for seven successive years from 1964 to 1970 and was also top in 1972. Bred by the late Mrs Henry C. Phipps' Wheatley Stable, he was a bay colt by Nasrullah out of Miss Disco by Discovery out of Outdone. He was the winner of 23 races from 33 starts value $764,204, including the Preakness Stakes, the Flamingo Stakes and the Wood Memorial Stakes.

Bold Ruler's son Bold Lad (Ire), who was bred by his owner, the late Beatrice Lady Granard, was the leading two-year-old in Great Britain and Ireland in 1966; he was also the leading sire of two-year-olds in 1971. His best winner is, however, the filly Waterloo, who won the 1,000 Guineas for the late Hon. Mrs Richard Stanley. Bold Lad (USA), who was out of Misty Morn by Princequillo, was the champion two-year-old of his year in U.S.A. and was the sire of Bold Fascinator, the winner of the French 1,000 Guineas and Sirlad (Italian Derby). Bold Bidder, who sired the Kentucky Derby winner Cannonade, was also responsible for Mount Hagen, the winner of the Prix du Moulin de Longchamp. Breakspear II was responsible for Trepan II, who won the Prince of Wales Stakes and Eclipse Stakes, only to suffer disqualification in both races. Boldnesian, a further son of Bold Ruler, was the sire of Bold Reasoning, who in his turn got Seattle Slew, the winner of nine races value $717,720 including the American Triple Crown. Seattle Slew was syndicated as a stallion for $12,000,000. The outstanding horse to be sired by Bold Ruler was, however, Secretariat.

Foaled in 1970, bred by Mr L. Chenery and owned by his daughter Mrs Penny Tweedie, Secretariat was a chestnut colt by Bold Ruler out of Somethingroyal, the mother of Sir Gaylord (the sire of Sir Ivor). He must be rated the greatest horse to race in America since Man O'War, and being, like Man O'War, a big red chestnut, earned like him, the nickname of 'Big Red'. Secretariat is the only horse in the history of the American Turf to have received the title of 'Horse of the Year' at two years, and he received the award again at three years. He was the winner of 16 races, value $1,316,808, including the American Triple Crown of the Preakness Stakes, Kentucky Derby and the Belmont Stakes, breaking the record for the track in all three cases. He also broke the track record in the Marlboro Cup. He was syndicated as a stallion for $6,000,000, and his first crop included Dactylographer, the winner of the Observer Gold Cup, the most valuable two-year-old race to be run over a mile in England.

Mill Reef

There is no doubt, however, that the outstanding member of the Nearco male line was Mill Reef. Bred in the USA by his owner Mr Paul Mellon, Mill Reef was a bay colt by Never Bend out of Milan Mill by Princequillo out of Virginia Water by

Count Fleet out of Red Ray by Hyperion out of Infra Red by Ethnarch, who traced at three removes to Our Lassie, the winner of the Oaks. He was trained at Kingsclere by Ian Balding and ridden by G. Lewis. Mill Reef won 12 races and £309,225 from 14 starts. As a two-year-old he was the winner of five races, including the Coventry Stakes, Gimcrack Stakes and Imperial Stakes. At three years he won the Derby, the Eclipse Stakes by four lengths from Caro, the King George VI and Queen Elizabeth Stakes by 8 lengths, and the Prix de l'Arc de Triomphe in the record time of 2m. 28.30 secs, defeating the champion French trained filly Pistol Packer by three lengths. At four years he won the Prix Ganay and the Coronation Cup, and the racing world eagerly awaited a confrontation between him and his arch-rival Brigadier Gerard, who had beaten him the previous season in the 2,000 Guineas. But Mill Reef was destined never to have the chance to avenge his defeat, for while in training for a second tilt at the Prix de l'Arc de Triomphe he shattered a sesamoid bone, and for a time his life hung in the balance. However, he was successfully saved for stud duties and Mr Mellon generously agreed that Mill Reef should stand at the National Stud at Newmarket, and made six nominations available to British breeders at 11,000 gns for a live foal, which was later increased to £7,500 plus £7,500 for a live foal. Mill Reef quickly established himself as a sire when, in 1978, his son Shirley Heights won the Derby and the Irish Sweeps Derby, in the colours of Lord Halifax, and another son, Acamas, won the French Derby in the colours of Monsieur Marcel Boussac. Acamas was sold as a stallion for the world record sum of £4,000,000 to a group of breeders, who included the Aga Khan and Captain A. D. D. Rogers. Mill Reef headed the sires' list in 1978.

Fairway (Chart 1B—*continued*)

Fairway, the best of the sons of Phalaris, who was bred and owned by the late Lord Derby, trained by Frank Butters and ridden by Tommy Weston, won 12 races and £42,722 in stakes. His victories included the St Leger, Newmarket Stakes, Princess of Wales's Stakes, Eclipse Stakes, Champion Stakes twice, and Jockey Club Cup. By Phalaris out of the Chaucer mare Scapa Flow, dam also of Pharos and the 1,000 Guineas winner

Fair Isle, the success of Fairway at the stud was outstanding. He was head of the list of winning sires in 1936, 1939, 1943, and 1944; second in 1935, 1937, and 1942; and third in 1946; among his best offspring being Fair Trial, Pay Up, Tide-Way, Blue Peter, Watling Street, Kingsway, Garden Path and Honeyway.

Blue Peter, a very fine racehorse, who died at the end of 1957, won the 2,000 Guineas, Derby and Eclipse Stakes, together with £31,963 in stakes for the late Lord Rosebery in 1939. Blue Peter, out of Jiffy, got Ocean Swell, winner of the war-time Derby in 1944 and the Ascot Gold Cup in 1945 for the same distinguished patron of the Turf, and out of Sun Chariot, got Blue Train, unbeaten winner of the Newmarket Stakes for King George VI. He was also the sire of the famous Italian racehorse Botticelli, winner of the Italian Triple Crown, and the Ascot Gold Cup. Botticelli was the sire of many classic winners in Italy.

Watling Street, bred by Lord Derby from the famous mare Ranai, won a war-time Derby; Garden Path, a full sister to Watling Street, won the 2,000 Guineas, which race was also won by Pay Up, in the colours of the late Lord Astor, and Kingsway. Tide-way won the 1,000 Guineas. Honeyway, a brilliant sprinter, and the winner of the July Cup and Victoria Cup, later revealed unsuspected depths of stamina when winning the Champion Stakes. Until his death in 1968 Honeyway stood at the Dalham Hall Stud of his owner, the late Lord Milford; the stud is now in the ownership of his son the Hon. James Philipps. Honeyway was the sire of Honeylight, who was out of Crepuscule, the mother of Crepello, and who won the 1,000 Guineas for the late Sir Victor Sassoon; Dictaway the winner of the French 1,000 Guineas; Great Nephew; and Sunny Way, the sire of Scottish Rifle, winner of the Eclipse Stakes. Great Nephew finished second in the 2,000 Guineas and was then sent to be trained in France, where he won the Prix de Paques, Prix Dollar and Prix du Moulin de Longchamp, bringing the total to £64,317. He headed the sires' list in 1975, largely as a result of the exploits of his brilliant son Grundy, of whom more presently.

Fair Trial, who was top of the winning sires' list in 1950, was the sire of Court Martial, winner of the 2,000 Guineas and Champion Stakes for the late Lord Astor; Lambert Simnel, winner of the 2,000 Guineas; Palestine, who won the 2,000 Guineas and £38,216 in stakes for the late Aga Khan; Festoon, the winner of the 1,000 Guineas and the Coronation Stakes, who was afterwards sold at the 1954 Newmarket December Sales for 40,000 guineas, then a record price for a broodmare; and Petition, the winner of the Eclipse Stakes for the late Sir Alfred Butt. Ki Ming, a further winner of the 2,000 Guineas, was by Ballyogan, a son of Fair Trial.

Court Martial, who was exported to the USA in 1958, headed the winning sires' list in 1956 and 1957, his best winners being Timandra, winner of the French 1,000 Guineas and French Oaks, and Major Portion, winner of the Middle Park Stakes, St James's Palace Stakes, Sussex Stakes and Queen Elizabeth II Stakes, who was bred and owned by Mr H. J. Joel, trained by Ted Leader and ridden by Eph Smith. Major Portion, who was exported to Australia in 1976, was the sire of Soleil, winner of the French 2,000 Guineas. Privy Councillor, a further grandson of Court Martial, won the 2,000 Guineas in 1962. However, it is probable that the best representative of Court Martial in Great Britain or Ireland is the grandson Tower Walk, a high class sprinter and a successful sire of fast two-year-olds.

Palestine was the sire of Pall Mall, who won the 2,000 Guineas for the Queen, and has the sire, in his turn, of Reform and of Sallust, the winner of the Richmond Stakes, Sussex Stakes, Goodwood Mile and Prix du Moulin de Longchamp. Sallust, who is the track record holder for a mile at both Goodwood and Longchamp, was the sire in his first crop of Sanedtki winner of the Prix de la Foret. Reform, who like Sallust was bred and raced by Sir Michael Sobell, won the St James's Palace Stakes, the Sussex Stakes, the Queen Elizabeth II Stakes and the Champion Stakes, by two lengths from Taj Dewan and Royal Palace. Reform's most successful winners are Polygamy, winner of the Oaks; Roi Lear, winner of the French Derby; Admetus, winner of the Washington International Stakes; and Catalpa, the winner of the Ribblesdale Stakes at the Royal meeting at Ascot in record time.

Petition was the leading sire in 1959, due to the victories of his brilliant daughter Petite Etoile. His most successful son on the racecourse was Petingo, who was owned by Captain Marcos Lemos. Petingo, who was the leading two-year-old of 1968, won the Craven Stakes, the St James's Palace Stakes and the Sussex Stakes as a three-year-old and finished second to Sir Ivor in the 2,000 Guineas. Petingo's most promising stud career (he was the leading first crop sire in Europe in 1972) was brought to an early end by his death in 1976. His best winners were English Prince, bred and owned by Mrs V. Hue-Williams, who was the winner of the White Rose Stakes, King Edward VII Stakes and Irish Sweeps Derby, and Fair Salinia, the winner of the Oaks, Irish Guinness Oaks and Yorkshire Oaks. Coup de Feu, a grandson of Petition, owned by Lloyds underwriter Mr T. Sasse and trained by his son Duncan Sasse, won the Eclipse Stakes.

Queen's Hussar, the winner of the Sussex Stakes and a grandson of Petition, headed the sires' list in 1972, due to his magnificent son Brigadier Gerard. He was also the sire of Highclere, who won the 1,000 Guineas and the French Oaks in the colours of the Queen. Highclere was bred at the Sandringham Stud, and was out of Highlight, by Borealis out of Hypericum, who won the 1,000 Guineas of 1946 for King George VI.

Sweet Solera, who won the Oaks and 1,000 Guineas in 1961, was a great granddaughter of Fairway.

Grundy

Bred by the Overbury Stud, by Great Nephew out of Word from Lundy by Worden II out of Lundy Princess by Princely Gift out of Lundy Parrot by Flamingo, Grundy was sold for 11,000 guineas as a yearling to Dr Carlo Vittadini, the owner of industries based in Milan, was trained by Peter Walwyn and ridden by Pat Eddery. He was the winner of £326,421 in stake money. As a two-year-old in 1974, Grundy was unbeaten, his victories including the Champagne Stakes and the Dewhurst Stakes which he won by six lengths. At three years in 1975 he became the champion of Europe, winning the Irish 2,000 Guineas, by 1½ lengths, the Epsom Derby, by two lengths, the Irish Sweeps Derby by two lengths and the King George VI and Queen Elizabeth Stakes. The latter race, in which Grundy finally came out the better of a long drawn out battle with Bustino, was one of the most exciting races ever to have been run on the Turf. Grundy triumphed by three quarters of a length, with Dahlia, who had won the King George VI and Queen Elizabeth Stakes in 1973 and 1974, a further five lengths away in third place. Grundy's time of 2 minutes 26.98 seconds was 2.36 seconds better than the previous record. In his other three starts, Grundy finished second in the Greenham Stakes and the 2,000 Guineas and fourth in the Benson and Hedges Gold Cup. He was retired to the National Stud at Newmarket.

Petite Etoile

Petite Etoile, grey filly by Petition out of Star of Iran by Bois Roussel out of Mah Iran, by Bahram out of Mah Mahal, by Gainsborough out of Mumtaz Mahal by The Tetrarch, one of the best fillies in the history of the Turf, won more money in stakes than any other animal of her sex had previously done, a total of £67,786.

Her victories included the Oaks, 1,000 Guineas, Champion Stakes, Yorkshire Oaks and Sussex Stakes in 1959, when she won all her six races, and the Coronation Cup in 1960, when she beat the previous year's Derby winner Parthia. Her own defeat by Aggressor, in the King George VI and Queen Elizabeth Stakes, was one of the saddest sights to see, particularly as many blamed her jockey and not her stout-hearted self for the humiliation. She also won the Coronation Cup again in 1961.

Petite Etoile was bred by the late Aga Khan, owned by the late Aly Khan, trained by Noel Murless and ridden in all her races (with the exception of the 1,000 Guineas, in which she was ridden by Douglas Smith) by Lester Piggott.

Brigadier Gerard

Brigadier Gerard is without question the outstanding member of the Fairway male line, and is indeed one of the most brilliant horses to have raced in England. He was bred by Mr John Hislop, a racing journalist of distinction, the author of many books on racing and breeding, and a former leading amateur rider, by Queen's Hussar out of La Paiva by Prince Chevalier out of Brazen Molly by Horus out of Molly Adare by Phalaris out of Molly Desmond by Desmond out of Pretty Polly. He was owned by Mrs John Hislop, trained by W. R. Hern, and ridden in all his races by J. Mercer.

He was the winner of seventeen races from eighteen starts,

amassing a total of £243,926 in stakes money. He was unbeaten in his four starts as a two-year-old, including the Middle Park Stakes, which he won by three lengths from Mummy's Pet. As a three-year-old he maintained his unbeaten sequence, winning the 2,000 Guineas, by three lengths from his main rival Mill Reef, the St James's Palace Stakes, the Sussex Stakes by five lengths, the Queen Elizabeth II Stakes and the Champion Stakes.

At four years Brigadier Gerard won the Lockinge Stakes at Newbury, the Westbury Stakes at Sandown Park, the Prince of Wales's Stakes and the Royal Ascot meeting in the time of 2 minutes 6.32 seconds (beating the previous record by 2.28 seconds), the Eclipse Stakes, the King George VI and Queen Elizabeth Stakes by a length and a half, the Queen Elizabeth II Stakes at Ascot by six lengths in the record time of 1 minute 39.96 seconds (a time 2.64 seconds faster than the previous best) and the Champion Stakes for the second time. The only defeat of his career came about in the Benson and Hedges Gold Cup, in which he finished second to Roberto. Brigadier Gerard was retired to the Egerton Stud at Newmarket. Twenty-four shares were sold to selected breeders for £25,000 each, which placed a value on him of £1,000,000.

Pharamond and Sickle

These two full-brothers, the first of whom was placed third in the 2,000 Guineas and the second the winner of the Middle Park Stakes were both exported to the United States. However, the lines descending from both horses have become successfully revived in Great Britain.

Pharamond II was the sire of Menow, who in his turn was responsible for Tom Fool. The latter sired Silly Season, the winner of the Champion Stakes in the colours of Mr Paul Mellon; Tompion, the sire of the French 2,000 Guineas winner Blue Tom; and Buckpasser. Bred and raced by Ogden Phipps, out of Busanda by War Admiral out of Businesslike by Blue Larkspur out of the famous mare La Troienne, Buckpasser was the winner of 25 races from 31 starts, value $1,462,014, including the American Derby, Arlington Classic and Jockey Club Gold Cup. He was syndicated for stud purposes at the then record price of $4,800,000.

Sickle was the sire of Unbreakable, the winner of the Victoria Cup, who in his turn sired Polynesian, the progenitor of Native Dancer, known as the 'Gray Ghost of Sagamore'. Bred and owned by J. G. Vanderbilt out of Geisha by Discovery out of Miyako, Native Dancer won 22 races from 23 starts, value $780,240, including the Preakness Stakes, Belmont Stakes, Arlington Classic, American Derby and Travers Stakes. His only defeat came in the Kentucky Derby, in which he finished second.

Native Dancer was the sire of that fine filly Hula Dancer, the winner of the 1,000 Guineas, the Champion Stakes and Prix Jacques Le Marois, the Prix du Moulin de Longchamp and the Grand Criterium in the colours of Mr P. A. B. Widener. Native Dancer also sired Raise a Native, champion American two-year-old of 1963 and sire of Crowned Prince (sold for a record price of $510,000 as a yearling and the leading two-year-old in England of 1971), and grandsire of Affirmed, winner of the American Triple Crown of the Preakness Stakes, Kentucky Derby and Belmont Stakes, the latter race in 2m.26.8 seconds – a time more than two seconds faster than that recorded by Secretariat. Affirmed was syndicated as a stallion for $17,000,000, a world record figure. Dancer's Image, the winner of the Wood Memorial Stakes, was disqualified after winning the Kentucky Derby and was sire of European sprint champion Lianga. The most important link in the chain of male descent from Sickle was however Dan Cupid, the sire of the great Sea-Bird II.

Sea Bird II

A chesnut colt, bred by his owner Monsieur Jean Ternynck, and foaled in France in 1962, Sea Bird II was by Dan Cupid out of Sicalade by Sicambre out of Marmalade by Maurepas out of Couleur, the dam of Camaree, winner of the 1,000 Guineas. Sea-Bird was the greatest of all the male-line descendants of Phalaris, and in the opinion of many good judges, one of the greatest horses to race on the Turf. Trained by Etienne Pollet and ridden by Pat Glennon, he was the winner of seven races from eight starts in England and France worth the equivalent of £285,000, including the Prix Greffulhe, Prix Lupin, the Derby, by 5 lengths from Meadow Court; the Grand Prix de Saint-

Cloud and the Prix de l'Arc de Triomphe by 5 lengths from Reliance II and Diatome. The latter performance was all the more meritorious since he swerved entering the straight.

The American breeder Mr Dan Galbreath leased Sea-Bird for the sum of $1,350,000 to stand at his Darby Dan Farm in Kentucky. He was repatriated to Europe prior to the 1973 stud season, but died early that year.

His most successful son in the USA was Little Current, winner of the Preakness Stakes. The outstanding member of his progeny was, however, Allez France.

Foaled in 1970, Allez France was a chestnut filly, bred by Bieber-Jacobs Ltd, by Sea Bird II out of Priceless Gem by Hail to Reason out of Searching by War Admiral out of Big Hurry by Black Toney out of La Troienne. She raced in the colours of Daniel Wildenstein and was trained by Angel Penna. She was the winner of 13 races worth the equivalent of £587,474 including the French 1,000 Guineas, French Oaks and Prix de l'Arc de Triomphe, Prix Ganay (twice) and Prix Vermeille. She finished in front of Dahlia on all the nine occasions in which they met.

Thus the male line descending from Phalaris has evolved as the most powerful in the world to-day.

Swynford to Bahram, Brantome, Alycidon and Crepello (Chart 1C)

Swynford sired the filly Keysoe, out of the Oaks winner Keystone II, winner of the St Leger, and the great-granddam of Ballymoss; Sansovino, winner of the Derby and the sire of Sandwich, winner of the St Leger for the late Lord Rosebery, who was out of Gondolette; Ferry, also out of Gondolette, winner of the 1,000 Guineas; and Tranquil winner of the 1,000 Guineas and the St Leger, who was out of Gondolette's daughter Serenissima, dam also of Bosworth and of Selene, the mother Hyperion. All these were owned by the late Lord Derby. Swynford was also the sire of Saucy Sue, winner of the 1,000 Guineas, Oaks and Coronation Stakes for the late Lord Astor; Bettina winner of the 1,000 Guineas; and St Germans, who was out of the famous broodmare Hamoaze, who won the Doncaster Cup and was second in the Derby. St Germans was exported to the United States, and his line descends through The Rhymer, Vertex and the Kentucky Derby winner Lucky

Debonair to Malacate, who defeated Empery in the Irish Sweeps Derby of 1976.

There is no doubt however that the most influential son of Swynford was Blandford, who was bred at the National Stud out of Blanche by White Eagle out of Black Cherry, the dam of Cherry Lass, winner of the 1,000 Guineas and Oaks. Blandford, who was bought by Mr R. C. Dawson as a yearling for 730 guineas, proved a wonderful bargain. He won the Princess of Wales's Stakes and other good races before going to stud, where he sired among many good horses such notable performers as Trigo, Blenhim, Windsor Lad, Bahram, Brantome, Pasch, Umidwar, Udaipur and Campanula. Trigo won the Derby and the St Leger; Pasch, the 2,000 Guineas and Eclipse Stakes for Mr H. E. Morris; Udaipur, bred by the Aga Khan out of Uganda, winner of the French Oaks, was the winner of the Oaks; Campanula won the 1,000 Guineas for her owner, the late Sir George Bullough; Umidwar, also out of Uganda, won the Jockey Club Stakes and Champion Stakes; and Blenheim won the Derby. Umidwar was the sire of Ujiji, winner of the substitute Gold Cup run at Newmarket during the war, and of Norseman, sire of the King George VI and Queen Elizabeth Stakes winner Montaval.

Out of Mah Mahal, a daughter of Gainsborough and Mumtaz Mahal, Blenheim sired Mahmoud, winner of the Derby in the existing record time of 2 minutes 4/5 seconds in 1936. Both horses were owned by the Aga Khan, who eventually sold them to breeders in the United States, Blenheim in 1936 for £45,000 and Mahmoud in 1940 for £20,000. Donatello II, another son of Blenheim, bought by Monsieur E. Esmond for £45,000 and brought to England from Italy in 1938; and Whirlaway, also sired by Blenheim, won the Kentucky Derby, Preakness, Withers, Belmont and Travers Stakes, American Derby and Jockey Club Cup in the United States, together with the world record sum in stakes money at that time of $560,911 (over £100,000).

Donatello II became the sire of Picture Play, winner of a war time substitute 1,000 Guineas for Mr H. J. Joel; two winners of the Ascot Gold Cup in Alycidon and Supertello; and Crepello. Acropolis, an own brother to Alycidon, won the Great Voltigeur Stakes and became the grandsire, through Espresso, twice winner of the Grosser Preis Von Baden-Baden in Germany, of Sagaro. This chesnut horse bred by his owner Mr Gerry Oldham, out of Zambara by Mossborough out of Grischuna and trained in France by F. Boutin, was the winner of ten races and the equivalent of £226,855. Besides winning the Grand Prix de Paris and the Prix du Cadran, he became the only horse in the history of the Turf to win the Ascot Gold Cup three times. He was retired to the National Stud at Newmarket.

A branch of the Blenheim line has been revived in England to produce horses of top class sprinting ability. It descends via Wyndham, Windy City II, Restless Wind and Tumble Wind to Tumbledownwind, winner of the Gimcrack Stakes in the colours of Mr Julian Wilson, racing correspondent to B.B.C. Television.

Windsor Lad and Bahram were, however, the best offspring of Blandford in terms of racing merit. Windsor Lad, after winning the Chester Vase, Newmarket Stakes and Derby for the Maharajah of Rajpipla, was sold by him for £50,000 to Mr Martin Benson, in whose colours he won the St Leger, Coronation Cup and Eclipse Stakes. Altogether Windsor Lad won 10 races and £36,257 and it was a tragic loss to his owner when this fine thoroughbred became sick at the stud and had to be destroyed on humanitarian grounds in 1943. His best son was Windsor Slipper, winner of the Irish 2,000 Guineas, Irish Derby and Irish St Leger in 1942, who was bred by the late Viscount Furness, and whose son, the Champion Stakes winner Solar Slipper, got Pandofell, who won the Ascot Gold Cup, Doncaster Cup and Yorkshire Cup in 1961.

Bahram

Bahram, by Blandford out of Friar's Daughter (dam also of Dastur), by Friar Marcus, was foaled in 1932, bred and owned by the Aga Khan, trained by Frank Butters and ridden by Freddie Fox, and Charlie Smirke. He was very lazy by temperament but a champion racehorse. He was an unbeaten winner of 9 races to the value of £43,086 and was also the first horse to win the Triple Crown of 2,000 Guineas, Derby and St Leger since Rock Sand performed the rare feat in 1903. There can be little doubt that Bahram was about the best thoroughbred to appear on the English Turf between the two World Wars and it was with feelings of dismay, indeed of anger, that British bloodstock breeders learned in 1940 that the Aga Khan had sold his famous horse to an American syndicate for £40,000.

However, before his export to the United States, Bahram got Turkhan, winner of a war-time substitute St Leger; Persian Gulf, half brother to Precipitation, and winner of a war-time substitute Coronation Cup; and Big Game (out of Myrobella, by Tetratema out of Dolabella, a daughter of Gondolette), winner of the 2,000 Guineas and the Champion Stakes of 1942, when carrying the colours of His Majesty King George VI, who had leased the colt from the National Stud where he was bred.

Turkhan achieved a measure of success as a sire of fillies but left no son capable of carrying on his line. Big Game, who headed the sires' list in 1948, was the sire of Ambiguity, winner of the Oaks and the Jockey Club Cup for the late Lord Astor, who was out of the Jockey Club Cup winner Amber Flash; Queenpot, who won the 1,000 Guineas for the late Sir Percy Loraine; and Combat, an unbeaten winner of all his 9 races whose dam was the Oaks winner Commotion, by Mieuxce out of Riot by Colorado out of Lady Juror, by Son-in-Law. Combat in his turn was the sire of Aggressor, who as a five-year-old defeated the famous Petite Etoile, in the 1960 King George VI Queen Elizabeth Stakes by ¾ length, having already defeated the previous year's Derby winner Parthia by 1½ lengths in the Hardwicke Stakes over the same course at Ascot only a month previously; Aggressor being a bay horse by Combat out of Phaetonia, by Nearco out of Phaetusa, by Hyperion, owned by Sir Harold Wernher, trained by J. Gosden at Lewes and ridden by J. Lindley. Aggressor was the sire of that very good filly Dibidale, owned by Mr Nicholas Robinson and trained by Barry Hills, who won the Irish Guinness Oaks.

Persian Gulf was the sire of Parthia, who was out of Lightning, by Hyperion out of Chenille, dam of the St Leger winner Alcide, who won the Derby; Zarathustra, winner of the Ascot Gold Cup and Goodwood Cup; Zabara, out of Samovar by Caerleon, winner of the 1,000 Guineas and Coronation Stakes; Agreement, winner of two Doncaster Cups in the colours of Her Majesty the Queen; Rustam, an own-brother to Zabara, who won the National Breeders' Produce Stakes and was the sire of Talahasse and Double Jump, the leading two-year-olds of their respectives years (1963 and 1964); and Gulf Pearl, winner of the Chester Vase and the sire of Deep Diver, one of the outstanding sprinters of the post-war years, and the winner of nine races, £44,566, including the Nunthorpe Stakes (in record time) and the Prix de l'Abbaye de Long-champ (in which he covered the 5 furlongs in 57 seconds).

Parthia became the sire of Sleeping Partner, who won the Oaks and the Ribblesdale Stakes for the late Lord Rosebery, and of Parthian Glance, who won the Yorkshire Oaks and Park Hill Stakes. He was exported to Japan in 1968. It seems however that the line of Bahram is more likely to survive in England through Persian Gulf than through his other two sons.

Brantome

The Swynford male line has become very strong in France through Brantome, bred and owned by Baron Edouard de Rothschild. Brantome won the French 2,000 Guineas, French St Leger, Prix de l'Arc de Triomphe and Prix du Cadran.

Brantome was the sire of Veiux Manoir, who won the Grand Prix de Paris in the colours of Baron Guy de Rothschild. Vieux Manoir was the sire of Val de Loir, a really outstanding horse bred by M. R. Forget out of Vali, also dam of the Epsom Oaks winner Valoris, the winner of seven races value 1,082,003 francs, including the French Derby, Grand Prix de Deauville and Prix Hocquart; Mourne, bred by the late Mr R. B. Strassburger, out of Ballynash (also dam of Montaval) winner of the Prix Daphnis; Le Haar, winner of the Prix Jean Prat, and third in the French Derby; and San Roman, winner of the Grand Prix de Paris.

Val de Loir was the sire of La Lagune, winner of the Oaks by seven lengths in the colours of Monsieur H. Berlin; Val de l'Orne, winner of the French Derby; Tennyson and Chaparral, both winners of the Grand Prix de Paris; and Lagunette, an own-sister to La Lagune, who won the Irish Guinness Oaks.

Mourne, whose very promising career was cut short by his breaking down in training, was the sire of Snob, who in his turn sired the French Derby winner Goodly. The best horse to be sired by Mourne was however Rock Roi, who was owned by Mrs V. Hue-Williams and trained by Peter Walwyn. Rock Roi was the winner of nine races value £42,582, including the Gordon Stakes at Goodwood, the Goodwood Cup, the Doncaster Cup, the Prix du Cadran and the John Porter Stakes. He also suffered the rare misfortune of twice finishing first the Ascot Gold Cup, only to lose the race on a disqualification on both occasions.

Le Haar was the sire of Niksar, who won the 1965 2,000 Guineas for Mr Wilfrid Harvey, and of Veronese, an outstanding horse in Italy and winner of the Gran Premio di Milano. His most important winner was, however, Exbury, a chesnut horse bred by Baron Guy de Rothschild, out of Greensward, by Mossborough out of Stargrass. Exbury was the winner of eight races and the equivalent of £156,186, being the unbeaten champion of Europe as a four-year-old in 1963. His successes included the Prix de l'Arc de Triomphe, the Coronation Cup, in which he easily defeated the St Leger winner Hethersett, also the Grand Prix de Saint-Cloud and Prix Ganay, defeating Val de Loir on both occasions. Exbury is the sire of Crow, the winner of the St Leger, Prix Eugene Adam and Coronation Cup for Mr Daniel Wildenstein; Example, winner of the Park Hill Stakes and Prix de Royallieu in the colours of Her Majesty the Queen; and Smuggler, bred and owned by Lord Porchester and winner of the Princess of Wales's Stakes, the Gordon Stakes and the Yorkshire Cup and the Henry II Stakes at Sandown Park. The male line of Brantome seems set to continue for many years to come.

Alycidon, Meld, Alcide and Park Top

Alycidon, bred by the late Lord Derby and owned by the present peer, trained by Walter Earl and ridden by Douglas Smith, won the Ascot, Goodwood and Doncaster Cups, the King George VI Stakes, Jockey Club Stakes and £37,206 in stakes money. He was foaled in 1945 and was by Donatello II out of Aurora by Hyperion out of Rose Red by Swynford out of Marchetta by Marco. He was a magnificent racehorse and proved a splendid sire at stud.

His daughter Meld was the finest filly to be seen on a racecourse since Pretty Polly. By Alycidon out of Daily Double by Fair Trial out of Doubleton by Bahram out of Double Life, dam also of Persian Gulf and Precipitation, she was bred and owned by Lady Zia Wernher, trained by Sir Cecil Boyd-Rochfort and ridden in all her races by W. Carr.

She won the Oaks by six lengths, St Leger, 1000 Guineas and Coronation Stakes in 1955, together with £43,051 in stakes. Her final victory in the St Leger, by three-quarters of a length, was a most gallant feat as she was a sick filly at the time and was found to have a high temperature after the race. At stud, when mated to the French Derby and Grand Prix de Paris winner Charlottesville, she bred Charlottown, winner of the Derby and the Coronation Cup.

Another outstanding horse to be sired by Alycidon was the colt Alcide, who was out of King Salmon's daughter Chenille, grandam of Parthia (Persian Gulf-Lightning by Hyperion-Chenille), and like the latter was bred and raced by the late Sir Humphrey de Trafford, trained by Captain Boyd-Rochfort and ridden by Harry Carr. He won the King George VI and Queen Elizabeth Stakes and Winston Churchill Stakes in 1959, and was only beaten by a short head in the Ascot Gold Cup and Jockey Club Cup. In the previous year he had won the St Leger by 8 lengths, the Great Voltigear Stakes and the Derby Trial Stakes by 12 lengths and the Chester Vase. He had, most unfortunately, to be scratched from the Derby owing to temporary indisposition. It was hoped that he would prove the next link in the great male line of Isonomy, but unfortunately he proved a disappointing sire. However he was responsible for Oncidium, who won the Coronation Cup for Lord Howard de Walden and became a very successful stallion in New Zealand.

Alycidon was also the sire of Homeward Bound, who won the Oaks and the Ribblesdale Stakes in the colours of the late Sir Foster Robinson; the Ascot Gold Cup winner, Twilight Alley, who was out of Crepuscule, the dam of Crepello, winner of the 2,000 Guineas and Derby, and of Honeylight, winner of the 1,000 Guineas; and Kalydon, winner of the Oxfordshire Stakes and the sire of that very game and high class mare Park Top.

The last named mare was bred by Mrs L. Scott out of Nellie Park, by Arctic Prince out of Oola Hills by Denturius. Park Top was secured as a yearling for a mere 500 guineas by the Duke of Devonshire, who had previously owned her dam. She was trained by the late Bernard Van Cutsem and partnered in her races by Lester Piggott and Willie Carson. Park Top was given the accolade of Horse of the Year in 1969 as a five-year-old during which year she won the King George VI and Queen Elizabeth Stakes, the Coronation Cup and the Hardwicke Stakes and was second in the Prix de l'Arc de Triomphe, Eclipse Stakes and Champion Stakes. She had previously won the Ribblesdale Stakes as a three-year-old and was to win the Cumberland Lodge Stakes at six years, during her final racing season. In all, Park Top won the equivalent of £137,500 in England and France, which made her, at that time, the second highest stakes winning mare in European Turf history.

Crepello

Crepello, however, seems likely to prove the strongest link in the Isonomy male line. One of the outstanding horses to race since the war, he was bred and owned by the late Sir Victor Sassoon, by Donatello II out of Crepuscule, by Mieuxce out of Red Sunset by Solario out of Dulce II by Asterus out of Dorina. He was trained by Sir Noel Murless and ridden in all his races by Lester Piggott.

Crepello raced only five times, winning three races value £34,201, the Dewhurst Stakes, the 2,000 Guineas and the Derby, in which he defeated Ballymoss by a length and a half. In his only other starts he was second in the Windsor Castle Stakes and fourth in the Middle Park Stakes. Unfortunately he broke down in training shortly before the St Leger and could not be raced again.

Crepello, who died in 1974, headed the sires' list in 1969, occupying third place in 1967 and 1973. His most successful son was undoubtedly Busted, who was unbeaten as a four-year-old in 1967, winning the Coronation Stakes at Sandown Park, the Eclipse Stakes, the King George VI and Queen Elizabeth Stakes by three lengths from the Hardwicke Stakes winner Salvo and the Doncaster St Leger and Irish Sweeps Derby winner Ribocco, and the Prix Henry Foy. Busted, who was bred and owned by Mr Stanhope Joel, won a total of £58,937.

At stud Busted is the sire of Bustino, who won five races, value £145,858 for Lady Beaverbrook, including the Derby Trial Stakes, the Great Voltigeur Stakes, the St Leger, and the Cornation Cup (in the record time of 2 m 33.31 sec.). Bustino was also second to Grundy in one of the most exciting finishes ever to be seen for the King George VI and Queen Elizabeth Stakes, which was won in the record time of 2 minutes 26.98 seconds. Busted was also responsible for Weaver's Hall, the winner of the Irish Sweeps Derby, and for Busaca, winner of the Yorkshire Oaks.

In addition to Busted, Crepello is the sire of Mysterious, out of Hill Shade by Hillary II, who won the 1,000 Guineas Oaks and Yorkshire Oaks for Mr George Pope, junior; Caergwrle who won the 1,000 Guineas for Lady Murless and was trained by her husband; Crepellana, winner of the French Oaks; Celina, winner of the Irish Guinness Oaks; and Soderini, winner of the Hardwicke Stakes.

Sunstar to Buchan and Craig-an-Eran (Chart 2—continued)

Sunstar had two good sons in Buchan and Craig-an-Eran, who were both owned by Lord Astor and trained by Alec Taylor. After being beaten by a neck in the 2,000 Guineas, Buchan, who was out of Sceptre's granddaughter Hamoaze, ran second in the Derby and third in the St Leger, winning the Chester Vase, Princess of Wales's Stakes, Eclipse Stakes twice, Champion Stakes, and Doncaster Cup, and he also finished first in the Ascot Gold Cup but was disqualified. Craig-an-Eran, who was out of Sceptre's daughter Maid of the Mist, won the 2,000 Guineas and the Eclipse Stakes and only lost the Derby by a neck.

The best of the offspring of Buchan was a filly out of Popingaol called Book Law, also owned by Lord Astor and trained by Alec Taylor. This beautiful filly won the St Leger, Coronation Stakes, and Jockey Club Stakes, finishing second in the Oaks, beaten only by a head, and second in the 1,000 Guineas. Her stake total was £31,875.

The best of the offspring of Craig-an-Eran were April the Fifth, who won the Derby for Mr Tom Walls, the actor, Mon Talisman, who won the French Derby and Prix de l'Arc de Triomphe, and Admiral Drake, who won the Grand Prix de Paris and who was out of Plucky Liege, dam also of Sir Gallahad III and Bois Roussel. The male line of Sunstar is having some difficulty in holding its own at the moment, although Monsieur l'Amiral, a son of Admiral Drake, won the

Cesarewitch, Queen Alexandra Stakes, and Goodwood Cup, and Phil Drake, another son of Admiral Drake, the Derby and Grand Prix de Paris, while Clairvoyant, a son of Talisman, won the Grand Prix de Paris and the French Derby.

St Simon to Tulyar, Sicambre, Round Table, Ribot and Worden 11
(Chart 2 *continued*)

St Simon, as already noted, was probably the greatest thoroughbred sire of all time, but, after only two generations, the male lines descending from him virtually ceased to produce any outstanding racehorses in England, and many years went by without any animal tracing back in tail male line to St Simon, winning one of the English classic races. However, with the reintroduction of the blood from France, Italy and America, the St Simon sire line has now revived in this country.

The two most prominent chains were formerly through Florizel II, Doricles, Consols and Massine, winner of the Ascot Gold Cup and Prix de l'Arc de Triomphe, to Mieuxce, winner of the French Derby and Grand Prix de Paris in 1936 and sire of Commotion, winner of a wartime substitute Oaks; (Massine also got Maravedis, the sire of Souverain, winner of the Grand Prix de Paris, French St Leger, King George VI Stakes and Ascot Gold Cup); and through Chaucer, a son of St Simon and Canterbury Pilgrim, dam also of Swynford.

Chaucer was a very good sire of broodmares and fillies, being responsible for the 1,000 Guineas winners Canyon and Pillion (the former being the dam of the 2,000 Guineas winner Colorado). He sired one outstanding son in Stedfast, winner of the Hardwicke Stakes, Jockey Club Stakes, Champion Stakes and Coronation Cup, who finished second to Sunstar in the 2,000 Guineas and Derby and was only beaten by a head by Prince Palatine in the Eclipse Stakes. Stedfast was the sire of Brownhylda, winner of the Oaks. The male line of Chaucer was however, carried on by another of his sons, Prince Chimay, winner of the Jockey Club Stakes. Prince Chimay's son Vatout won the French 2,000 Guineas and sired Atout Maitre, who won the Jockey Club Cup, and Vatellor. The last named horse sired Pearl Diver, winner of the Derby for Baron Geoffrey de Waldner, whose dam was the famous French racing mare Pearl Cap; My Love, jointly owned by the late Aga Khan and the late

Monsieur Leon Volterra, winner of the Derby and Grand Prix de Paris; Nikellora, winner of the French 1,000 Guineas, French Oaks and Prix de l'Arc de Triomphe; and Felix II, winner of the Jockey Club Cup. Vatout's most successful son was, however, Bois Roussel, winner of the 1938 English Derby for the late Hon Peter Beatty. Bois Roussel was the sire of Tehran, who won a war-time St Leger, and who in turn got Tulyar, and finished at the top of the list of winning sires in 1952, as well as Mystery IX, winner of the Eclipse Stakes, and Tabriz, whose son Taboun won the 2,000 Guineas. Other sons of Bois Roussel were Migoli, who won the Eclipse Stakes, the Champion Stakes and the Prix de l'Arc de Triomphe for the late Aga Khan, Ridge Wood, who won the St Leger. Migoli was the sire of Gallant Man, winner of the Belmont Stakes in the United States of America and a successful sire there. Bois Roussel also proved himself to be a brilliant sire of brood-mares, including the dams of St Paddy, Petite Etoile and Cantelo.

Tulyar

It was Tulyar, however, who was the oustanding male line descendant of Chaucer. He was a brown colt, the first foal of his dam, by Tehran out of Neocracy, by Nearco. Foaled in 1949, bred and owned by the Aga Khan, trained by Marcus Marsh, and ridden by Charlie Smirke, Tulyar won two Nursery Stakes, each over a mile, under top-weight as a two-year-old, and in the following year won the Henry VIII Stakes at Hurst Park, the Ormonde Stakes at Chester, the Derby Trial Stakes at Lingfield, the Derby at Epsom, the King George VI and Queen Elizabeth Stakes at Ascot, the Eclipse Stakes at Sandown Park and the St Leger at Doncaster, being unbeaten as a three-year-old, when his stake total for the seven races was £75,173 and his overall winnings £76,417, then a record for the English Turf. At the end of his three-year-old career, the late Aga Khan sold Tulyar to the Eire Government for the world record price for a thoroughbred of £250,000 to stand at the Irish National Stud. Unfortunately Tulyar proved something of a disappointment as a stallion and was sold to the United States in 1956. Both the Chaucer and Florizel II branches of the St Simon line are having a struggle to hold their own at present.

Persimmon to Sicambre and Round Table (Chart 2 *continued*)

Persimmon's great grandson Prince Rose (by Rose Prince, by Prince Palatine) founded a sire line that has been prominent in England, Ireland, France and the United States. His line was propagated by Prince Chevalier, Prince Bio and Princequillo.

Prince Chevalier, out of Chevalerie, by Abbot's Speed, was the winner of the French Derby and was second in the Grand Prix de Paris, beaten a head by Souverain, and in the Prix de l'Arc de Triomphe, beaten a neck by Caracalla II. He was imported into England in 1947 and was the sire of Arctic Prince, winner of the Derby for the late Mr Joseph McGrath and sire of Arctic Explorer, winner of the Eclipse Stakes; Soltikoff, winner of the Prix de l'Arc de Triomphe; Charlottesville, who was out of Noorani, the dam of the Ascot Gold Cup winner Sheshoon, who won the French Derby and Grand Prix de Paris for the late Aga Khan; Doutelle, bred and owned by Her Majesty the Queen, out of Above Board, the winner of the Yorkshire Oaks, who won the John Porter Stakes; Court Harwell, winner of the Oxfordshire Stakes at Newbury; and Pirate King, winner of the St James's Palace Stakes and the sire of Random Shot, who was awarded the Ascot Gold Cup on the disqualification of Rock Roi. Prince Chevalier was also sire of the dam of Brigadier Gerard.

Charlottesville was the leading sire of 1966, the year in which his son Charlottown, who was out of Meld, winner of the 1,000 Guineas, Oaks and St Leger, triumphed in the Derby. Charlottown also won the Coronation Cup and John Porter Stakes as a four-year-old. Charlottesville was also the sire of Carlemont, winner of the Sussex Stakes and of Gaia, winner of the Irish Guinness Oaks. Court Harwell was responsible for Meadow Court, owned by Mr G. M. Bell who won the King George VI and Queen Elizabeth Stakes and the Irish Sweeps Derby. Doutelle was the sire of Pretendre, who was second to Charlottown in the Derby and who sired Canonero II, the winner of the Kentucky Derby and Preakness Stakes; and of Canisbay, who won the Eclipse Stakes in the colours of Her Majesty and became a very successful sire in Italy. His son Weimar was the champion horse of his year in Italy, winning the Gran Premio d'Italia, Gran Premio di Milano, Gran Premio del Jockey Club and Italian St Leger. It is however through Orange Bay, another son of Canisbay, that the line of Prince Chevalier seems likely to survive in England. Owned by Dr Carlo Vittadini, he was the winner of the Italian Derby, the Hardwicke Stakes, the Jockey Club Stakes and the Cumberland Lodge Stakes and was beaten a short head by The Minstrel in the King George VI and Queen Elizabeth Stakes. He retired to stud in England in 1978.

Prince Bio, who won the French 2,000 Guineas, headed the list of winning sires in France in 1951. He was the sire of Northern Light II (Grand Prix de Paris and French Derby) and Rose Royale II, who won the 1,000 Guineas and Champion Stakes. His son Prince Taj, who headed the sires' list in France in 1967 and 1968, was the sire of Astec (French Derby). He was also the sire of Taj Dewan, winner of the Prix Ganay and beaten a short head by Royal Palace in both the 2,000 Guineas and the Eclipse Stakes.

Sicambre, however, was the outstanding son of Prince Bio, both on the racecourse and at stud. Bred by the late M. Jean Stern, out of Sif by Rialot-Suavita, he was the winner of the Grand Criterium at two years and the French Derby and Grand Prix de Paris at three years. His most successful progeny were Sicarelle, the winner of the Oaks for Madame Suzy Volterra; Celtic Ash, winner of the Belmont Stakes and sire of the St Leger winner Athens Wood; Diatome, who won the Washington International Stakes for Baron Guy de Rothschild, and whose son Steel Pulse won the Irish Sweeps Derby; Phaeton, winner of the Grand Prix de Paris and the sire of Vitiges, winner of the Champion Stakes; Roi Dagobert, the champion two-year-old in France; Tiziano, winner of the Italian St Leger and sire of the Epsom Oaks winner Valoris, whose dam Vali was the dam of Val de Loir; and Shantung. The last named horse, who won the Prix la Rochette and was third in the Derby, was the leading sire in Europe in 1969. He was responsible for Full Dress II, the winner of the 1,000 Guineas for Mr R. B. Moller; Ginevra, the winner of the Oaks, who was sold at the Newmarket December Sales for the then record sum, for a filly out of training, of 106,000 guineas; Lacquer, winner of the Irish 1,000 Guineas; and Saraca, winner of the Prix Vermeille.

Princequillo, who won the American Jockey Club Gold Cup, was a leading stallion in America. He was the sire of

Tambourine II, who was out of La Mirambule, the dam of Nasram II, winner of the King George VI and Queen Elizabeth Stakes, and who won the very first running of the Irish Sweeps Derby in 1962; and Prince John, whose son Stage Door Johnny won the Belmont Stakes and has sired some horses of near top class ability in England. Princequillo's outstanding son was, however, Round Table.

Bred at the Claiborne Stud, out of Knight's Daughter by Sir Cosmo out of Feola, the dam of the 1,000 Guineas winner Hypericum, Round Table won over $1,000,000, including the American Derby and Hollywood Gold Cup. He was voted 'Horse of the Year' in America and gained the accolade of 'champion grass horse' in three successive years. At stud he is the sire of Baldric II, the winner of the 2,000 Guineas and the Champion Stakes, and himself the sire of Irish Ball (Irish Sweeps Derby) and Favoletta (Irish 1,000 Guineas); Artaius, winner of the Eclipse Stakes and the Sussex Stakes, who was syndicated as a stallion in Ireland in 1977 for £55,000 per share; Apalachee, the champion two-year-old in England and Ireland in 1973; and Targowice, the champion two-year-old of his year in France.

Rabelais to Ribot and Worden II

Rabelais, the winner of the Goodwood Cup, was exported to France, where he sired Durbar, the winner of the English Derby for Mr H. Duryea; Biribi, the winner of the Prix de l'Arc de Triomphe and the sire of Le Pacha, winner of the Grand Prix de Paris, French Derby, French St Leger and Prix de l'Arc de Triomphe; Rialto, winner of the Grand International d'Ostend; and Havresac II, sire of Cavaliere d'Arpino, winner of the Gran Premio di Milano, and considered by his owner, the late Signor Federico Tesio, to have been the best horse that he ever owned.

The line of Rialto was carried on through his son Wild Risk, the leading French stallion of 1961 who, like his sire, was bred by the late Monsieur Jean Couturié. Wild Risk was the sire of Le Fabuleux, the winner of the French Derby and the sire of Meneval, winner of the Irish St Leger and the Hardwicke Stakes; Vimy, the winner of the King George VI and Queen Elizabeth Stakes for M. Pierre Wertheimer and the sire of

Khalkis, winner of the Eclipse Stakes; Balto, winner of the Grand Prix de Paris and Ascot Gold Cup; and Worden II. The last named horse, bred by his owner Mr R. B. Strassburger, out of Sans Tares by Sind out of Tara, the dam of Norseman, won six races in France, Italy and America, including the Washington International Stakes, the Premio Roma, and Prix du Conseil Municipal, and was twice placed third in the King George VI and Queen Elizabeth Stakes. After standing for six seasons in France, he was imported into England in 1960. Worden II's most successful progeny were Bon Mot III, the winner of the Prix de l'Arc de Triomphe and the sire of Lassalle, winner of the Ascot Gold Cup and Prix du Cadran in the same year; Armistice, winner of the Grand Prix de Paris; Just Great, winner of the Great Voltigeur Stakes, and Karabas, the winner of eleven races and the equivalent of £103,387 including the Washington International Stakes, the Hardwicke Stakes and the Prix du Conseil Municipal. Worden II was also the great grandsire, through Marino and Carvin, of that very high class filly Pawneese, raced in the colours of M. Daniel Wildenstein, Pawneese won six races and the equivalent of £237,821 including the Epsom Oaks, the French Oaks and the King George VI and Queen Elizabeth Stakes; Pawneese's winnings in England alone amounted to £131,626, a total that no filly with the exception of Dahlia has equalled in that country. Worden II was also a successful sire of broodmares, being the maternal grandsire of Grundy, Wollow and Juliette Marny.

Cavaliere d'Arpino was the sire of Traghetto, the winner of the Italian 2,000 Guineas and Derby, and the sire of Nuccio, winner of the Coronation Cup and the Prix de l'Arc de Triomphe; and of Bellini, the winner of the Italian Derby and St Leger. The latter's son Tenerani was the winner of the Italian Derby, the Queen Elizabeth Stakes and the Goodwood Cup. He was leased as a stallion by the English National Stud where he stayed until his return to Italy in 1960. Tenerani sired Fighting Charlie, twice winner of the Ascot Gold Cup, and the Milan Gold Cup winner Tissot, who sired Ortis, winner of the Italian Derby and the Hardwicke Stakes. Tenerani's greatest achievement, however, was to be the progenitor of the mighty Ribot.

Ribot

In the opinion of many good judges, Ribot was the greatest horse to have raced in the entire history of the Turf. Bred by the late Signor Federico Tesio, by Tenerani out of the Romanella by El Greco out of Barbara Burrini by Papyrus out of Bucolic by Buchan out of Volcanic, Tenerani raced in the colours of Signor Tesio's partner, the Marchese Mario Incisa della Rocchetta, was trained by Ugo Penco and ridden by Enrico Camici. He was the unbeaten winner of sixteen races in Italy, France and England, from two to four years, including the Gran Criterium, Premio del Jockey Club, defeating Norman by 15 lengths, the Gran Premio di Milano, by eight lengths from Tissot, the King George VI and Queen Elizabeth Stakes and the Prix de l'Arc de Triomphe, twice.

Ribot stood his first stud season at Lord Derby's Woodland Stud at Newmarket, being returned to Italy at the end of the season. In 1960 he was leased for a five year term to Mr J. W. Galbreath, for the sum of $1,350,000 to stand at his Darby Dan Farm in Kentucky. When the lease expired, no satisfactory arrangement could be made for his return to Italy, and he remained in Kentucky until his death in 1973.

Ribot headed the list of sires in Great Britain and Ireland in 1963, 1967 and 1968, and was in second place in 1972. In Europe his most successful son was Ragusa, bred by Mr H. Guggenheim and owned by Mr J. R. Mullion, trained by Paddy Prendergast and ridden by Garnet Bougoure. He was the winner of seven races, value £146,650, including the Irish Sweeps Derby, the Doncaster St Leger, the King George VI and Queen Elizabeth Stakes by three lengths from Miralgo, and the Eclipse Stakes. Ragusa's death in 1973 was a great blow to the bloodstock breeding industry since he was the sire of Morston, the winner of the Derby that year. Owned and trained by Mr A. M. Budgett, Morston was out of Windmill Girl, also the dam of the Derby winner Blakeney. Ragusa also sired Ragstone, the winner of the Ascot Gold Cup and the most successful racehorse to be owned by the late Duke of Norfolk; Ballymore, winner of the Irish 2,000 Guineas and the sire of More So (Irish 1,000 Guineas); and Caliban, the winner of the Coronation Cup, defeating Park Top.

Ribot was also the sire of the full brothers Ribocco and

Ribero, both out of Libra, by Hyperion-Weighbridge; both owned by the late Mr C. W. Engelhard, and both winners of the Irish Sweeps Derby and Doncaster St Leger; Boucher, another winner of the St Leger, owned by Mr Ogden Phipps; Long Look, winner of the Oaks; Molvedo, winner of the Grand Prix de Deauville and Prix de l'Arc de Triomphe; and Prince Royal II, also winner of the Prix de l'Arc de Triomphe. Ribot was also the grandsire of Hurry Harriet, who inflicted a surprise defeat on Allez France in the Champion Stakes at 33 to 1.

In America, Ribot sired Graustark, the sire of the French Derby winner Caracolero; Arts and Letters, owned by Mr Paul Mellon, the horse of the year in America and the winner of 23 races value $262,404, including the Belmont, Blue Grass and Woodward Stakes; and Tom Rolfe, who was the sire of Run the Gantlet and Droll Role, stakes winners of the Washington International Stakes, and Hoist the Flag, who would have been unbeaten as a two-year-old in America, but for a disqualification in the Group 1 Champagne Stakes. Hoist the Flag fractured his off hind pastern and could not be trained as a four-year-old. He is the sire of Alleged, who was owned by a syndicate of breeders, headed by Robert Sangster, the chairman of Vernons Pools. Alleged was rated top of the three-year-old Free Handicap in 1977 in which he won six races, worth the equivalent of £170,822, including the Great Voltigeur Stakes and the Prix de l'Arc de Triomphe. His only defeat came in the St Leger in which he finished second to Dunfermline, with whom he was to reverse the placings in the Prix de l'Arc de Triomphe. As a four-year-old he won all his three races, including the Prix de l'Arc de Triomphe for the second time. He was syndicated as a stallion for $16,000,000.

The future of the St Simon line, now successfully revived in Great Britain, looks assured for many years to come.

The Tetrarch to King Salmon (Chart 3—continued)

The Tetrarch was bought as a yearling for 1,300 guineas by Major Dermot McCalmont and created a sensation in the racing world by his succession of victories as a two-year-old in 1913, when he was the unbeaten winner of 7 races and £11,336 in stakes. But during the winter and again in the following spring The Tetrarch rapped his off fore fetlock joint and never appeared on a race-course again. He was nicknamed 'The Rocking Horse' because of his spotted grey coat covered with white patches and he was altogether a phenomenal horse and a great favourite with the public.

At stud he sired Tetratema, winner of the 2,000 Guineas; Caligula, Polemarch and Salmon Trout, who all won the St Leger; and Mumtaz Mahal, 'the flying filly, who also created a sensation when she won the Queen Mary Stakes at Ascot very easily by ten lengths in 1923.

Royal Ministrel, winner of the Eclipse Stakes, and Mr Jinks, winner of the 2,000 Guineas; Tiffin, an unbeaten winner of eight races for the late Lord Ellesmere; Four Course, winner of the 1,000 Guineas; and Myrobella, who was leased from the National Stud by the late Lord Lonsdale and later became the dam of Big Game, were the best of the progeny of Tetratema. There is also a line of Tetratema, extant in France, which traces through Bacteriophage, Teleferique and Alizier to Tapalque, winner of the French Derby.

Salmon Trout sired King Salmon, winner of the Eclipse Stakes in record time and the Coronation Cup, who was exported to Brazil in 1943 after first getting Herringbone, winner of the 1,000 Guineas and war-time substitute St Leger in 1943.

The Castrel branch of the Herod male line, which at one time it seemed that The Tetrarch had succeeded in reviving again, appears to have faded out in England.

Bruleur to Djebel (Chart 3—continued)

Bruleur kept the Herod line alive in France. One of his sons, Ksar, won the French Derby, French St Leger and Prix de l'Arc de Triomphe, twice, and another, Hotweed, the French Derby and Grand Prix de Paris. His daughter Brulette won the English Oaks, Goodwood Cup and Jockey Club Cup.

Ksar in turn produced Tourbillon, winner of the French Derby, and Le Ksar, winner of the English 2,000 Guineas. Tourbillon proved to be one of the most successful sires in the history of the French Turf, and it is largely due to him that the male line of Herod has survived to-day. For eleven consecutive years, he was in the top four in the French sires' list, being leading sire on four occasions.

Owing to the fact that Tourbillon's pedigree contained horses of doubtful origin, he and his progeny were barred from the General Stud Book by the terms of the Jersey Act (see page 000). So successful, however, was Tourbillon as a stallion, that he was largely responsible for the decision, taken in 1949, to repeal the act.

Tourbillon was raced by Monsieur Marcel Boussac and stood at the latter's stud, until his death in 1954. He was the sire of Djebel, who was out of Loika by Gay Crusader, and won the English substitute 2,000 Guineas and Prix de l'Arc de Triomphe, twice; Caracalla II, out of the great broodmare Astronomie, who was never beaten and who won the Ascot Gold Cup, Grand Prix de Paris, Prix de l'Arc de Triomphe and French St Leger; Coaraze, the winner of the French Derby, who was out of that wonderful mare Corrida (twice winner of the Prix de l'Arc de Triomphe), and who became a successful sire in Brazil; Cillas, winner of the French Derby; Turmoil II, winner of the Prix du Cadran, and the sire of Popof, winner of the Grand Prix de Paris; Goya II, out of the famous broodmare Zariba, winner of the St James's Palace Stakes and Braunes Band at Munich; Ambiorix, winner of the Grand Criterium and a very successful stallion in the United States; and Tornado, winner of the Prix Lupin. All these horses with the exception of Tornado (who belonged to Monsieur Jean Couturié) and Turmoil II, were the property of Monsieur Boussac.

Goya II was the sire of Asmena, out of Astronomie (the dam of Caracalla II) who won the Oaks; the French Derby winners Good Luck and Sandjar; and Goyama, winner of the Coronation Cup at Epsom and grandsire of Nelcius, winner of the French Derby. Tornado was the sire of Aquino II, winner of the Ascot Gold Cup and champion sire in Poland; Tahiti (French Oaks); Tyrone (French 2,000 Guineas) and Thymus (French 2,000 Guineas). He was also grandsire of Tropique (Eclipse and Coronation Cup), the sire in his turn of Paveh (Irish 2,000 Guineas and Sussex Stakes).

Djebel to Blakeney, Levmoss and Klairon (Chart 3—*continued*)
Djebel proved, however, to be by far the most successful of Tourbillon's sons at stud. By the time he died, in 1958, he had headed the French sires' list three times. Djebel sired the

VAGUELY NOBLE

NIJINSKY

BRIGADIER GERARD

Courtesy: W. W. Rouch & Co. Ltd.

MILL REEF

Courtesy: W. W. Rouch & Co. Ltd.

outstanding filly Coronation V, winner of the French 1,000 Guineas and the Prix de l'Arc de Triomphe. Coronation V represented an example of very close inbreeding to Tourbillon, since her dam, Esmeralda, was a daughter of that stallion. But although a brilliant racemare, she never succeeded in breeding a single foal when she was retired to stud.

Djebel also sired Arbar, the winner of the King George VI Stakes and Ascot Gold Cup, who was out of Astronomie; Galcador, who was out of Pharyva by Pharos, winner of the Derby; Argur, winner of the Eclipse Stakes and the champion sire in the Argentine; and Djeddah, winner of the Eclipse Stakes and Champion Stakes, and a successful stallion in the United States; all of whom were owned by Monsieur Boussac. Djebel was also the sire of My Babu, out of the famous broodmare Perfume II, who won the 2,000 Guineas in record time; and High Lupus, winner of the Irish 2,000 Guineas and the Champion Stakes.

My Babu was responsible for Our Babu, winner of the 2,000 Guineas and for Primera, winner of the Princess of Wales's Stakes. The last named was the sire of that fine mare Aunt Edith, who was bred by her owner, Colonel B. Hornung, from Fair Edith, by Hyperion, who was a granddaughter of Lord Rosebery's 1,000 Guineas winner Plack. Aunt Edith was successful in the King George VI and Queen Elizabeth Stakes. Primera was also the sire of Lupe, who won the Oaks and the Coronation Cup in the colours of Mrs Stanhope Joel, and of Attica Meli, the winner of the Yorkshire Oaks and Park Hill Stakes.

Hugh Lupus was the sire of Hethersett, who was out of the good racemare Bridge Elect, and who won the St Leger, Great Voltigeur Stakes and Brighton Derby Trial Stakes for his breeder, the late Major L. B. Holliday; and of Pourparler, winner of the 1,000 Guineas, who was bred by her owner, the late Beatrice, Lady Granard, out of Review, by Panorama, also the dam of the 1,000 Guineas winner Fleet.

Hethersett was the sire of Blakeney, who was out of Windmill Girl, by Hornbeam (also the dam of Derby winner Morston), who won the Derby; and of Highest Hopes, the champion filly of her year in Europe. Blakeney was in his turn sire of Juliette Marny, who won the Oaks and Irish Guinness Oaks for the Hon. James Morrison, also of Julio Mariner, her own brother, who won the St Leger.

Successful attempts to revive the male line of Herod in England and Ireland have been made through two grandsons of Djebel; Klairon and Le Levanstell. Klairon, the winner of the French 2,000 Guineas, was imported into England in 1962. He was the sire of Monade, winner of the Oaks; Shangamuzo, winner of the Ascot Gold Cup and Doncaster Cup; Lorenzaccio, winner of the Champion Stakes, defeating Nijinsky, and Luthier, winner of the Prix Jacques le Marois. Luthier, son of the famous mare Flute Enchantee, was champion sire in France in 1976, his earnings that season having surpassed the previous earnings of any other stallion in the history of the French thoroughbred breeding. His best winners are Riverqueen, winner of the French 1,000 Guineas, Galiani (Grand Prix de Paris) and Montcontour, winner of the Hardwicke Stakes. Another of his sons, Ashmore, twice winner of the Grand Prix de Deauville, was imported to stand at stud in Ireland.

Le Levanstell won the Queen Elizabeth II Stakes at Ascot, defeating the brilliant filly Petita Etoile. His most successful son was Levmoss, bred by Mr Joseph McGrath out of Feemoss, by Ballymoss out of Feevagh, winner of the Yorkshire Oaks. Levmoss won the Ascot Gold Cup, the Prix du Cadran and the Prix de l'Arc de Triomphe and the equivalent of £143,483 in stake money. Levmoss's own-sister Sweet Mimosa won the French Oaks. Le Levanstell also sired My Swallow, the champion two-year-old of 1970; Allangrange, winner of the Irish St Leger and sire of Miralla (Irish 1,000 Guineas); and Sarah Siddons, winner of the Irish 1,000 Guineas and Yorkshire Oaks. Le Levanstell died in 1975.

Although this is strictly speaking a French sire line, it has been purposely included in this summary, in view of the fact that many winners of important races in England and Ireland belong to it; because successful attempts have been made to revive it in England and Ireland; and because it may well prove to be the only enduring male stirp of Herod left in this part of the world.

Hurry On to Precipitation (Chart 4— continued)

Hurry On, the sole surviving link connecting with the male lines of Matchem, was bred by Mr W. Murland and bought as a yearling for 500 guineas by Mr Fred Darling, who passed him on to Mr James Buchanan, later Lord Woolavington. Trained by Fred Darling at Beckhampton and ridden by Joe Childs, he was the unbeaten winner of six races, including the substitute St Leger and Jockey Club Cup in 1916.

Hurry On was an exceptionally big and powerful horse, standing just 17 hands, and before he died in 1936 he had got Captain Cuttle, Coronach, Call Boy, Toboggan, Pennycomequick, Plack, Cresta Run and Precipitation.

Captain Cuttle won the Derby in record time and sired Scuttle, winner of the 1,000 Guineas for King George V in 1928. Coronach, bred and owned by Lord Woolavington, trained by Fred Darling and ridden by Joe Childs, won the Derby in a canter by 5 lengths, the St Leger in the record time of 3 minutes 13/5 seconds, the Eclipse Stakes, Coronation Cup, Hardwicke Stakes and £48,224, and sired that fine mare Corrida, winner of the equivalent of over £47,000 in stakes, mostly on the continent, who subsequently became the dam of the French Derby winner Coaraze. Call Boy won the Derby, and, on the death of his owner, was sold to his brother-in-law for a sum not disclosed, but rumoured to have been about £60,000. Toboggan won the Oaks, Coronation Stakes and Jockey Club Stakes, and when mated to Hyperion produced Hydroplane, dam of the American wonder horse Citation. Pennycomequick, who also won the Oaks, was bred and owned by the late Lord Astor, and was out of Plymstock, a daughter of Polymelus and the 1,000 Guineas winner Winkipop. Plack, who won the 1,000 Guineas and Jockey Club Cup, was owned by the late Lord Rosebery. She became the dam of Afterthought, winner of the Jockey Club Cup and grandam of that fine mare Aunt Edith, winner of the King George VI and Queen Elizabeth Stakes. Cresta Run, who won the 1,000 Guineas, was owned by Lt-Col. Giles Loder, and was a great-great granddaughter of Admiration, the dam of Pretty Polly.

Precipitation, who was out of Double Life, dam also of Persian Gulf, won the Jockey Club Stakes and Ascot Gold Cup. He sired Chamossaire, winner of the substitute St Leger run at

York in 1945, who was out of Snowberry, by Cameronian-Myrobella, and who sired the St Leger winner Cambremer and that very good horse Santa Claus; Airborne, winner of the first post-war Derby run at Epsom and St Leger run at Doncaster in 1946, who was out of Bouquet, by Buchan-Hellespont; Supreme Court, winner of the King George VI and Queen Elizabeth Stakes in 1951 in record time for the course, together with £36,950 in stakes, for his owner Mrs T. Lilley (now Mrs V. Hue-Williams), when he was trained by E. Williams and ridden by C. Elliott. He was by Persian Gulf or Precipitation (almost certainly the latter) out of Forecourt, by Fair Trial out of Overture, by Dastur out of Overmantle, by Apron (a son of Son-in-Law) out of Arabella, by Buchan out of Polly Flinders, by Polymelus out of the famous mare Pretty Polly. Supreme Court left no son good enough to carry on his line in England, but is represented in France by Cadmus, the sire of the top-class miler Gravelines, the winner of the Prix du Moulin de Longchamp.

Precipitation also sired Premonition, who won the St Leger for his owner Brigadier W. P. Wyatt, a member of the Jockey Club, who also traced in tail female line to Pretty Polly; Why Hurry, winner of a war-time Oaks for the late Mr J. V. Rank, who was out of Cybiane by Blandford and was descended in tail-female line from Petty Polly's dam, Admiration; and Sheshoon, bred by the late Aga Khan and the late Aly Khan and owned by the late Aly Khan's executors, who won the Ascot Gold Cup, the Grand Prix de Saint-Cloud in France, and the Grosser Preis von Baden in Germany. Sheshoon's dam Noorani by Nearco was also dam of Charlottesville, winner in 1960 of the Grand Prix de Paris and French Derby.

The Matchem male line, in spite of the splendid opportunities afforded by the brilliance of Hurry On at the stud, was at one time having a fierce struggle for existence. Captain Cuttle had been sold for £50,000 and went to Italy in 1928 where he died in 1932; Coronach went to New Zealand in 1940, without leaving any famous son behind him, except perhaps Niccolo Dell'Arca, who was imported from Italy, but was sent to France in 1957; Call Boy was almost sterile at the stud before he died in 1939. Precipitation alone remained to perpetuate through his sons the male stirp of Matchen in England.

Santa Claus

Santa Claus, who was foaled in 1961, seemed for a long time to be the horse most likely to ensure the survival of the Matchem line. Bred by the late Doctor F. A. Smorfitt, he was out of Aunt Clara, by Arctic Prince out of Sister Clara, by Scarlet Tiger out of Clarence, dam of Sun Chariot, winner of the 1,000 Guineas, Oaks and St Leger. Santa Claus was owned by Mr John Ismay and trained throughout his career by J. M. Rogers. Santa Claus won four races. As a two-year-old he won the National Stakes at the Curragh, easily beating the Chesham Stakes winner Mesopotamia. At three years he won the Irish 2,000 Guineas, the Epsom Derby, in which he defeated the St Leger winner Indiana, and the Irish Sweeps Derby, becoming the first horse in hstory to win the English and Irish Derbies. He was unable to act on the firm going when defeated by Nasram in the King George VI and Queen Elizabeth Stakes. However he ran an excellent race when second to Prince Royal II in the Prix de l'Arc de Triomphe. In all, Santa Claus won a total of £153,814 in stakes money, a figure far in excess of that previously earned by any other horse trained in England or Ireland. With the exception of the Derby when he was ridden by Scobie Breasley and the Prix de l'Arc de Triomphe, when he was ridden by Jimmy Lindley, William Burke rode him in all his races.

Santa Claus stood at stud for five seasons. Then, on the day before the 1970 covering season, he died of a blood clot. His first two crops yielded Santa Tina, winner of the Irish Guinness Oaks and her full-brother Reindeer, winner of the Irish St Leger. Reindeer was exported to New Zealand in 1974 and Santa Claus left no other son good enough to carry on his line.

Sheshoon

The year in which Santa Claus died was, however, to see the phenomenal emergence as a sire of Sheshoon, who was fourteen years old at the time, and had stood in England for ten years, largely neglected by the principal breeders. During that year Sheshoon was to head the list of sires in Europe, his progeny winning the equivalent of £362,313 in stakes money.

The horse primarily responsible for Sheshoon's position at the head of the list of European sires was Sassafras. Bred in

Ireland by his owner, the late Mrs Arpad Plesch, he is a bay horse out of Ratification mare Ruta, whose third dam was Schiaparelli, dam of Herringbone, winner of the 1,000 Guineas and St Leger. Sassafras raced in France throughout his career, being trained by Francois Mathet. He was the winner of six races, worth the equivalent of £249,544, including the French Derby, beating the Grand Prix winner Roll of Honour, the French St Leger and the Prix de l'Arc de Triomphe, in which he defeated the hitherto unbeaten Nijinsky. Sassafras has sired winners of top-class races over a wide range of distances, his progeny including Henri le Balafre, winner of the French St Leger and Galway Bay, winner of the Coventry Stakes at Ascot. He also sired Dom Alaric, winner of the Grand Prix Prince Rose, the most valuable race ever to be contested in Belgium.

Sheshoon was to sire his first English classic winner three years later when his son Mon Fils was successful in the 2,000 Guineas of 1973. Other sons of Sheshoon include Pleben, winner of the Grand Prix de Paris and French St Leger, Samos, winner of the French St Leger and Stintino, winner of the Prix Lupin. His daughter Vela was the leading two-year-old in France in 1969, being the winner of the Criterium de Pouliches that year. There now seems a strong likelihood that a descendant of Sheshoon will emerge to perpetuate the Matchem line in England.

Man O'War

The Matchem line survives in the United States through Australian (a son of West Australian), Spendthrift, Hastings, Fair Play and Man O'War, the most famous of all American racehorses. 'Big Red', as he was affectionately dubbed, only suffered one unfortunate defeat in 21 races, winning all the others without difficulty, including the Hopeful and Futurity Stakes as a two-year-old, and the Preakness, Withers, Belmont, Dwyer, Travers and Lawrence Realization Stakes and the Jockey Club and Kenilworth Park Gold Cups as a three-year-old in 1920. Man O'War died in 1947.

War Admiral, who was one of the few horses to win the Preakness Stakes, the Kentucky Derby and the Belmont Stakes, the three races that comprise the American Triple Crown, was Man O'War's most successful son in America. He was to become the sire of Singing Grass, the dam of the English Derby and St Leger winner Never Say Die.

Many attempts have been made, which may well meet with success, to revive the Australian branch of the Matchem line in England. Relic, a son of War Relic, by Man O'War, and the winner of five of his seven races, including the Hopeful Stakes at two years and the Hibiscus Stakes at three years, was imported to England in 1957, having previously stood for six seasons in France.

Relic, who died in 1970, was the sire of Pieces of Eight (Eclipse Stakes and Champion Stakes), who is the sire of Stateff, winner of the Gran Premio del Jockey Club in Italy; Buisson Ardent, owned by the late Aga Khan, winner of the Middle Park Stakes and French 2,000 Guineas; and Venture VII, an own-brother to Buisson Ardent, who won the Middle Park Stakes, St James's Palace Stakes and Sussex Stakes. Polic, a further son of Relic who won the Prix d'Arenberg, one of the most important events in France for two-year-olds, has exerted a powerful sprinting influence through his son Polyfoto (Nunthorpe Stakes), sire of Bay Express (King's Stand Stakes). Relic was also grandsire of Behistoun (Washington International Stakes).

Buisson Ardent, who died in 1963 after only seven seasons at stud, was the sire of Atherstone Wood and Ardent Dancer, winners respectively of the Irish 2,000 Guineas and Irish 1,000 Guineas. His most important winners, however, were Roan Rocket and Silver Shark.

Silver Shark, who was raced and bred by the Aga Khan, being out of Palsaka, by Palestine out of the Oaks winner Masaka, was the winner of ten races in France, including the Prix d'Ispahan. He was exported to Japan in 1972, his son Sharp Edge, winner of the Irish 2,000 Guineas, being sent to Australia in 1974. Roan Rocket was the winner of five races, value £28,882, including the St James's Palace Stakes and Sussex Stakes. He has proved a most successful sire of two-year-olds and it is through him that the Australian line of Matchem is most likely to be perpetuated in England.

CHAPTER V

Famous Thoroughbreds: The Dam Lines and Leading Brood-mares

When mares with foal at foot flee down the glades.
Dorothy Wellesley, *Horses.*

The 'Jersey Act'

IN Volume XXII of the General Stud Book, issued in 1913, it was laid down that the qualification for registration in the Stud Book should read as follows: 'No horse or mare can after this date be considered as eligible for admission unless it can be traced without flaw on both sire's and dam's side of its pedigree to horses and mares themselves already accepted in the earlier volumes of the book'.

This was known as the 'Jersey Act' after Lord Jersey, who sponsored the regulation, but, as many good racehorses, both in France and in the United States, were debarred from entry in the Stud Book as a consequence of this rule, some French and American owners suggested that the 'Act' should be repealed or at any rate modified, and the Jockey Club accordingly set up a committee to consider the matter.

After this committee had submitted its report, Messrs Weatherby announced in the introduction to Volume XXXI of the General Stud Book, issued in 1947, that 'any animal claiming admission from now onwards must be able to prove satisfactorily some eight or nine crosses of pure blood, to trace back for at least a century, and to show such performances of its immediate family, on the Turf as to warrant the belief in the purity of its blood.' In the introduction to Volume XXXVI, published in 1969, the words 'to trace back for at least a century' were deleted.

It has already been seen that out of the 174 Eastern sires mentioned in Volume I of the General Stud Book only three have survived through direct male lines to the present day, namely the Darley Arabian through Eclipse, the Byerly Turk through Herod, and the Godolphin Arabian through Matchem, and their respective descendants.

It is now time to turn to the other side of the pedigree of the thoroughbred and to consider the dam lines, tracing down through the mother to daughter chain from what are known as the foundation mares in the Stud Book.

The Tap-Root Mares and the Bruce Lowe Family Numbers

At the end of the last century Mr Bruce Lowe, who was assisted in his researches by Mr William Allison, listed some 50 tap-root mares in numerical order, based on the number of direct descendants of each mare, through the female line who had won the Derby, Oaks, and St Leger up to that time; the number 1 being allotted to the family whose foundation mare could claim the most winners of these three classic races among her descendants in tail female at the time the system was compiled by Bruce Lowe; the number 2 to the family with the second largest number of these classic winners among its offspring; and so on down the scale.

According to this figure system, therefore, each female line was given a family number by which it is now usually known, and the principal tap-root mares, with their Bruce Lowe family numbers, and some of their more famous descendants through the direct female line, are as follows:

No. 1. Natural Barb Mare of Mr Tregonwell. This celebrated foundation mare lived in the reign of Charles II, and up to the end of 1978 was the female ancestress of no less than 86 out of the 600 winners of the Derby, Oaks and St Leger; many more than any other tap-root mare could claim. Whalebone, Bay Middleton, Melbourne, Lord Lyon, Bend Or, Robert the Devil, Swynford, Prince Palatine, Phalaris, Gay Crusader, Book Law, Cameronian, Ocean Swell, Alycidon, Never Say

Die, Altesse Royale, Bustino, Sodium, Madelia, Royal Palace, Tudor Melody, Buckpasser, Allez France and Vaguely Noble were descended from her in tail female.

No. 2. Burton Barb Mare. One of the most prolific mares in the number of her descendants now living. She also was alive in the days of the Merry Monarch, when she was located at the Hampton Court Stud. Thoroughbreds who traced back to her were Crucifix, Voltigeur, Lord Clifden, Carbine, The Tetrarch, Hurry On, Gainsborough, Precipitation, Aureole, Meld, Alcide, Norther Dancer, Sea-Bird II, Highclere, Charlottown, Busted, Secretariat and Alleged.

No. 3. Bowes' Mare by the Byerley Turk, dam of the two True Blues. A famous mare who was foaled in about 1695. Among her descendants were The Flying Dutchman, Stockwell, Hannah, Galopin, Memoir and La Fleche, Isinglass, Bay Ronald, Polymelus, Blandford, Sun Chariot, Dante, Palestine, Pinza, Santa Claus.

No. 4. Layton Barb Mare. This mare was foaled in about 1685, and famous horses who traced to her were Matchem, Thormanby, Apology, Common, Rock Sand, Coronach, Nearco, Ribot, Never Too Late II, Sagaro, Ribocco, Ribero and Habitat.

No. 5. Old Ebony, daughter of the Duke of Rutland's Mare by The Massey Barb. She was bred in 1714 and claims among her descendants Gladiateur, Hermit, Doncaster, Galtee More, Sunstar, Son-in-Law, Reform, and Val de Loir.

No. 6. Old Bald Peg. This is the earliest known mare in the Stud Book, as she was alive in 1650. King Fergus and Priam traced to her and Hyperion, Myrobella, Big Game, Nimbus, Chamossaire, Snow Knight, Juliette Marny, Julio Marner and Grey Sovereign all belong to this family.

No. 7. Lord Darcy's Black-Legged Royal Mare. She was probably a daughter of one of the royal mares at Hampton Court at the time of the death of Queen Anne, and was possibly an offshoot of the No. 13 family stem. Famous horses coming down from this mare were West Australian, Donovan, Persimmon, Flying Fox, Diamond Jubilee, Sicambre, Pall Mall and La Lagune.

No. 8 Hatton's Mare by Bustler. She lived in about 1680 and numbered among her descendants Orville, Sultan, Newminster, Ayrshire, Gulf Stream, Heliopolis, Sir Ivor, Nijinsky, Grundy and The Minstrel.

No. 9 Vintner Mare. Cyllene was her most notable descendant. Fair Trial, Tudor Minstrel, Caracalla II, Migoli, Petite Etoile, Nasrullah, Royal Charger, Prince Taj, Pawneese, and Ragusa also belong to this family.

No. 10 Fair Helen by William's Squirrel. This mare lived in about 1730, and Blair Athol, Hampton, Bayardo and Lemberg, Orwell, Owen Tudor, Airborne, Prince Rose and Rheingold traced to her.

No less than 418 out of the 600 winners of the Derby, Oaks and St Leger up to the end of 1978 are descended from these ten foundation mares and over half the thoroughbred mares alive in this country today trace back to them in direct female line. Other tap-root mares and their descendants were:

No. 11 Miss Betty Darcy's Pet Mare, probably a daughter of Old Grey Royal, No. 13 family; Birdcatcher, St Simon and Orme.

No. 12 Sedbury Royal Mare, dam of Darcy's Brimmer mare; Eclipse and Roberto.

No. 13 Sedbury Royal Mare, dam of Darcy's Yellow Turk Mare and grandam of Old Grey Royal; Highflyer, Orlando, Pharos and Fairway, Tourbillon, Norseman, Worden II, Djeddah, Dahlia and Seattle Slew.

No. 14 Oldfield Mare; Touchstone, Pretty Polly, Tetratema, Supreme Court, St Paddy, Psidium, Nearctic, Court Harwell, Luthier, Brigadier Gerard, Artaius, Only For Life and Flying Water.

No. 15 Royal Mare, dam of Grey Whynot.

No. 16 Sister to Stripling; Ormonde, Sceptre, Pommern, Buchan, Bahram, Bois Roussel, Sir Gallahad III, Bull Dog, Crepello, Sunny Boy III, Pia, Match III, Relko and Reliance II.

No. 17 Byerley Turk Mare, grand-dam of the Wharton Mare.

No. 18 Old Woodcock Mare (circa 1695); Waxy and Formosa.

No. 19 Old Woodcock Mare (circa 1690); Vedette, Isonomy, Tracery, Windsor Lad, Our Babu, King of the Tudors and Never Bend.

No. 20   Mare by Sir Thomas Gascoigne's Foreign horse;
Blue Peter, Pharis II, Blakeney and Morston.

No. 21   Queen Anne's Moonam Barb Mare.

No. 22   Belgrade Turk Mare; Mill Reef, Khaled, Wollow
and Blushing Groom.

Note: These foundation mares have been given the names by
which they are now usually known, but this is not to deny that
some of them may have been Arabians; that is to say that some
of them may have been got by imported pure-bred Arab sires
although they were not necessarily thrown by pure-bred Arab
dams.

Convenient Classification of Brood-mares but Unsound Theory of Sire Families

The researches of Bruce Lowe and William Allison were of
considerable importance at the time they were published, in
that they represented the first serious attempt to give to the
dam's side of a thoroughbred's pedigree some share of the
credit for the development of the racehorse, which hitherto had
been assigned almost entirely to the sire lines.

But, however useful the facts presented and however conve-
nient the classification of the female families may have been,
there is little doubt that the theories deduced from the facts
were in many respects unsound.

For instance Bruce Lowe considered that the No. 1 family
was the best female line because it produced the most classic
winners, apparently ignoring the fact that it also produced
more bad selling-platers than any other family.

Again, Bruce Lowe considered that certain maternal families were particularly strong in what he called the 'sire element',
viz.: Nos. 3, 8, 11, 12, and 14, and he accordingly named these
the 'Sire Families'. Modern critics clearly cannot support this
theory, in view of the fact that the best sires of recent times
belong to other families not regarded by Bruce Lowe as 'Sire
Families'. For instance, as already shown, Swynford, Phalaris,
Alycidon and Vaguely Noble belonged to No. 1 family; The
Tetrarch, Hurry On, Gainsborough, Aureole, Sea-Bird II,
Busted and Northern Dancer to No. 2 family; Nearco and Ribot
to No. 4; Son-in-Law, and Reform to No. 5; Hyperion was an
offspring of No. 6 family; Cyllene was No. 9; Bayardo No. 10;

Pharos and Fairway to No. 13; and Crepello belonged to No. 16 family.

Dam Lines Prominent in Recent Years

It would require a separate volume to trace in detail all the female families from the original tap-root mares down to the present day, but some of the more important dam lines will be considered. These are the lines descending through Paraffin, Conjure and Paradoxical, all three of whom trace in direct female chain to the Tregonwell Barb Mare, the No. 1 foundation mare; Altoviscar, from the No. 2 family, tracing to the Burton Barb Mare; Gondolette, who belongs to the No. 6 family and so goes back to Old Bald Peg; Lady Josephine, who comes down from the Vintner Mare, No. 9 Family; Admiration, who belongs to the No. 14 family, coming down from the Oldfield Mare; and Miss Agnes, who is a direct descendant of the Sister to Stripling, who stands at the head of No. 16 family.

Paraffin (Chart 5)

This famous brood-mare of the No. 1 family was a daughter of Paradigm, the dam of Lord Lyon (Triple Crown) and Achievement (St Leger and 1,000 Guineas) and the grandam of Jannette (St Leger and Oaks), and she herself was the dam of Footlight, Illuminata, and Almondell.

Paradigm was a daughter of Ellen Horne, another of whose daughters, Rouge Rose, was the dam of Bend Or and the third dam of Roi Herode.

Footlight was the dam of Glare, whose daughters were Lady Lightfoot, dam of Prince Palatine (St Leger, Eclipse, and two Ascot Cups); Flair (1,000 Guineas); and Lesbia (Coronation Stakes).

Among the offspring of Illuminata were Ladas (Derby and 2,000 Guineas) by Hampton; Gas (by Ayrshire, son of Hampton), dam of Cicero (Derby); and Chelandry (1,000 Guineas) by Goldfinch (son of Ormonde, and Thistle, dam of Common), dam of Neil Gow (2,000 Guineas and Eclipse); all winners for the first Lord Rosebery.

Popinjay. This daughter of Chelandry by St Frusquin was bought by Lord Astor for 1,000 guineas and became one of the three foundation mares who made the Cliveden Stud, perhaps the most famous establishment in the world for the breeding of successful mares. Out of Popingay came Popingaol, dam of Book Law (St Leger and Coronation Stakes), mother of Rhodes Scholar (Eclipse); Book Debt, mother of Pay Up (2,000 Guineas) and of Bread Card, the dam of Rising Light (Jockey Club Stakes); and Pogrom (Oaks and Coronation Stakes). Good and Gay, another daughter of Popinjay, was the dam of Saucy Sue (Oaks, 1,000 Guineas and Coronation Stakes). All these winners ran in the colours of the first Lord Astor, who bred them himself, with the exception of Rising Light, who was bred and owned by the late King George VI. Popingaol was also fourth dam of Tudor Melody, the sire of Kashmir II (2,000 Guineas), and fifth dam of Provoke (St Leger).

Samphire. Another daughter of Chelandry, she was the dam of Juniata, mother of Jiffy, dam of Ocean Swell (Derby and Ascot Gold Cup), bred and owned by the late Lord Rosebery, while Galady II, a great-great-grandaughter of Chelandry, was the dam of Galatea II, (Oaks and 1,000 Guineas) and third dam of Never Say Die (Derby and St Leger).

The other dam line from Paraffin through Almondell comes down to the mare Mistrella, two of whose daughters were Beam (Oaks) and Trimestral, dam of Trimdon (two Gold Cups), Foxhunter (Gold Cup) and Trilogy, mother of Light Brocade (Oaks).

Happy Climax, dam of Panorama and fourth dam of Cantelo (St Leger); and those good race mares Vaucluse (1,000 Guineas), her daughter Bongrace (Doncaster Cup and Jockey Club Cup), and her grandaughter Ribbon were also descended from Paraffin, as was Shirley Heights (Derby and Irish Sweeps Derby).

Conjure (Chart 6)

This is another brood-mare whose offspring have added such lustre to the No. 1 dam line in recent years, and she was the first mare to be bought by the first Lord Astor, who paid £100 for her in 1900. Third Trick and Winkipop (1,000 Guineas and Coronation Stakes) were full sisters out of Conjure. Third Trick was dam of Pinprick and Long Suit; the former dam of Point Duty, mother of Traffic Light (Coronation Stakes), the dam of Amber Flash (Jockey Club Cup), whose daughter was Ambiguity (Oaks and Jockey Club Cup); the latter dam of Short Story (Oaks). Winkipop was dam of Plymstock, mother of Pennycomequick (Oaks), Sunny Devon (Coronation Stakes), and Picture, dam of Instantaneous, the mother of Court Martial (2,000 Guineas). All these brilliant fillies and the colt Court Martial were bred and raced by the second and third Lord Astors. Amber Flash was also grandam of Sodium (Irish Sweeps Derby and English St Leger). Other daughters of Point Duty were Sun Helmet, dam of Woodburn (Cesarewitch) and fourth dam of Quiet Fling (Coronation Cup); Thorn Wood, dam of Thicket, mother of Hornbeam (Great Voltigeur Stakes); and Fair Ranger, dam of Sunset, mother of Moonmadness, dam of Madelia (French 1,000 Guineas and French Oaks).

Paradoxical (Chart 7)

The third brood-mare from No. 1 family. Her line descends through her daughters Absurdity and Doxa, both own-sisters by Melton. Absurdity was the dam of Black Jester (St Leger); and Jest (Oaks and 1,000 Guineas) and mother of Humorist (Derby). All these classic winners were owned by the late Mr J. B. Joel. Absurdity's daughter Gesture was the dam of Amuse, the mother of Picture Play (1,000 Guineas). Picture Play, bred Queen of Light, dam of Crystal Palace, the mother of Royal Palace (2,000 Guineas, Derby, Coronation Cup, Eclipse Stakes and King George VI and Queen Elizabeth Stakes); and of Chandelier, the dam of Crocket (Champion Two-Year-Old).

Doxa was the dam of Lady of Pedigree, the mother of Helene de Troie, mother of Adargatis (French Oaks). Adargatis bred Ardan (French Derby, Prix de l'Arc de Triomphe and Coronation Cup) and Pardal (Princess of Wales's Stakes and Jockey Club Stakes) and sire of Psidium (Derby). Helene de Troie also bred La Troienne, who was exported to the United States of America where she bred Bimelech (Preakness Stakes and Belmont Stakes) and Black Helen (Coaching Club American Oaks). Other daughters of La Troienne were Baby League, third dam of Boucher (English St Leger); Businesslike, dam of Busanda, the mother of Buckpasser (American Derby and Jockey Club Gold Cup); and Big Hurry, the mother of Searching, dam of Priceless Gem, the mother of Allez France

(French 1,000 Guineas, French Oaks and Prix de l'Arc de Triomphe).

Altoviscar (Chart 8)

This branch of the No. 2 family has emerged in recent years as a most prepotent influence in the breed of the thoroughbred. Altoviscar's two daughters Alope, dam of Foxlaw (Ascot Gold Cup) and Comedienne, dam of Call Boy (Derby) first drew attention to its merits. Since then other descendants of Comedienne, namely Dancing Time (1,000 Guineas) and Umberto (Knights Royal Stakes), and two daughters of Aloe, full sister to Foxlaw, namely Feola and Sweet Aloe, have added further lustre to the family.

The royal mare, Feola, produced Knight's Daugther, dam of the dollar millionaire winner Round Table, Kingstone (Great Yorkshire Stakes), Hypericum (1,000 Guineas), Angelola (Yorkshire Oaks and Oaks Trial Stakes) and Above Board (Yorkshire Oaks and Cesarewitch). Hypericum was the mother of Restoration (King Edward VII Stakes) and of Highlight, the dam of Highclere (1,000 Guineas and French Oaks); Angelola, the mother of Aureole (King George VI and Queen Elizabeth Stakes, Hardwicke Stakes and Coronation Cup) the leading sire in 1960 and 1961; and Above Board being the mother of Above Suspicion (St James's Palace Stakes and Gordon Stakes) and Doutelle (Cumberland Lodge Stakes), all these thoroughbreds (except Round Table) being bred and owned by the Queen or her father and grandfather.

Sweet Aloe's daughter Chenille is not only the dam of Alcide (King George VI and Queen Elizabeth Stakes, St Leger and Great Voltigeur Stakes), but also of Lightning, whose son was Parthia (Derby and Jockey Club Cup), both these colts having been bred and owned by the late Sir Humphrey de Trafford.

Gondolette (Chart 9)

The most celebrated broodmare of the No. 6 family was Gondolette, who was bred by Mr Waring and sold to Mr George Edwardes for 75 guineas as a yearling, bought by Mr Hall Walker (late Lord Wavertree) in 1905 for 360 guineas and later resold to the late Lord Derby in 1912 for 1,500 guineas.

Together with Anchora, Bridget and Canterbury Pilgrim, she founded the fortunes of the famous Stanley Stud where she became the dam of Sansovino (Derby), Ferry (1,000 Guineas), Dolabella and Serenissima.

Dolabella. This mare was bought for the National Stud and produced the speedy Myrobella, dam of Big Game (2,000 Guineas); and of Snowberry, mother of Chamossaire (St Leger), grandmother of Hopeful Venture (Grand Prix de Saint-Cloud and Hardwicke Stakes) and great-grandmother of Snow Knight (Derby).

Serenissima. This mare was the dam of Tranquil (St Leger and 1,000 Guineas), Bosworth (Gold Cup), and that wonderful mare Selene, mother of Hyperion (Derby and St Leger). These were all winners for the late Lord Derby. Selene was also the maternal grandam of Mossborough, sire of the mighty Ballymoss. Double Jump (Champion Two-Year-Old), Collyria (Park Hill Stakes) and Raise You Ten (Goodwood Cup) also trace to Gondolette.

Lady Josephine (Chart 10).

This broodmare of the No. 9 family was bought by the Sledmere Stud for 1,200 guineas and became the dam of the flying filly Mumtaz Mahal and of Lady Juror, winner of the Jockey Club Stakes. Mumtaz Mahal was the mother of Mah Mahal, dam of Mahmoud (Derby) and of Mah Iran, dam of Migoli (Eclipse) and Star of Iran, mother of Petite Etoile (Oaks, 1,000 Guineas, Champion Stakes, Yorkshire Oaks and Coronation Cup); and all these thoroughbreds were owned by the Aga Khan. Other daughters of Mumtaz Mahal were Mumtaz Begum, mother of Nasrullah, grandmother of Royal Charger and Prince Taj, third dam of Ginetta (French 1,000 Guineas) and fourth dam of Kalamoun (French 2,000 Guineas); and Rustom Mahal, mother of Abernant. Lady Juror was the mother of Fair Trial; Riot, dam of Commotion (Oaks) mother of unbeaten Combat; and Sansonnet, dam of Neolight (Coronation Stakes) and of Tudor Minstrel (2,000 Guineas), all owned by the late Mr J. A. Dewar. Lady Juror also bred Jurisdiction, third dam of Kashmir II (2,000 Guineas) and fourth dam of Erimo Hawk (Gold Cup).

Admiration (Chart 10)

This is one of the most prolific families of the present day and many good racehorses of recent times belong to it.

Admiration had several daughters who carried on her female line, among them Veneration II, Pretty Polly, Adula and Miranda.

Veneration II was the dam of Craganour (who finished first in the Derby of 1913 but was disqualified by the Stewards), fifth dam of Why Hurry (Oaks) and sixth dam of Marguerite Vernaut (Champion Stakes).

Adula (Park Hill Stakes) was the dam of Knockfreena (Coronation Stakes) and of Mountain Mint, second dam of Cresta Run (1,000 Guineas) and of Foxbridge, an outstanding successful sire in the Antipodes. Cresta Run was fifth dam of Magic Flute (Coronation Stakes).

Miranda was the third dam of Tehran (St Leger), the sire of Tulyar (Derby and St Leger). She was also ancestress of Argur (Eclipse Stakes) a very successful sire in the Argentine, Hard to Beat (French Derby), Highest Hopes (Prix Vermeille) and Mrs McArdy (1,000 Guineas).

But the most famous of all the daughters of Admiration was the brilliant Pretty Polly (Oaks, St Leger and 1,000 Guineas), who herself became a broodmare of high distinction. Her four daughters, Molly Desmond, Dutch Mary, Polly Flinders and Baby Polly have between them produced in tail female line such notable performers as Brigadier Gerard (2,000 Guineas, Eclipse Stakes, King George VI and Queen Elizabeth Stakes and Champion Stakes, twice); St Paddy (Derby, St Leger and Eclipse Stakes); Flying Water (1,000 Guineas and Champion Stakes); Psidium (Derby); Premonition (St Leger); Only For Life (2,000 Guineas); Supreme Court (King George VI and Queen Elizabeth Stakes); Donatello II (Italian Grand Prix and Italian Derby), who was sire of Alycidon (Ascot, Goodwood and Doncaster Cups) and Crepello (2,000 Guineas and Derby); Vienna, sire of Vaguely Noble (Prix de l'Arc de Triomphe); Great Nephew, sire of Grundy (Derby, Irish Sweeps Derby and King George VI and Queen Elizabeth Stakes); Luthier, leading sire in France in 1976; Court Harwell, sire of Meadow Court (King George VI and Queen Elizabeth Stakes); Nearctic, sire of Nonoalco (2,000 Guineas) and grandsire of Nijinsky

(2,000 Guineas, Derby and St Leger); Pardao (Princess of Wales's Stakes); Artaius (Eclipse Stakes and Sussex Stakes); Arctic Explorer (Eclipse Stakes); Colorado Kid (Doncaster Cup); Cappiello (Grand Prix de Paris), Crimea II (Cheveley Park Stakes); Don II (French 2,000 Guineas); Fearless Fox (Goodwood Cup); Challenge and Black Peter (both winners of the Jockey Club Stakes); Orthodox (Newmarket Stakes); Guersant (French 2,000 Guineas and Hardwicke Stakes), Double Bore (Goodwood Cup); The Cobbler (Middle Park Stakes); Huntercombe (Middle Park Stakes); Hyperbole (Knights Royal Stakes); Eastern Emperor (Jockey Club Cup); Lucyrowe (Coronation Stakes); Thymus (French 2,000 Guineas) and Sea Parrot (Yorkshire Oaks).

This is the No. 14 family and the brood-mares concerned all originated from the Eyrefield Lodge Stud, now owned by Mr Edmund Loder, who inherited the stud on the death of his father, the late Lieutenant-Colonel Giles Loder, in 1966. The stud had been in the ownership of Colonel Loder since 1917.

Miss Agness (Chart 12)

Four well-known female families come down from this famous broodmare, one through Polly Agnes and one through Frivolity, the third through Little Agnes, and the fourth through Windermere.

Polly Agnes produced Lily Agnes (Doncaster Cup) dam of the mighty Ormonde (Triple Crown) and of his full-sister Ornament, mother of the wonderful racing mare Sceptre (2,000 Guineas, 1,000 Guineas, Oaks and St Leger) and ancestress of Long Look (Oaks). She also bred Orphan Agnes, third dam of Pommern (2,000 Guineas, Derby and St Leger) and ancestress of Night Off (1,000 Guineas).

Maid of the Mist. This daughter of Sceptre was bought by Lord Astor for 4,500 guineas in 1911 and became the third of the celebrated matrons of the Cliveden Stud together with Conjure and Popinjay. She became the dam of Craig an Eran (2,000 Guineas and Eclipse); Sunny Jane (Oaks), the grandam of Betty (Coronation Stakes); Jura, dam of Glenabatrick, the mother of Tiberius (Gold Cup), and Keener, the fifth dam of Full Dress II (1,000 Guineas); and Hamoaze, the dam of Buchan (Eclipse), Saltash (Eclipse) and St Germans (Doncaster Cup). All these were winners for Lord Astor, except Tiberius, who was owned by Sir Abe Bailey, and Full Dress II, who was owned by Mr R. B. Moller. Petition (Eclipse), sire of the famous filly Petite Etoile, was also descended in tail female line from Sceptre, as were Match III (King George VI and Queen Elizabeth Stakes, French St Leger and Washington International Stakes), Relko (Derby, Coronation Cup, French 2,000 Guineas and French St Leger), Reliance II (French Derby and French St Leger), Taboun (2,000 Guineas), Zucchero (Coronation Cup) Never Say (Park Hill Stakes) and Grey of Falloden (Doncaster Cup).

The second branch of the Miss Agnes line comes down through Frivolity and Comic Song to Concertina, whose dam was 25 years old at the time of her birth.

Concertina. This mare produced Plucky Liege and Garron Lass. The former was dam of Sir Gallahad III (French 2,000 Guineas), Admiral Drake (Grand Prix) and Bois Roussel (English Derby) and ancestress of Pia (Oaks) and Sanctus (French Derby and Grand Prix de Paris). The latter was dam of Friar's Daughter, mother of Dastur (Coronation Cup) and that undefeated champion Bahram (Triple Crown), both bred and owned by the Aga Khan. She was also third dam of Sunny Boy III.

Little Agnes was ancestress of that great broodmare Crepuscule, the dam of Honeylight (1,000 Guineas), Crepello (2,000 Guineas and Derby) and Twilight Alley (Ascot Gold Cup). She was also ancestress of Vedas (2,000 Guineas), Zinfandel (Ascot Gold Cup), Desmond, sire of The White Knight, and Sardanapale (Grand Prix de Paris).

Windermere, was the dam of Rydal, the mother of Rydal Mount, dam of Troutbeck (St Leger). Rydal also bred Rydal Fell, the third dam of Pearl Cap (French 1,000 Guineas, French Oaks and French St Leger) fourth dam of Pearl Diver (Derby), and fifth dam of Flocon (Eclipse Stakes) and Tourment (French 2,000 Guineas and French St Leger). Other top class winners who belong to this branch of the family are Sleeping Partner (Oaks), Molvedo (Prix de l'Arc de Triomphe) and Salvo (Hardwicke Stakes).

Famous Brood-mares

To conclude this chapter on the dam lines of thoroughbred pedigrees it may be of interest to give the names of some of the most famous broodmares in the history of the English Turf. These are Penelope, dam of Whalebone and Whisker; Barbelle, dam of The Flying Dutchman and Van Tromp; Pocahontas, dam of Stockwell, Rataplan and King Tom; Paradigm, dam of Lord Lyon and Achievement and grandam of Jannette; Quiver, dam of the full sisters Memoir and La Fleche, both got by St Simon, and of Maid Marian (dam of Polymelus), got by Hampton; Morganette, dam of Galtee More and Ard Patrick; Vista, dam of Bona Vista, Sir Visto and Velasquez; Perdita II, dam of the full brothers Florizel II, Persimmon and Diamond Jubilee, all got by St Simon; Canterbury Pilgrim, dam of Swynford and Chaucer; Galicia, dam of Bayardo and Lemberg; and Scapa Flow, who produced the winners of 63 races value £86,084, including Pharos, Fairway and Fair Isle. To these may now be added Double Life, dam of Precipitation and Persian Gulf; Rosy Legend, dam of Dante and Sayajirao; Astronomie, dam of Marsyas II, Caracalla II, Arbar and Asmena; Neocracy, dam of Tulyar and Saint Crespin III; Crepuscule, dam of Crepello, Honeylight and Twilight Alley; Relance III, dam of Match III, Reliance II and Relko; Noorani, dam of Charlottesville and Sheshoon; Review, dam of Pourparler and Fleet; La Mirambule, dam of Tambourine II and Nasram II; Libra, dam of the full-brothers Ribocco and Ribero, both by Ribot; Windmill Girl, dam of Blakeney and Morston; Flaming Page, dam of Nijinsky and grandam of The Minstrel; and Set Free, dam of Juliette Marny and Julio Mariner.

CHAPTER VI

The Pedigrees of Some Famous Thoroughbreds

Look back into your mighty ancestors.
Shakespeare, *King Henry V.*

A CLOSE study of the pedigrees of some famous racehorses will show how the sire lines and the dam lines, discussed in the two previous chapters, enter into the composition of the modern thoroughbred.

Stockwell

The 'Emperor of Stallions' was a chestnut horse foaled in 1849, his sire The Baron (chestnut) and his dam Pocahontas (bay).

Whalebone; a grandson of Woodpecker; Whisker; Blacklock; Selim; Tramp; Orville; and a grandson of Saltram; these were the eight sires who moulded this celebrated thoroughbred; six lines of Eclipse and two of Herod.

Fused with them was the purest female blood, flowing down from Bowes' Mare by the Byerley Turk, dam of the two True Blues (No. 3 family), through Miss Belsea, Hyaena, Everlasting, and her daughter by Woodpecker, Fractious, Amazon, Harpalice, Clare, and Marpessa to Pocahontas, dam also to Rataplan and King Tom.

Bend Or

Bend Or was also a chestnut horse and was foaled in 1877, both his parents being chestnuts; Doncaster, his sire, by Stockwell (son of Pocahontas) out of Marigold by Teddington; and Rouge Rose, his dam, by Thormanby (son of Alice Hawthorn) out of Ellen Horne, who traced back in tail female through Delhi (by Plenipotentiary, son of Emilius), Pawn Junior (by

Waxy), Pawn (sister to Penelope, dam of Whalebone and Whisker), Prunella (by Highflyer), Promise, and Julia, to the Tregonwell Barb Mare (No. 1 family).

St Simon

This famous thoroughbred was a brown horse foaled in 1881; his sire Galopin being by Vedette out of Flying Duchess by The Flying Dutchman (son of Bay Middleton and Barbelle); and his dam St Angela being by King Tom (son of Harkaway and Pocahontas) out of Adeline, by Ion out of Little Fairy, who traced back in the female line to Miss Betty Darcy's Pet Mare (No. 11 family).

Memoir and La Fleche

These two champion fillies were full sisters by St Simon out of Quiver. The male blood which flowed in their veins was contributed to by four lines of Eclipse (3 from Pot8os; 1 from King Fergus), three lines of Herod (2 from Woodpecker; 1 from Highflyer), and one line of Matchem; a very well-balanced pedigree. The female line went back through a daughter of Young Melbourne (by Melbourne) and Brown Bess, via Everlasting, Hyaena, and Miss Belsea, to the dam of the two True Blues; one of the most outstanding dam lines in the Stud Book.

Quiver, when mated with Hampton, also produced Maid Marian, mother of Polymelus, the sire of Phalaris; and Brown Bess, when mated with West Australian, also produced the mother of Musket, the sire of Carbine.

Florizel II, Persimmon, and Diamond Jubilee

These three good colts were full brothers by St Simon out of Perdita II. An analysis of the sixteen sire lines which contributed to the blood of these famous racehorses at the fourth remove shows that Eclipse was responsible for ten of them (5 through Pot8os; 4 through King Fergus; 1 through Joe Andrews), Herod for four of them (3 through Woodpecker; 1 through Highflyer), and Matchem for two of them. Perdita II, their dam, was by Hampton out of Hermione, by Young Melbourne out of La Belle Helene, by St Albans out of Teterrima, by Voltigeur out of Ellen Middleton, by Bay Middleton out of a mare descended from Lord Darcy's Black-legged Royal Mare, who stands at the head of the No. 7 family.

Isinglass

This bay colt, foaled in 1890, was perhaps the greatest racehorse that ever ran. His racing record has already been dealt with in an earlier chapter and it now remains to 'read' his pedigree.

His sire was Isonomy, and so he was descended from Eclipse in the male line through Whalebone. His dam was Deadlock, who came down from Bowes' Mare by the Byerley Turk (No. 3 family) tracing, like Stockwell, Memoir, and La Fleche to Miss Belsea.

The male lines which enter the family tree of Isinglass through the sires of the fourth remove are Birdcatcher; Flatcatcher by Touchstone; The Baron by Birdcatcher; Ethelbert by Faugh a Ballagh, full brother to Birdcatcher; Newminister by Touchstone out of Beeswing; Rataplan by The Baron out of Pocahontas; Orlando by Touchstone; and The Flying Dutchman by Bay Middleton out of Barbelle; and through the dams at the fourth remove are Plenipotentiary by Emilius, son of Orville; Melbourne; Glencoe; The Prime Warden by Cadland, grandson of Orville; Melbourne; Birdcatcher; Priam, grandson of Orville; and Rubini by St Patrick, son of Walton, grandson of Highflyer.

Summarized this represents, through the sires, 7 lines of Eclipse through Whalebone and one of Herod through Woodpecker, and, through the dams, three lines of Eclipse through Orville, one line of Eclipse through Whalebone, one line of Herod through Woodpecker, one line of Herod through Highflyer, and two lines of Matchem through Melbourne; a final score of 11 Eclipse, 3 Herod, and 2 Matchem. But the most remarkable factor of all is that no less than 8 lines, exactly half the pedigree of Isinglass at the fourth remove, are male lines of Whalebone.

Hyperion

Turning now to more recent times, let us examine the pedigree of the most outstanding sire of the first half of the twentieth century.

Hyperion, a chestnut colt foaled on April 18th, 1930, was by Gainsborough out of Selene, by Chaucer out of Serenissima, by Minoru out of Gondolette.

He was therefore descended from Eclipse through Touchstone; Newminster (out of Beeswing); Lord Clifden; Hampton; Bay Ronald (out of Black Duchess); Bayardo (out of Galicia, by Galopin-Isoletta by Isonomy); and Gainsborough (out of Rosedrop, by St Frusquin, son of St Simon).

His dam line was one of the best in the stud book. Chaucer was by St Simon out of Canterbury Pilgrim (dam also of Swynford) by Tristan (son of Hermit and Thrift) out of Pilgrimage. Minoru was by Cyllene out of Mother Siegel (by a son of Hermit out of a Galopin mare). Gondolette, herself, goes back in direct female line to Old Bald Peg, the No. 6 foundation mare.

Big Game

A brown colt foaled on January 24th, 1939, who won the substitute races for the 2,000 Guineas and the Champion Stakes in 1942 in the colours of King George VI, Big Game was bred at the National Stud and is by Bahram, unbeaten winner of the Triple Crown of 2,000 Guineas, Derby, and St Leger, out of speedy Myrobella. He is therefore descended in direct male line from Eclipse through Whalebone, Birdcatcher, and Isonomy, and in direct female line from Old Bald Peg, No. 6 family. His maternal grandsire was Tetratema by The Tetrarch, a direct male descendant of Herod through Thormanby.

Bahram was out of Friar's Daughter, who comes down in No. 16 family from the Sister to Stripling through Miss Agnes, her sire being Friar Marcus, a descendant of Stockwell through Doncaster, Bend Or, Bona Vista, Cyllene, and Cicero.

The maternal grandam of Big Game, namely Dolabella, was by White Eagle (a son of Gallinule by Isonomy) out of Gondolette, great grandam of Hyperion.

St Simon comes into the pedigree as the sire of the famous mare La Fleche, dam of John O' Gaunt by Isinglass. John O' Gaunt, mated with Canterbury Pilgrim, produced Swynford, sire of Blandford, who got Bahram, the sire of Big Game.

Sun Chariot

A brown filly, foaled on March 5th, 1939, who won the substitute races for the 1,000 Guineas, Oaks, and St Leger in 1942, also in the royal racing colours, Sun Chariot was likewise bred at the National Stud and is by Hyperion, winner of the Derby and St Leger, out of Clarence, who never raced. She is therefore descended in direct male line from Eclipse through Whalebone, Touchstone, and Hampton, and in direct female line from Bowes' Mare by the Byerley Turk, No. 3 family. Her maternal grandsire was Diligence by Hurry On, a direct descendant of Matchem through West Australian.

Hyperion was out of Selene, who was by Chaucer (a son of St Simon and Canterbury Pilgrim) out of Serenissima, by Minoru out of Gondolette, great grandam of Big Game.

The maternal grandam of Sun Chariot, namely Nun's Veil, was by Friar Marcus (a son of Cicero by Cyllene) out of Blanche (dam of Blandford) by White Eagle out of Black Cherry, by Bendigo out of Black Duchess, the dam of Bay Ronald.

Dante and Sayajirao

Dante, a brown colt foaled in March 1942 who won the Derby, and Sayajirao, another brown colt foaled in April 1944 who won the St Leger, are full brothers by unbeaten Grand Prix winner Nearco out of Rosy Legend. They therefore belong to the Eclipse, Stockwell, Bend Or, Cyllene, Phalaris male line; while on the female side they are descended from Bowes' Mare by the Byerley Turk, dam of the two True Blues, No. 3 family.

Rosy Legend was by Dark Legend (a son of Dark Ronald) out of Rosy Cheeks, by St Just (a son of St Frusquin) out of Purity, by Gallinule (a son of Isonomy) out of Sanctimony, by St Serf (a son of St Simon) from Golden Iris, by Bend Or out of Gardenia (sister of Camelia, winner of the Oaks and the 1,000 Guineas) by Macaroni out of Araucaria, daughter of the famous brood-mare Pocahontas, dam of Stockwell.

The pedigree of these two splendid thoroughbreds is worthy of close study. The eight sires of the fourth generation back are Polymelus (Stockwell), Chaucer (Vedette), Rabelais (Vedette), Spearmint (Touchstone), Bay Ronald (Touchstone), Amphion (Vedette), St Frusquin (Vedette), and Gallinule

(Isonomy); all eight male stirps of Eclipse, with a considerable amount of St Simon blood in the middle of both halves of the pedigree.

Alycidon

A colt foaled in 1945 by Donatello II out of Aurora by Hyperion, Alycidon was bred by the late Lord Derby and won the Ascot, Goodwood, and Doncaster Cups for the present peer.

His male line from Eclipse descends through Isonomy, Isinglass, John O' Gaunt, Swynford, Blandford, and Blenheim to Donatello II, and his female line from the Tregonwell Barb Mare (No. 1 family) comes down via Penelope and Queen Bertha through Marchetta by Marco and Rose Red by Swynford to Aurora by Hyperion.

The important factor in the pedigree of Alycidon is the complete absence of Phalaris blood, which no doubt accounted to some extent for his stamina.

Tulyar

The most brilliant racehorse of recent years, Tulyar is a brown colt bred and owned by H.H. the Aga Khan and foaled in 1949, being by Tehran out of Neocracy by Nearco. He won the Derby, St Leger, Eclipse Stakes, and King George VI and Queen Elizabeth Stakes in 1952.

Tulyar is descended on the male side from Eclipse via St Simon, the sire line passing down through Chaucer, Prince Chimay, Vatout, and Bois Roussel to Tehran.

Bois Roussel was out of Plucky Liege, by Spearmint (son of Carbine) out of Concertina by St Simon, and Tehran was out of Stafaralla by Solario (son of Gainsborough) out of Mirawala, by Phalaris out of Miranda, full sister to Pretty Polly.

On the female side Tulyar comes from the No. 22 family, whose tap-root is the Belgrade Turk Mare. His third dam was Athasi, a famous brood-mare who, when mated with Blandford, produced Trigo, Athford, Primero, Harinero, and Harina. The latter was put to Nearco, the resultant offspring being Neocracy.

It will thus be seen that the pedigree of Tulyar contains most of the best male and female thoroughbred blood lines of the last thirty years, and it is interesting to note that, like Dante and Sayajirao, all eight sire lines at the fourth remove are male stirps of Eclipse.

Petite Etoile

Bred by the late Aga Khan and his son the late Aly Khan, Petite Etoile is a grey filly thrown in 1956 as the third foal of her dam, Star of Iran, who had been mated to Petition.

With a pedigree containing Lady Juror, Sceptre, Concertina, and Mumtaz Mahal as its four main female lines, and with Bois Roussel, Bahram, Gainsborough, and The Tetrarch as the link sires on the distaff side (No. 9 family), it is not surprising that Petite Etoile, endowed with such a pedigree, proved to be one of the great racing mares in the history of the Turf, with victories to her credit in the Oaks, 1,000 Guineas, Yorkshire Oaks, Sussex Stakes, Champion Stakes, and Coronation Cup twice.

St Paddy

A bay colt, bred by the Eve Stud Ltd., St Paddy, winner of the Derby and St Leger in 1960, is by Aureole out of Edic Kelly and is the third foal of his dam.

Aureole, the best son of the famous sire Hyperion, was bred by Her Majesty the Queen from the Royal Stud mare Angelola, by Donatello II out of Feola, by Friar Marcus out of Aloe, by Son-in-Law out of Alope, by Gallinule out of Altoviscar.

Edie Kelly was by Bois Roussel out of Caerleon's daughter Caerlissa, the next dam being Sister Sarah, by Tracery's son Abbots Trace out of Sarita, by Swynford out of Molly Desmond, daughter of the famous Pretty Polly.

This is an open pedigree derived from the four main sire lines of Eclipse, viz.: Gainsborough, Phalaris, Swynford, and Chaucer, reinforced by four more lines of St Simon, lacking Hurry On or Tetrarch blood, and tracing to Admiration (No. 14 family), at present the most successful foundation mare in the Stud Book.

Relko

A bay horse foaled in France in 1960 and bred and owned by the late M. Francois Dupré, Relko was the winner of the

English Derby, French 2,000 Guineas, French St Leger and Coronation Cup. He was by Tanerko (son of Tantieme) out of Relance III, also the dam of Match III and Reliance II. In male line he descends from Eclipse via Stockwell, Bend Or and Flying Fox, the male line coming down through Ajax, Teddy, Aethelstan, Deiri and Deux Pour Cent to Tantieme. Tanerko was out of La Divine, by Fair Copy (a son of Fairway and Composure, a granddaughter of Gondolette).

Relance III was a daughter of Relic (a son of War Relic by Man O' War) and was out of Polaire, by Le Volcan (son of Tourbillon) out of Stella Polaris, by Papyrus (by Tracery) out of Crepuscule by Galloper Light out of Terra d'Ombra by Thrush out of Coronation IV by Isinglass out of the great broodmare Sceptre. Relko therefore belongs to No. 16 family, whose tap-root mare is the Sister to Stripling.

Relko is possessed of a true international pedigree, whose four main sire lines are those of Teddy, Phalaris, Man O' War and Tourbillon.

Sea-Bird II

In the opinion of many good judges the greatest horse to race in Europe since the second World War, Sea Bird II was the winner of the Prix Lupin, the Epsom Derby and the Prix de l'Arc de Triomphe. A chesnut colt, foaled in France in 1962, he was bred by his owner Monsieur Jean Ternyck, by Dan Cupid (son of Native Dancer) out of Sicalade by Sicambre. In male line he descends from Eclipse through Stockwell, Bend Or and Phalaris the line coming down via Sickle, Unbreakable and Polynesian to Native Dancer. Dam of Dan Cupid is Vixenette, also by Sickle (by Phalaris out of Selene, mother of Hyperion); Dan Cupid is therefore inbred to Sickle in the fourth and second removes of his pedigree.

Sicambre, the maternal grandsire of Sea-Bird II, belongs to the male line of St Simon. Marmalade, the second dam of Sea Bird, is an own-sister to Camaree, the winner of the 1,000 Guineas, being by Maurepas (by Aethelstan, son of Teddy) out of Couleur, by Biribi (by Rabelais, son of St Simon) out of Colour Bar by Colorado, tracing at four removes to Donnetta, the dam of Diophon (2,000 Guineas) and Diadem (1,000

Guineas). The line goes back to the Burton Barb Mare, the foundation mare of No. 2 family.

The main sire lines in the pedigree are Phalaris, Phalaris, St Simon and Teddy. Perhaps, however the most interesting aspect about Sea-Bird II's pedigree is the fact that both his sire and dam, though not closely related to one another, are both the products of matings between closely related animals. Dan Cupid is in-bred to Sickle; Sicalade has three lines in her pedigree of the St Simon horse Rabelais. The pedigree of Sea-Bird II therefore represents an interesting mating of in-bred lines.

Royal Palace

The winner of the 2,000 Guineas, the Derby, the Coronation Cup, the Eclipse Stakes and the King George VI and Queen Elizabeth Stakes, Royal Palace is a bay horse, foaled in ·1964, bred and owned by Mr H. J. Joel, and is by Ballymoss out of Crystal Palace by Solar Slipper. In male line he descends from Eclipse, the line descending through Phalaris, Pharos, Nearco and Mossborough (who was out of All Moonshine out of Selene). His maternal grandsire is Solar Slipper (by Windsor Slipper, a son of Windsor Lad by Blandford).

Crystal Palace, the dam of Royal Palace, is out of Queen of Light by Borealis (by Brumeux, by Teddy, out of Aurora, dam of Alycidon) out of the 1,000 Guineas winner Picture Play, by Donatello II. The female stirp traces through Paradoxical, to the Natural Barb mare of Mr Tregonwell, the foundation mare of No. 1 family. The four main lines in the pedigree, viz. Phalaris, Gainsborough, Swynford and Teddy, are all male stirps of Eclipse. Gainsborough features no less than four times in the first six removes of his pedigree.

Sir Ivor

The winner of the 2,000 Guineas, the Derby, the Champion Stakes and the Washington International Stakes, Sir Ivor is a bay colt foaled in 1965, bred in the United States of America by Mrs Reynolds W. Bell and owned by Mr Raymond Guest, by Sir Gaylord (by Turn-To, son of Royal Charger) out of Something royal, (by Princequillo), dam of Secretariat, out of Attica by Mr Trouble, son of Mahmoud.

In male line Sir Ivor descends from Eclipse through Phalaris and Nearco. His maternal grandsire Mr Trouble, is a son of Mahmoud (a grandson of Mumtaz Mahal) and Motto by Sir Gallahad III (out of Plucky Liege).

His dam Attica, is out of Athenia, by Pharamond II (by Phalaris out of Selene, mother of Hyperion) out of Salaminia by Man O' War out of Alcibiades by Supremus. The line traces via Bridget, one of the foundation mares of the Stanley Stud, to Hutton's mare by Bustle, the tap-root mare of No. 8 family. All the main lines in the pedigree trace to Eclipse, through Phalaris, St Simon, Swynford and Phalaris.

Nijinsky

The first and only horse to win the Triple Crown of the 2,000 Guineas, Derby and St Leger since Bahram accomplished this feat in 1935, Nijinsky was also the winner of the Irish Sweeps Derby and King George VI and Queen Elizabeth Stakes. He was bred in Canada by Mr E. P. Taylor and owned by the late Mr C. W. Engelhard. A bay colt, foaled in 1967, he is by Northern Dancer, out of Flaming Page. Northern Dancer's sire Nearctic was by Nearco out of Lady Angela, by Hyperion, who traced to Pretty Polly. His dam Natalma is by Native Dancer out of Almahmoud by Mahmoud (grandson of Mumtaz Mahal).

Flaming Page is by Bull Page (son of Bull Lea, by Bull Dog by Teddy out of Plucky Liege) out of Flaring Top, by Menow (by Pharamond who is out of Selene) out of Flaming Top by Omaha (grandson of Sir Gallahad III, by Teddy out of Plucky Liege). The female family is that of No. 8, whose foundation mare is Hatton's mare by Bustle.

All the main male lines in the pedigree of Nijinsky trace to Eclipse. Three of these lines trace through Phalaris, with the exception of that of Bull Page, Nijinsky's maternal grandsire, which traces through Teddy. Selene appears twice in the pedigree, Mumtaz Mahal and Pretty Polly once each.

Mill Reef

Mill Reef, the winner of the Derby, Eclipse Stakes, King George VI and Queen Elizabeth Stakes, Prix de l'Arc de Triomphe and Coronation Cup, is a bay colt, who was foaled in the United States of America in 1968. His sire is Never Bend, by Nasrullah (grandson of Mumtaz Mahal) out of Lalun, by Djeddah (son of Djebel, by Tourbillon). His dam, Milan Mill, by Princequillo (by Prince Rose).

In male line he descends from Eclipse through Phalaris and Nearco. Milan Mill, his dam, is out of Virginia Water by Count Fleet (by Reigh Count, by Sunreigh, by Sundridge) out of Red Ray by Hyperion out of Infra Red by Ethnarch, tracing at three generations to the Oaks winner Our Lassie. The female family is No. 22, whose foundation mare was the Belgrade Turk mare. The four main male lines in the pedigree consist of Phalaris, Tourbillon, St Simon and Speculum.

The extended pedigree of Mill Reef is given on page 000.

Brigadier Gerard

The winner of the 2,000 Guineas, Eclipse Stakes, King George VI and Queen Elizabeth Stakes, Brigadier Gerard is a bay colt foaled in 1968, who was bred by Mr J. L. Hislop and owned by Mrs J. L. Hislop. He is by Queen's Hussar out of La Paiva. In male line he is descended from Eclipse, through Phalaris, the line coming down through Fairway, Fair Trial, Petition, and March Past to Queen's Hussar. The latter's dam Jojo is by Vilmorin (by Gold Bridge) out of Fairy Jane by Fair Trial.

La Paiva is by Prince Chevalier (son of Prince Rose) out of Brazen Molly, by Horus (by Papyrus, son of Tracery) out of Molly Adare by Phalaris out of Molly Desmond by Desmond out of that great race mare Pretty Polly.

The four main male lines in Brigadier Gerard's pedigree trace to Eclipse via Phalaris, Orby, St Simon and Rock Sand. Brigadier Gerard has two crosses of Fair Trial in the fourth remove and three lines of Fairway in the fifth remove of his pedigree. He also carries a line of Sceptre through his great-grandsire Petition.

Grundy

The winner of the Derby, Irish Sweeps Derby and King George VI and Queen Elizabeth Stakes, Grundy is a chestnut colt, foaled in 1972, bred by the Overbury Stud and owned by Dr Carlo Vittadini, by Great Nephew out of Word From Lundy by Worden II. In male line he is descended from Eclipse through Phalaris and descends through Fairway and Honeyway to Great Nephew. The dam of Great Nephew is Sybil's Niece by Admiral's Walk (son of Hyperion) out of Sybil's Sister, by Nearco out of Sister Sarah, a great-grandaughter of Pretty Polly.

Word from Lundy is out of Lundy Princess by Princely Gift (son of Nasrullah, by Nearco) out of Lundy Parrot by Flamingo (by Flamboyant, son of Tracery) out of Waterval by Friar Marcus (son of Cicero, by Cyllene). The line traces to Hutton's mare by Bustle, the foundation mare of No. 8 family.

The four main male lines, all of which trace to Eclipse, are Phalaris, Gainsborough, St Simon and Phalaris.

CHAPTER VII

Theories of Bloodstock Breeding

Fine gold will not wear well without an alloy.
William Crimson.

Robertson's Theory of Male Dominance

IT has been shown how both the male and the female sides, the top half and the bottom half of the pedigree of a thoroughbred racehorse can be traced back for over two hundred years, but experts still differ as to the relative importance of the sire line and the dam line in the heredity of the racehorse.

The opinion of one of the greatest authorities on the subject, the late 'Professor' J. B. Robertson, M.R.C.V.S., 'Mankato', is worth quoting from the volume on *Flat Racing* in the Lonsdale Library. He wrote 'The Y (male) chromosone *only* passes along the direct male line father to son chain. It is no part of the female equipment. On the other hand the male derives his X (female) chromosome from his mother and passes it to his daughter. The daughter at the same time receives an X chromosome from her mother. The male is thus YX and the female XX. It is the dominance of Y over X which results in maleness. . . . Though the Y chromosome is anchored to the direct male chain, there is no definite anchorage of the X chromosome to the direct mother to daughter path. . . . Although the Y and X chromosomes in the horse are the bearers of few, if any, of the genes which determine characters not strictly correlated with sex, their respective paths furnish clear evidence that the male line chain is a safer guide than the devious paths by which an X chromosome may reach a mare from either side of her pedigree.'

The same expert authority wrote in the *Bloodstock Breeders' Review* for 1937: 'The alternative souces of the X chromosome, the crossing over of the genes in the ordinary chromosomes, and also the fact that none of the ordinary chromosomes is chained, as it were, to either the male or female lines, renders absolutely nugatory the Bruce Lowe doctrine of perpetual anchorage in the direct female line of those characters and qualities which make or mar a racehorse.'

Becker's Theory of Female Influence

On the other hand the late Friedrich Becker, in *The Breed of the Racehorse*, stated categorically that 'Those sons of great sires which eventually succeeded in carrying on their lines bore very little if any resemblance to them and mostly were racehorses of an altogether different type. This feature, more perhaps than any other, demonstrates that a Sire Line does not thrive on the properties inherited from ancestors in straight male lineage, but that its continuation is determined by the qualities of the maternal lines with which it is crossed.'

He expressed the view that the factors which are being handed on in straight male descent, when consolidated by inbreeding, foster decay of the sire line, hence the failure of the St Simon male line.

Certainly the virtual extinction in this country of the St Simon male stirp remains one of the most profound mysteries of bloodstock breeding. In spite of his outstanding success as possibly the most brilliant stallion of all time and his evident ability to transmit his sterling qualities through the best broodmares at the stud to sons and daughters of the highest class on the race-course, the direct male descendants of St Simon below the second or third generation failed to win classic races and proved altogether unsatisfactory at the stud.

On the other hand, as already noted in another chapter, one of the sons of St Simon, namely Chaucer, became a very successful sire of broodmares, and practically no good thoroughbred pedigree exists to-day without St Simon blood somewhere on the female side.

Galton's Law of Ancestral Contribution

Sir Francis Galton, in a more dialectical approach to the subject, laid down a rule of ancestral contribution under which on the average both parents together contribute one half to their offspring; the four grandparents, one quarter; the eight great-grandparents, one eighth; and so on to infinity; and this has proved a quite satisfactory theory in the estimation of the probable stamina capacity of a racehorse.

If one half of the average distance of the races won by the sire and the dam, excluding two-year-olds races, is added to one quarter of the similar averages for the four grandparents and one eighth for the eight great-grandparents, plus one eighth for the sixteen sires and dams of the next previous generation, a stamina index can be obtained which will serve as an approximate guide to the potential distance up to which any particular horse can be expected to win races.

Vuillier's System of Dosages

Colonel J. Vuillier, in *Les Croisments Rationnels*, propounded a system of dosages based on Galton's law. He carefully analysed to the 4,096 ancestors in the twelfth generation of a pedigree the number of times different sires appeared in the pedigrees of the best winners and concluded therefrom that certain sires and, oddly enough, one mare, in definite proportions, were desirable in the make-up of a first-class racehorse. He recommended that if a stallion or a brood-mare was deficient in any of the indicated strains, this deficiency should be made good by the brood-mare or the stallion with whom the animal concerned was to be mated.

Mr H. E. Keylock, F.R.C.V.S., in the *Bloodstock Breeders' Review* for 1938, voiced the opinion that the Vuillier system of dosages is the most clearly defined system that has yet been propounded for the mating of thoroughbreds. He suggested, however, that some modification is now necessary. 'If one accepts Galton's law of ancestral contribution,' he wrote, 'the unit value of an ancestor beyond the sixth generation can have but an infinitesimal value in a pedigree, and the ancestors from the sixth to the first generation must predominate. . . . Applying this contention to Vuillier's "standard horse", the only sires which need be considered are Stockwell, Newminster, St Simon, Galopin, Isonomy, Hampton, Hermit, and Bend Or.' The others, which made up Vuillier's 'dough', namely Birdcatcher, Touchstone, the mare Pocahontas, Voltaire, Pantaloon, Melbourne, Bay Middleton, and Gladiator, will, in the opinion of this expert, now be dominated by the more recent ancestors in a pedigree.

Chismon's Adage

The late Mr William Chismon, who was secretary to the late Lord Wavertree, founder of the National Stud, and an adviser to the Aga Khan on breeding, once made a profoundly important statement to the effect that 'fine gold will not wear well without an alloy; neither will the progeny of finely bred mares be very robust or sturdy if got by stallions whose pedigrees contain too much fine blood'.

Breeding not an Exact Science

It must never be forgotten that breeding is not an exact science, although the late Lord Wavertree was an ardent believer in astrology and its application, through the medium of horoscopes, to the mating and racing of thoroughbreds. There is, of course, no certain method for the breeding of classic winners, but by a process of 'trial and error' some lines have been found to 'nick' well together and others to be less successful when mated.

It must be admitted that many thoroughbreds, apparently of the bluest blood, are a failure both on the race-course and at the stud, although conversely practically all classic winners and successful sires or brood-mares are themselves well-bred animals.

In some rare cases full brothers, like Persimmon and Diamond Jubilee, and full sisters, like Memoir and La Fleche, have been almost equally brilliant on the race-course, but more often than not, as they inherit different genes from their parents, there is a considerable difference in racing ability between them, in spite of the fact that they are bred on precisely the same lines. The conspicuous success of both the full brothers, Pharos and Fairway, as stallions at the stud is also exceptional.

Senator Tesio's Views

Mr John Hislop, in his foreword to the English translation of the late Senator Federico Tesio's notes on *Breeding the Racehorse* wrote 'Senator Tesio produced his many great race-horses, sires, and brood-mares from comparatively limited resources. He never had a large number of mares in his stud at any given time, did not spend a great deal of money on bloodstock and sold most of the best horses he bred. Senator Tesio was a genius.'

Another writer has maintained that this famous Italian breeder 'produced all the right results for all the wrong reasons'. Be that as it may, the results included such celebrated thoroughbreds as Nearco (1935), Niccolo Dell' Arca (1938), Tenerani (1944), Botticelli (1951), and mighty Ribot (1952), considered by some good judges to have been the best racehorse in the entire history of the Turf.

In the circumstances, at least some of the views expressed by 'the wizard of Dormello' ought to be well worth while paying heed to, and his final conclusions are therefore reproduced for the benefit of my readers:

'All life is based on the consumption of energy to gain supremacy and on rest to restore that energy. In the rivalry for the selection of racing stock, no thoroughbred family can hold the supremacy of success for more than a small number of generations in direct line. This number of generations and the degree of their attainment are irrevocably limited by nature. When these limits are reached, the top producer of the moment must surrender his supremacy to another producer slightly inferior as an individual, who may occasionally belong to a collateral branch but in most instances will represent another family altogether. He in turn will start a new line of top stars. After running its cycle this line too will surrender the sceptre—which it may eventually regain after a period of rest.'

'Breeders have always concentrated on improving the speed of the thoroughbred, which is not a Mendelian character but is derived from a combination of many Mendelian characters under the influence of nervous energy. These characters, by selection through the severe test of the races, have all been stamped with the mark of quality. But through successive generations the degree of nervous energy and of selected quality can only reach a certain limit. When this limit is reached the "bubble" must burst.'

General Conclusions on the Breeding of Thoroughbreds

When considering the conflicting claims of the sire and the dam as the preponderating influence in the evolution of the thoroughbred two important compensating factors must be borne in mind. Firstly, that generally speaking only those colts who have proved themselves on the race-course to be the very best of their age are subsequently used as stallions and serve the cream of the brood-mares, whereas nearly all fillies, whatever their racing record, good or bad, end up in the paddocks as brood-mares; and secondly, that a successful stallion has far more progeny than a successful brood-mare, because in any single year a sire may get more than forty offspring whereas a dam can only produce one.

After the most careful consideration of all the factors involved and the most profound study of the many differing opinions expressed and conflicting theories held by experts on the subject of bloodstock breeding, one arrives at the following general conclusions:

1. The best racing colt of to-day is the best stallion of to-morrow, provided that he is also the finest physical specimen of his sire line alive when he goes to the stud.

2. The best bred filly of to-day is the best brood-mare of to-morrow, irrespective of her performance on the race-course, provided that she has not been over-raced and once she has proved that she can throw a good winner.

3. The aggregate excellence of all the sires in the last few generations is of more importance than the aggregate excellence of all the dams in the pedigree of a thoroughbred.

4. The bottom half of a pedigree should contain some inbreeding for speed to the top half, but with at least one outcross of good stout blood for stamina. 'Breed in to fix type, breed out to secure vigour,' is the maxim propounded by Mr Watson in his book *Heredity*, quoted by Mr John Loder in his interesting chapter on the British Racing Thoroughbred in *The Book of the Horse*.

5. As about 75 per cent of the leading stallions of to-day are direct male descendants of Gainsborough, Phalaris, or Swynford, we may perhaps propound a new theory by reversing Mr Chismon's adage and stating categorically that 'the progeny of finely bred *stallions* will not be very robust or sturdy if thrown by *mares* whose pedigree contain too much fine blood'.

CHAPTER VIII

Origins of Horse-Racing

I have heard of riding wagers
Where horses have been nimbler than sands.

Shakespeare, *Cymbeline.*

HORSE-RACING is derived from warfare, chariot racing, and the chase, and it is not without significance that, at the time of the Roman occupation of Britain, Queen Boadicea and her people, the trible of the Iceni, lived on Newmarket Heath and that their gold and silver coins were stamped on the reverse side with the effigy of a horse.

The earliest horse-race in England of which a record still exists took place at Netherby in Yorkshore about A.D. 210 between Arabian steeds brought to this country by the Roman Emperor Septimus Severus Alexander, who made special arrangements for the shelter and training of these delicate horses.

Matches Between Running Horses

Another early description of a match between running horses was given by the Venerable Bede, and King Alfred the Great had a Master of the Horse. The secretary to Thomas Becket, Archbishop of Canterbury in the reign of Henry II, refers to some rough-and-ready races at 'Smoothfield' in which, "the jockies inspired with thoughts of applause, and in the hope of victory, clap spurs to the willing horses, brandish their whips, and cheer them with their cries"; but it was not until the reign of King Richard I that racing first became a fashionable pastime for the barons and knights who followed the King to the Crusades.

It is known that in 1377 the Prince of Wales, afterwards Richard II, raced against the Earl of Arundel, later Lord High Admiral of England, 'owners up', and most of the early history of horse-racing consists of matches of this kind between two horses, when one proud possessor of a 'horse of price', which perhaps he has brought back with him from the Holy Land, wagers that his steed is swifter than that of another knight-at-arms, issues a challenge to his rival, and the matter is put to the test over a course of some miles before the King and Court.

Racing in Tudor Times

However, it was not until the reign of King Henry VIII that the first race-course was officially established, on the Roodee at Chester in 1540, and an annual prize first instituted, which took the form of a silver bell; and moreover this monarch did much to improve the royal studs and the breed of the horse in general throughout the country.

In 1574 Queen Elizabeth attended the races at Croydon and a grandstand was later built on the course for her convenience. She was also present at the races held on Salisbury Plain at about the same time.

King James I and the Markham Arabian

On 20th December 1616 a payment of £154 was made out of the Royal Exchequer to Master Markham for an Arabian horse for the use of His Majesty, and this small bay stallion became the first ancestor, through the royal mares, of the modern thoroughbred.

King James I greatly improved the royal palace at Newmarket, adding new stables and a grandstand on the Heath. He had royal studs at Cole Park and Tutbury and other establishments at Hampton Court and Eltham. The Duke of Buckingham was Master of the Horse, there were two Surveyors of the Races, and four child riders in the Royal Household received sixpence a day board wages and about £60 a year for their expenses, together with one 'horse livery' each. Race-meetings were held at Newmarket, Doncaster, York, Chester, Liverpool, Lincoln, Salisbury, Winchester, Croydon, and elsewhere, even in Hyde Park.

Cups had by now been generally adopted as prizes in place of the gold and silver bells previously awarded, and up to six or more horses competed in heats, followed by a deciding race between the winners of the heats, over long distances up to six

miles, from three to five times round the race-course, the horses
carrying weights of from eight to seventeen stone on their backs.
In addition matches between two horses were still a popular
feature of the racing, with wages of £1,000 or more a side.

Regular meetings in the spring and autumn were established at Newmarket by King Charles I, and the Newmarket
Gold Cup was first run for in 1634, but twenty years later the
Council of State under the Commonwealth prohibited horse-
racing, although it did not succeed in suppressing it altogether,
and it was not until after the Restoration that the sport again
flourished, when:

> *A hound and hawk no longer*
> *Shall be tokens of disaffection,*
> *A cockfight shall cease*
> *To be a breach of the peace,*
> *And a horse-race an insurrection.*

Old Rowley and Newmarket

King Charles II made Newmarket the headquarters of the
Turf, which it has remained ever since. Pope was to write later:

> *Then peers grew proud in horsemanship t'excell,*
> *Newmarket's glory rose, as Britain's fell.*

The Merry Monarch rode his own horse first past the winning
post in the Plate at Newmarket on 14th October 1671. His
favourite hack was called Old Rowley, which became the
King's own nickname, and this is still remembered to this day
in the famous Rowley Mile at Newmarket, the finest straight
mile race-course in the world. In the days of Charles II the
course at Newmarket was a tract of land extending four miles
round the level Heath, the grass of which was kept short and
which was marked out by tall wooden posts painted white, the
last post having a flag on it to denote the end of the course.

In addition to the meetings already mentioned races were
run on Epsom Downs and Burford Downs.

> *Here has been rode many a race.*
> *King Charles II I saw here;*
> *But I've forgotten in what year.*

Queen Anne and Ascot

Queen Anne owned and raced horses with the keenest zest, and in a letter to Stella, dated 10th August 1711, Dean Jonathan Swift records that the Queen and her consort were at Ascot. The opening race at the Royal Meeting is named after her the Queen Anne Stakes. She gave a number of Queen's Plates, for horses, mares, or geldings, carrying 12 stone each, to be run in three heats over a four-mile course.

Some of the racehorses of this period had curious names; 'Tickle-me-quickly', 'Jenny-come-tie-me', 'Peggy grieves me', 'Kill 'em and eat 'em', 'Patch Buttocks', 'Louse', and 'Pig' are a few of the more bizarre examples; and in addition to the usual bay, brown, black, chestnut, and grey colours of to-day, race-horses of the seventeenth and eighteenth centuries were white, yellow-dun, mouse-coloured, sorrel, piebald, and skewbald.

Horses hardly raced at all as three-year-olds in those days before the advent of the 'classic' races, and many of the best thoroughbreds did not run until they were six-year-olds and then went on running matches until they were ten or even twelve years of age.

Furthermore, the distances they ran were far more punishing than is now the case, as much as six or even eight miles in some cases, while four heats of a mile each was a common performance for one horse on the same day.

CHAPTER IX

Dictators of the Turf and the Jockey Club— leading Owners and Breeders

He attended to his game commonly, and didn't much meddle with the conversation except when it was about horses and betting.

William Makepeace Thackeray, *Vanity Fair*.

Tregonwell Frampton

Mr Tregonwell Frampton (1641–1727) has been called 'The Father of the English Turf'. This extraordinary man was appointed Supervisor of the royal race-horses at Newmarket by King William III and held the same appointment in the reigns of Queen Anne and the first two Georges. He took up his abode at Heath House in 1689 and was paid the sum of £1,000 per annum for the maintenance of ten boys and the provision of ten racehorses.

Frampton raced his favourite horse against one sponsored by Sir William Strickland in the most famous trial match of the period, on the result of which large sums were wagered; whereupon Parliament, 'in order to put a stop to such ruinous proceedings', enacted a law to prevent the recovery of any sum exceeding ten pounds betted upon a horse-race.

Sir Charles Bunbury

Sir Charles Bunbury (1740–1821), who married the most beautiful woman in England and at various times held the post of Chief Secretary for Ireland, was the leading figure on the Turf at the end of the eighteenth century. He became a kind of perpetual president of the Jockey Club for more than forty years and was the owner of Diomed, winner of the first Derby; Eleanor, the first filly to win the Derby and the Oaks; and Smolensko, the first colt to win the Derby and the 2,000 Guineas. The Bunbury Mile course at Newmarket is named after him.

The Prince Regent

King George IV as Prince of Wales won the Derby in 1788 and his brother the Duke of York won it in 1816 and 1822. The latter founded the first handicap race, the Oatlands Stakes, for 2,950 guineas, run at Ascot in 1791, the most valuable race of its time, which was won by the Prince of Wales's Baronet before a crowd of 40,000 racing enthusiasts. The First Gentleman in Europe is reputed to have won £17,000 over the victory of his horse.

When, after the 'in and out' running of Escape, the Stewards of the Jockey Club let is be known that if Sam Chifney continued to ride the Prince's horses 'no gentlemen would start again them,' 'Prinny' withdrew his royal patronage from the Turf.

Some Georgian Owners

Famous owners and breeders of Georgian times were Lord Egremont, who won the Derby five times and the Oaks five times, his last winner of the Derby being Lapdog, who 'swam home in fine style', at odds of 33 to 1 against, on a pouring wet day in 1826; and the Duke of Bedford, Lord Grosvenor (who won the Oaks six times), Sir Frederick Standish, the 3rd Duke of Grafton, and the 5th Earl of Jersey, who all won the Derby three times. Other keen supporters of racing were Lord Chesterfield, Sir John Shelley, and Charles James Fox, who was a member of the Jockey Club and kept some thirty 'running horses' in training.

Lord George Bentinck

Lord George Bentinck (1802–48) succeeded Sir Charles Bunbury as the most outstanding figure in racing circles.

Known as 'The Napoleon of the Turf', he was probably the ablest administrator in the annals of horse-racing. His father, the Duke of Portland, had secured the legal right of the Jockey Club to warn off Newmarket Heath any undesirable characters, and the son continued to carry out many reforms in his campaign to clean up and improve the Turf.

In 1844 the Derby was won by Running Rein, who, as a two-year-old named Maccabeus, had been surreptitiously exchanged with a colt in the yearling's paddock and was therefore in reality a four-year-old when he won the premier classic. Lord George Bentinck, after long and patient investigation, successfully exposed this fraud and the race was awarded to Orlando, who had finished second to Running Rein.

Lord George introduced the practice of parading the runners in the paddock before a race and numbering the horses to facilitate their indentification; he was responsible for inaugurating the system of starting races by means of a flag and laid out a model race-course at Goodwood. Furthermore, he abolished the peculiar custom whereby the owner of a winning horse was expected to give a present to the Judge, and was also the first person to send a racehorse by road, instead of the animal being ridden or led to the meeting, when Elis was conveyed in a van drawn by six horses from Goodwood to Doncaster, at the 'unheard of pace' of 95 miles in under 12 hours, to win the St Leger in 1836, an incident which caused some alarmed spectators to declare that a wild beast of fearful ferocity was locked up inside.

The best horse owned by Lord George Bentinck was Crucifix, whom he bought for £60 and with whom he won the 2,000 Guineas, 1,000 Guineas, and Oaks in 1840. He was a very heavy gambler and won £30,000 on Cotherstone in the Derby of 1843 and two years later cleared over £100,000 by betting alone.

In 1846 Lord George sold his entire racing interests for £10,000 in order to devote himself to his political duties, and among the horses sold was Surplice, destined to win the Derby and the St Leger in 1848 in the colours of Lord Clifden.

Now Lord George Bentinck had never fulfilled his life's ambition to own the winner of the Derby, and when he heard that a horse which he had actually once himself possessed had won the great race 'he gave a sort of superb groan' according to the description given of the incident by Disraeli. 'All my life I have been trying for this.' It was in vain to offer solace. 'You do not know what the Derby is,' moaned out Lord George. 'Yes I do,' replied Lord Beaconsfield, 'it is the Blue Riband of the Turf.'

Four months later Lord George Bentinck was dead 'by the visitation of God, to wit, a spasm of the heart'.

Admiral Rous

Vice-Admiral the Honourable Henry James Rous (1795 –1877) followed as the next 'Dictator of the Turf'. He showed that it was not necessary to breed and own racehorses on a large scale or to be a heavy gambler in order to control and improve the affairs of the Turf. It was Admiral Rous who first propounded the theory that the power of the Jockey Club should be based upon its moral force. 'Racing has always been, and will always be, a gambling speculation' he once wrote, but he was not going to let it degenerate into a blackguardly conspiracy.

In 1855 he was appointed official Handicapper to the Jockey Club and he was responsible for drawing up the scale of weight for Age which was in use until 1973, when it was revised by Major David Swannell, M.B.E., the Jockey Club Handicapper. The Admiral is commemorated in two races, at Ascot and Goodwood, named after him, the Rous Memorial Stakes.

Sir Randle Fielden

Major General Sir Randle Fielden, C.B., C.B.E., K.C.V.O., has been a leading figure in the administration and modernisation of the English Turf in recent years. A former Senior Steward of the Jockey Club, he was also chairman of the Joint Racing Board.

The Jockey Club

Under the direction of men like Sir Charles Bunbury, Lord George Bentinck, and Admiral Rous the whole system of horse-racing in this country gradually evolved and the Jockey Club slowly grew in importance, until the Stewards became the all-powerful central authority for the control and management of the Turf, and by degrees 'their actions became precedents, their advice grew into law.'

The Jockey Club was founded in 1750. At first its official meetings were held at the Star and Garter Coffee House in Pall Mall. Later Mr Richard Tattersall, founder of the famous firm of thorough-bred auctioneers, provided the Club with a cook and a private room at Hyde Park Corner, and subsequently Messrs Weatherby's rooms in Old Burlington Street became the recognised headquarters in London. At Newmarket the Club leased a Coffee Room in 1752, and eventually the freehold was bought in 1831.

The lands forming the actual race-course at Newmarket were acquired in 1798, 1807, 1808, and 1819 and adjoining lands later. This enabled the Jockey Club to establish its legal right by 1827 to 'warn off' undesirables from Newmarket Heath, with the exception of the Devil's Dyke, along which a coffin is wheeled once a year to preserve the public right of way.

In 1756 the Jockey Club abolished the established system of running heats for races followed by a deciding final, and directed that in future all horses would run against one another in a single race no matter how many entries might be made. By 1762 the practice of making jockeys wear distinctive racing colours had become standardized, and some ten years later the first official Judge was appointed, a Starter and a Clerk of the Scales coming soon afterwards, so that by the time Queen Victoria came to the throne horse-racing was very much as we know it to-day, the most noticeable difference being the method of riding, the jockeys of those days sitting upright in the saddle and using long stirrup-leathers and a long rein.

In 1970 the Jockey Club were granted a Royal Charter, and in 1977 it was decided to admit ladies to membership. The first ladies to become members were the Countess of Halifax, Mrs P. Hastings and Mrs H. T. Johnson-Houghton.

The Racing Calendar and the General Stud Book

As long ago as 1670 a Mr John Nelson had published the records of racing at Newmarket and in 1727 a Mr John Cheny first produced an annual volume entitled *An Historical List or Account of All Horse Matches run*. Mr James Weatherby, Keeper of the Match Book at Newmarket and Secretary of the Jockey

Club, first published the Racing Calendar in 1773, and ever since then Messrs Weatherbys have been solicitor, treasurer, agent, and shakeholder to the Jockey Club, Keeper of the Match Book, and publisher of the Racing Calendar. The first volume of the General Stud Book appeared in 1791.

Early Victorian Owners

Among well-known owners of the early Victorian era were Mr John Bowes and Sir Joseph Hawley, 'the lucky baronet', who both won the Derby four times; the former with Mundig, Cotherstone, Daniel O'Rourke, and West Australian; the latter with Teddington, Beadsman, Musjid, and Blue Gown. Mr Bowes celebrated his majority by winning the Derby for the first time in 1835 with Mundig, after a dispute with his trustees, and he won £50,000 on Cotherstone, when that horse won the premier classic in 1843, but the best thoroughbred he ever owned was West Australian, the first horse to win the Triple Crown, which he carried off in 1853, also winning the Ascot Gold Cup in record time in the following year.

Colonel Peel, owner of Orlando; Lord Eglinton, owner of Van Tromp and The Flying Dutchman, both out of the mare Barbelle; Lord Zetland, owner of Voltigeur; Mr James Merry, owner of Thormanby and Doncaster; Lord Chaplin, owner of Hermit; Lord Falmouth, owner of Kingcraft and Silvio; and Prince Batthyany, owner of Galopin, were other distinguished patrons of the Turf in those times.

Two remarkable characters of the nineteenth century, who were also keen racing men, were Squire Osbaldeston, who once rode 200 miles in under ten hours for a wager of 1,000 guineas, and John Gully, butcher, publican, champion bareknuckle prizefighter of England, bookmaker, and Member of Parliament, who won the Derby twice.

Late Victorian Owners

The four great pillars of the Turf at the turn of the last century were H.R.H. the Prince of Wales, afterwards King Edward VII; the 1st Duke of Westminster; the 6th Duke of Portland; and the 5th Earl of Rosebery.

The Prince of Wales won the Derby and the St Leger with Persimmon in 1896 and the Triple Crown and the Eclipse

Stakes with Diamond Jubilee in 1900, when he headed the list of winning owners and breeders and also won the Grand National of that year with Ambush II. After he had ascended the throne he again won the Derby with Minoru in 1909, when the monarch's horse, which started favourite for the race, won the Blue Riband of the Turf by a short head, amid scenes of utmost enthusiasm and to the accompaniment of the most tumultuous cheering ever heard on Epsom Downs.

The Duke of Westminster won the Triple Crown twice, once with the mighty, unbeaten Ormonde in 1886 and again with the famous Flying Fox in 1899. He also won the Derby with Bend Or in 1880 and Shotover in 1882.

The Duke of Portland, owner of St Simon and Carbine, won the Derby with Ayrshire in 1888, the Derby and the St Leger with Donovan in 1889, and the Oaks and the St Leger with Memoir in 1890.

The Earl of Rosebery is reputed to have made up his mind at an early age to marry an heiress, become Prime Minister, and win the Derby, all of which ambitions he subsequently achieved. He was in fact Prime Minister when his horse Ladas won him his first Derby in 1894. In the following year, wearing his colours, Sir Visto won the Derby and St Leger, and again in 1905 Lord Rosebery won the Derby with Cicero.

Baron Rothschild, owner of Hannah; Mr Leopold de Rothschild, owner of St Frusquin and St Amant; Baron de Hirsch, owner of La Fleche; Lord Alington and Sir Frederick Johnstone, owner of Common; Colonel H. McCalmont, owner of Isinglass; Mr J. Gubbins, owner of Galtee More and Ard Patrick; Sir James Miller, owner of Rock Sand; Major E. Loder, owner of Spearmint and Pretty Polly; Lord Wavertree; the brothers 'Solly' and 'Jack' Joel; and Mr A. W. Cox, owner of Bayardo, Lemberg, and Gay Crusader, were other keen supporters of the Turf during the Gay Nineties and Edwardian age.

Leading Owners and Breeders Between the Wars
The leading figures on the Turf between the wars and up to 1950 were King George V and his son King George VI; the 17th Earl of Derby; the 2nd Viscount Astor; the Aga Khan; and the 6th Earl of Rosebery; together with Lord Woolavington, Lord Glanely, Lord Dewar, and Sir Abe Bailey.

The best racehorse owned by King George V was the filly Scuttle, who won the 1,000 Guineas in 1928. King George VI, in addition to breeding his own racehorses, leased a number of yearlings from the National Stud, and two of these were Big Game and Sun Chariot, the former winner of the 2,000 Guineas and the Champion Stakes, the latter winner of the 1,000 Guineas, the Oaks, and the St Leger, all war-time substitute races in 1942, when His Majesty ended the season at the top of the list of winning owners. In 1946 Hypericum, after unseating his jockey, D. Smith, and bolting at the start, won the 1,000 Guineas and Rising Light the Jockey Club Stakes in the royal colours, both these horses having been bred by the King. In 1950 the monarch also won the Cesarewitch with his home-bred filly Above Board.

The late Lord Derby (black; white cap) was deservedly dubbed the doyen of the English Turf. When he won the Derby with Sansovino in 1924 he was the first peer of his line to win the premier classic since his ancestor, who founded the race, won it in 1787 with Sir Peter Teazle. The 17th Earl again won the Derby with Hyperion in 1933 and a war-substitute race in 1942 with Watling Street. His six winners of the St Leger were Swynford, Keysoe, Tranquil, Fairway, Hyperion, and Herringbone; and his other classic successes were with Colorado and Garden Path in the 2,000 Guineas; Canyon, Ferry, Tranquil, Fair Isle, Tideway, Herringbone, and Sun Stream in the 1,000 Guineas; and Toboggan and Sun Stream in the Oaks. Lord Derby also won the Eclipse Stakes with Swynford, Colorado, Fairway, Caerleon, and Gulf Stream, and the Gold Cup with Bosworth. A wonderful record indeed and, furthermore, as the owner of four of the best stallions of recent times, Swynford, Hyperion, Fairway, and Pharos, and of wonderful brood-mares like Selene and Scapa Flow, at the Stanley House Stud, Lord Derby was rightly regarded as the leading breeder of bloodstock in this country; a truly noble patron of the Turf who enjoyed the affection and esteem of the entire racing community. Alycidon, winner of the Ascot, Goodwood, and Doncaster Cups, was owned by the present Lord Derby.

The late Lord Astor (light blue; pink sash and cap) never succeeded in winning the Derby, although Blink, Buchan,

Craig-an-Eran, Tamar, and St Germans all finished second in the famous race; an astonishing run of ill fortune. Lord Astor won the St Leger with Book Law and the Oaks no less than five times, with Sunny Jane, Pogrom, Saucy Sue, Short Story, and Pennycomequick. He also owned such good colts as Buchan and three winners of the 2,000 Guineas, Craig-an-Eran, Pay Up, and Court Martial. In addition Buchan, Craig-an-Eran, Saltash, and Rhodes Scholar carried his colours to victory in the Eclipse Stakes. Lord Astor built up one of the finest studs in the world at Cliveden, the three foundation mares being Conjure, bought for £100 in 1900, Popinjay, bought for 1,000 guineas, and Maid of the Mist, brought for 4,500 guineas. Lord Astor was a non-betting owner-breeder like the late Lord Derby. His son, the third Viscount. who died in 1966 won the Oaks with Ambiguity.

The late Aga Khan (green and chocolate hoops; chocolate cap) was a lavish supporter of the Turf and won the Derby five times, with Blenheim, Bahram, Mahmoud, My Love, and Tulyar; the St Leger six times, with Salmon Trout, Firdaussi, Bahram, Turkan, Tehran, and Tulyar; the Oaks twice with Udaipur and Masaka; the 2,000 Guineas three times, with Diophon, Bahram, and Palestine; and the 1,000 Guineas once with Rose Royale II. He also won the Eclipse Stakes with Rustom Pasha, Migoli, and Tulyar, the Gold Cup with Felicitation and Umiddad, and the King George VI and Queen Elizabeth Stakes with Tulyar. In the St Leger of 1932 the Aga Khan actually owned four out of the first five horses, Firdaussi (1st) Dastur (2nd) Udaipur (4th) and Taj Masra (5th). In 1952 he headed the list of winning owners with what was then the record sum of £92,518 in stakes and the Aga Khan was the only man ever to win over a million pounds in stakes during his lifetime. As related elsewhere the Aga Khan sold three of his Derby winners to breeders in the United States; Blenheim for £45,000 in 1936, and unbeaten triple-crowned Bahram for £40,000, and Mahmoud for £20,000 in 1940. Early in 1953 it was announced that he had sold Tulyar to the Irish National Stud for £250,000.

The late Lord Rosebery (primrose and rose hoops; rose cap, who died in 1974) won the Derby twice: with Blue Peter in 1939 and with Ocean Swell in 1944, the former also winning the

2,000 Guineas and the Eclipse Stakes and the latter the Jockey Club Cub and Ascot Gold Cup. His other classic successes were the Oaks with Sleeping Partner and the St Leger with Sandwich, and he also won the Eclipse Stakes with Miracle. Lord Rosebery, like Lord Durham and Lord Hamilton of Dalzell before him, played a very important part in the administration of the Turf and sponsored many reforms for improving the amenities of racing.

The late Lord Woolavington won the Derby with Captain Cuttle and Coronach and the St Leger with Hurry On and Coronach, and his daughter, the Honourable Lady Macdonald-Buchanan, won the war-time Derby with Owen Tudor in 1941 and a substitute Gold Cup at Newmarket with the same good horse in 1942; she also owned the brilliant sprinter Abernant. The late Lord Glanely won the Derby with Grand Parade, the Oaks with Rose of England, the St Leger with Singapore and Chulmleigh, the 2,000 Guineas with Colombo, and the 1,000 Guineas with Dancing Time.

Lord Dewar never won a classic race, but his nephew, Mr J. A. Dewar, carried off the 2,000 Guineas and the Derby with a horse bred by his uncle, namely Cameronian, won a war-time Oaks with Commotion, a post-war 2,000 Guineas with Tudor Minstrel and 1,000 Guineas with Festoon. Sir Abe Bailey won the Oaks with Lovely Rosa and the Gold Cup twice, with Foxlaw and Tiberius.

Leading Owners and Breeders in Recent Times

Her Majesty Queen Elizabeth II (racing colours: purple, gold braid, scarlet sleeves, black velvet crop with gold fringe) has met with remarkable success as an owner and breeder since she ascended the throne in 1952.

As is well known, the Queen is an enthusiastic patron of the Turf and really loves horses. Among her winners have been the mighty Aureole (King George VI and Queen Elizabeth Stakes, Coronation Cup and Hardwicke Stakes), Pall Mall (2,000 Guineas), Highclere (1,000 Guineas and French Oaks), Carrozza (Oaks), Dunfermline (Oaks and St Leger), Canisbay (Eclipse Stakes), Above Suspicion (St James's Palace Stakes), Almeria (Yorkshire Oaks, Park Hill and Ribblesdale Stakes), Example (Park Hill Stakes and Prix de Royallieu), Escorial

(Musidora Stakes), Hopeful Venture (Grand Prix de Saint-Cloud, Hardwicke Stakes and Princess of Wales's Stakes), Pindari (Great Voltigeur Sweepstakes and King Edward VII Stakes) and Charlton (Henry II Stakes). She has won the Doncaster Cup four times, with Atlas in 1956, with Agreement in 1958 and 1959 and with Magna Carta in 1970. Her Majesty headed the list of winning owners in 1954 with £40,993 in stakes winnings and in 1957 with £62,212, the first reigning monarch ever to do so twice in the history of the Turf.

The late Sir Victor Sassoon (peacock blue, old gold hoops and sleeves) won the Derby four times: with Pinza in 1953, Crepello in 1957, Hard Ridden in 1958, and St Paddy in 1960. Pinza also won the King George VI and Queen Elizabeth Stakes, Crepello the 2,000 Guineas, Hard Ridden the Irish 2,000 Guineas, and St Paddy the St Leger, Eclipse, Jockey Club, and Voltigeur Stakes. Exhibitionist won the Oaks and the 1,000 Guineas, and Honeylight the 1,000 Guineas, for the same owner. Sir Victor was the leading owner in 1953 with £58,579 in stakes, and again in 1960 with £90,069.

Aly Khan inherited his father's racing interests when the old Aga Khan died in 1957, and until his own tragic death in a motor accident in 1960 met with the same brilliant successes as the Aga had enjoyed.

Among the racehorses he owned were the 1,000 Guineas winner Rose Royale II, in partnership with his father, the 2,000 Guineas winner Taboun, the Eclipse Stakes winner Saint Crespin III, the Gold Cup winner Sheshoon, and the wonderful filly Petite Etoile, winner of the Oaks, 1,000 Guineas, Champion Stakes, Yorkshire Oaks, Sussex Stakes, Coronation Cup twice, and over £60,000 in stake money. In 1959 Aly Khan beat his father's previous record winnings in a season by heading the list of winning owners with £100,688 in stakes.

Prominent owners during the fifties and sixties were the late Sir Humphrey de Trafford, owner of Parthia (Derby and Jockey Club Cup) and Alcide (King George VI and Queen Elizabeth Stakes, St Leger, Voltigeur and Winston Churchill Stakes); Lady Zia Wernher owner of Meld (Oaks, St Leger and 1,000 Guineas and Coronation Stakes) and of Meld's son Charlottown (Derby and Coronation Cup); the late Sir Harold Wernher, owner of Aggressor (King George VI and Queen

Elizabeth Stakes); the late Sir Winston Churchill, who owned the popular favourite Colonist II, winner of the Jockey Club Cup, as well as High Hat and Vienna; the late Mr William Hill, founder and chairman of the famous bookmaking establishment, who owned Cantelo (St Leger); the late Major Lionel Holliday, the owner of Hethersett, Neasham Belle, Night Off, Narrator and many other good horses; Mr H. J. Joel, owner of Royal Palace (2,000 Guineas, Derby, Eclipse Stakes and King George VI and Queen Elizabeth Stakes), Connaught (Eclipse Stakes), Henry the Seventh (Eclipse Stakes) and Major Portion (Sussex Stakes); Mrs V. Lilley, as she was then, owned Supreme Court and Aurelius. She has since remarried and as Mrs Hue-Williams owned English Prince (Irish Sweeps Derby). Her husband, Colonel R. Hue-Williams, is the owner of Altesse Royale (1,000 Guineas, Oaks, and Irish Guinness Oaks).

Mr Stanhope Joel owned Busted (Eclipse Stakes and King George VI and Queen Elizabeth Stakes), having won the St Leger with Chamossaire back in 1945. Mrs Joel was the owner of Lupe (Oaks and Coronation Cup).

Mr Louis Freedman, who bought the Cliveden Stud on the death of the late Lord Astor, and the Beech House Stud from Lady Sassoon, has been a very successful owner in more recent years, his best winners being Polygamy (Oaks), Lucyrowe (Coronation Stakes) and I Say (Coronation Cup). Mrs J. L. Hislop headed the owners' list in 1972 and was third in 1971, due to the success of Brigadier Gerard, who was bred by her husband Mr John Hislop, a former leading amateur rider and a journalist and author of distinction. Brigadier Gerard won the 2,000 Guineas, Eclipse Stakes, Champion Stakes, twice and King George VI and Queen Elizabeth Stakes.

Mr David Robinson owned Our Babu (2,000 Guineas); he was leading owner in 1969 and second in 1970 and 1971. Sir Michael Sobell, who purchased the late Dorothy Paget's bloodstock on her death in 1960, was the owner of Reform (Champion stakes) and Sun Prince (St James's Palace Stakes). Lady Beaverbrook was twice second on the owner's list, her most successful winners being Bustino (Coronation Cup in record time and St Leger) and Relkino (Benson and Hedges Gold Cup). The Duke of Devonshire owned that fine mare Park Top.

Mr G. A. Oldham was the owner of Sagaro, the only horse in Turf history to win the Ascot Gold Cup three times, and Intermezzo (St Leger). Mr C. A. B. St George has been owner or part owner of many high class horses, including Ginevra (Oaks), Bruni (St Leger) and Lorenzaccio (Champion Stakes). Mrs J. R. Mullion was the owner of Ragusa (Irish Sweeps Derby, King George VI and Queen Elizabeth Stakes, St Leger and Eclipse Stakes). Lord Halifax won the Derby and Irish Sweeps Derby with Shirley Heights and the late Duke of Norfolk the Ascot Gold Cup with Ragstone. Other owners include Colonel B. Hornung, owner of Aunt Edith (King George VI and Queen Elizabeth Stakes); Arthur Budgett, the owner and trainer of the Derby winners Blakeney and Morston; the Hon. James Morrison, owner of Juliette Marny (Oaks and Irish Guinness Oaks); and Mr David McCall, owner of Ile de Bourbon, winner of the King George VI and Queen Elizabeth Stakes.

But probably the most successful British owner of the present day is Mr Robert Sangster, the founder and chairman of Vernons Pools. Mr Sangster headed the list of winning owners in 1977, horses in his ownership having amassed the total of £348,023. His most successful horses were The Minstrel (Derby, Irish Sweeps Derby and King George VI and Queen Elizabeth Stakes) and Alleged (Great Voltigeur Stakes and Prix de l'Arc de Triomphe twice).

American Owners

The late Mr William Woodward was the most successful American owner in Britain in the third, fourth and fifth decades of the present century. He was the owner of Brown Betty (1,000 Guineas), Hycilla (Oaks), Boswell and Black Tarquin (both winners of the St Leger) and Flares (Ascot Gold Cup). The late Mr Robert Sterling Clark won the Derby and St Leger with Never Say Die, whom he most generously presented to the National Stud, when his racing days were over. Mrs Howell E. Jackson was the owner of Never Too Late II (1000 Guineas and Oaks), Baldric II (2,000 Guineas) and Nasram II (King George VI and Queen Elizabeth Stakes). Mr Raymond Guest, the United States Ambassador to the Republic of Ireland, headed the list of owners in Great Britain and Ireland in 1968 due to Sir Ivor (2,000 Guineas, Derby, Champion Stakes and Washington International Stakes), having also won the Derby in 1962 with Larkspur. Mr Paul Mellon was leading owner in 1971 due to the success of the mighty Mill Reef (Derby, Eclipse Stakes, King George VI and Queen Elizabeth Stakes and Prix de l'Arc de Triomphe). The late Mr C. W. Engelhard was the leading owner in 1970, when his colt Nijinsky became the first horse since Bahram to win the Triple Crown of the 2,000 Guineas, Derby and St Leger, also being successful in the Irish Sweeps Derby and King George VI and Queen Elizabeth Stakes. Mr Engelhard had previously won the St Leger three times with Indiana and the full brothers Ribocco and Ribero, both also winners of the Irish Sweeps Derby. Mr Nelson Bunker Hunt was the leading owner in 1973 and 1974, due principally to his fine mare Dahlia (King George VI and Queen Elizabeth Stakes, twice, Benson and Hedges Gold Cup, twice, and Irish Guinnes Oaks); he was also the owner of Empery (Derby).

Other leading American owners who have achieved success in Great Britain include Mr Dan Galbreath, owner of Roberto (Derby, Benson and Hedges Gold Cup and Coronation Cup), Mr P. A. Widener, owner of Hula Dancer (1,000 Guineas and Champion Stakes), Mr George Pope, junior, owner of Mysterious (1,000 Guineas, Oaks and Yorkshire Oaks); Mr Ogden Phipps, owner of Boucher (St Leger); Mr J. Cox Brady, owner of Long Look (Oaks); and Mrs George Getty II, owner of Artaius (Eclipse Stakes and Sussex Stakes).

French Owners

Monsieur Marcel Boussac, for many years the leading owner breeder in France, enjoyed an extraordinary run of success in this country. He won a war-time substitute 2,000 Guineas with Djebel, the Ascot Gold Cup with Caracalla II, Arbar, Elpenor and Macip, and other valuable prizes with horses like Goyescas, Corrida, Goya II, Marsyas II, Nirgal, Goyama, Pardal, Dynamiter, Coronation V, Argur and Djeddah. In 1950 he actually owned the winners of the Derby, Oaks and St Leger; Galcador, Asmena and Scratch II, winning the St Leger again in the following year with Talma II.

Madame Suzy Volterra, the glamorous owner of Phil Drake

(Derby) and Sicarelle (Oaks); M. Wertheimer, the owner of Vimy (King George VI and Queen Elizabeth Stakes) and Lavandin (Derby); the late Mr R. B. Strassburger, owner of Cambremer (St Leger) and Montaval (King George VI and Queen Elizabeth Stakes); Baron G. De Waldner, the owner of Wallaby II (Ascot Gold Cup), Javelot (Eclipse) and Pearl Diver (Derby); the late Monsieur F. Dupré, owner of Bella Paola (Oaks, 1,000 Guineas and Champion Stakes), Tantieme (Coronation Cup), Match III (King George VI and Queen Elizabeth Stakes) and Relko (Derby and Coronation Cup); Madame Jean Couturié, owner of Right Royal V (King George V and Queen Elizabeth Stakes); M. Eugene Constant, owner of Pan II (Ascot Gold Cup) and Thunderhead II (2,000 Guineas); M. Jean Ternynck, owner of that great horse Sea-Bird II (Derby) and of Cameree (1,000 Guineas); and M. Henri Berlin, owner of La Lagune (Oaks) are other French owners to have met with success in England.

However, the French owner who has enjoyed the most success in England in recent years is M. Daniel Wildenstein, a Paris art dealer. He was the leading owner in Great Britain in 1976, when winning the 1,000 Guineas with Flying Water, the Oaks and King George VI and Queen Elizabeth Stakes with Pawneese and the St Leger with Crow; the total stake money won by M. Wildenstein in England that year was £244,500.

Italian Owners

The late Senator Federicos Tesio, the famous Italian breeder, owner and trainer, some of whose theories have been discussed in an earlier chapter, died before the triumphs on the Turf of Botticelli, winner of the Ascot Gold Cup and the Italian Triple Crown, and the mighty Ribot, perhaps the greatest racehorse of all time, the unbeaten winner of 16 races, including in France the Prix de l'Arc de Triomphe, twice, in England the King George VI and Queen Elizabeth Stakes, and in Italy the Gran Premio di Milano and Premio del Jockey Club.

Botticelli and Ribot were both bred by Senator Tesio at the Razza Dormello Olgiata in Italy, and ran in the colours of the Marchese Mario Incisa Belle Rocchetta. The Italian owner who has enjoyed the most success in England in recent years is Dr Carlo Vittadini, who headed the list of winning owners in

1975 due to the success of Grundy in the Derby, Irish Sweeps Derby and King George VI and Queen Elizabeth Stakes. Carlo d'Alessio was a further Italian owner to achieve success in England, winning the 2,000 Guineas in two successive years with Bolkonski in 1975 and with Wollow in 1976.

Other Owners

German owners who have enjoyed success in Britain include Countess Margit Batthyany, owner of Pia (Oaks), and Dr Nils Schibbye, owner of Nebbiolo (2,000 Guineas). Mr Sven Hanson, a Swedish owner, has won the Oaks and Irish Guinness Oaks with Fair Salinia.

Indian owners to succeed in Britain have been Mr Ravi Tikkoo, a very successful owner whose principal win was gained with Steel Pulse (Irish Sweeps Derby). Mr. Tikkoo, who maintained a string of horses at Newmarket and engaged the former jockey Scobie Breasley as his private trainer, caused some consternation in racing circles when he decided, in 1975, owing to the excessive Value Added Tax that he was forced to pay, to move his whole string to France. Grecian-born Captain Marcos Lemos won the St Leger with Julio Mariner.

The National Stud

In 1915 the late Colonel Hall-Walker (afterwards Lord Wavertree) presented his famous Tully Stud in Ireland to the British nation, and this became what is now known as the National Stud and is administered by the Horserace Betting Levy Board.

Minoru, Prince Palatine and Blandford were bred at Tully, and among the broodmares who were transferred to the nation were Black Cherry, Blanche, Dolabella and Lady Lightfoot.

Sir Henry Greer became the first director and he was succeeded by Mr Noble Johnson, who in turn was followed by Mr Peter Burrell. Mr Burrell managed the stud most capably for 34 years, being in charge throughout the time when the stud was based at Gillingham in Dorset and for seven years following the move to Newmarket in 1964. Mr Burrell retired in 1971 to be succeeded by Lt-Col. Douglas Gray, who in his turn was succeeded by the present manager, Mr Michael Bramwell.

Myrobella, Big Game, Sun Chariot, Blue Train, Carrozza,

Chamossaire, Pindari and Hopeful Venture were the best horses bred at the National Stud, before it was decided to sell all the broodmares and foals at the Newmarket December Sales in 1964. Then 30 lots from the National Stud fetched a total of 271,920 guineas; a sum to be used in the foundation of a new stud at Newmarket, besides assisting in the buying of stallions which might otherwise be sold abroad.

The stallions standing at the National Stud in 1978 were Mill Reef, Grundy, Star Appeal, Sagaro, Blakeney and Habat.

CHAPTER X

Principal Trainers

Leathery limbs of Upper Lambourn,
Leathery skin from sun and wind,
Leathery breeches, spreading stables,
Shining saddles left behind,
To the down the string of horses,
Moving out of sight and mind.

John Betjaman, *Old Lights for New Chancels.*

John Scott

The most famous trainer of racehorses in the first half of the nineteenth century was John Scott of Whitewall, known to his contemporaries as 'The Wizard of the North'. Through his capable hands passed many of the crack thoroughbreds of the time, such as the mighty Touchstone, Charles XII, Canezou, West Australian, Imperieuse, and The Marquis. Altogether he trained the winners of 16 Legers, 6 Derbys, and 9 Oaks before he died in 1871.

Other successful trainers in those days were John Kent, who trained for Lord George Bentinck; William I'Anson, who trained his own horses Blink Bonny and Blair Athol to win the Derby and Oaks and the Derby and St Leger respectively; and old John Day of Danebury.

John Porter

In the second half of the nineteenth century John Porter and the Dawson family were the leading trainers. John Porter of Kingsclere was appointed private trainer to Sir Joseph Hawley at the age of 25 and trained Blue Gown to win the Derby for him in 1868. One of his first patrons was the Duke of Westminster, for whom he prepared Ormonde and Flying Fox to win their Triple Crowns. Porter had charge of Isonomy, whom he bought as a yearling for 360 guineas for Mr Gretton, and he also trained the horses owned by Lord Alington and Sir Frederick Johnstone, in whose colours Common won the Triple Crown.

For a short time the Prince of Wales and Baron de Hirsch, owner of that wonderful filly La Fleche, were also patrons of Kingsclere.

Porter retired in 1905 after a brilliant career, during which the horses trained by him at Kingsclere won over 1,000 races and over £720,000 in stakes, including seven Derbys and six St Legers.

Matthew Dawson

Matt Dawson of Heath House, Newmarket, numbered among his patrons at various times Mr Merry, Lord Falmouth, the Duke of Portland, Lord Hastings, and Lord Rosebery; and among the famous horses which passed through his stables were Thormanby, Silvio, Jannette, St Simon, Melton, Ladas, Sir Visto, and Velasquez.

Matt Dawson's father, George Dawson, trained Van Tromp for Lord Eglinton; his brother John, Galopin for Prince Batthyany and Petrarch for Lord Dupplin; and his nephew George, Ayrshire, Donovan, and Memoir for the Duke of Portland. Between them the Dawson family trained some fifty winners of classic races.

Robert Peck, who trained Doncaster for Mr Merry and Bend Or for the Duke of Westminster; and Captain Machell, who had charge of Seabreeze and Isinglass, were others in the forefront of their profession in those days.

Richard Marsh

At the turn of the century Richard Marsh of Egerton House, Newmarket, became the leading trainer, with the Prince of Wales as his principal patron, and he prepared Diamond Jubilee, Persimmon, and Minoru for their popular triumphs on the Turf in the royal racing colours.

Peter Gilpin, of Clarehaven Lodge, who was responsible for the brilliant career of Pretty Polly, was another prominent trainer of that period; and Charles Morton, who at various times had charge of the horses owned by Mr J. B. Joel, Bob Sievier, Boss Crocker, Abingdon Baird, and Lily Langtry, was another successful exponent of his profession.

Principal Trainers of Recent Times

The leading trainers between the two World Wars were Alec Taylor, George Lambton, Dick Dawson, and Atty Persse; and among those of recent years have been Fred Darling, Frank Butters, Joe Lawson, and Jack Jarvis, Walter Earl and Marcus Marsh, Cecil Boyd-Rochfort, and Noel Murless.

Alec Taylor

Alec Taylor, who was known as 'The Wizard of Manton', was the son of old Alec Taylor, who trained Teddington to win the Derby and Ascot Gold Cup for Sir Joseph Hawley. Young Alec had charge of Bayardo, Lemberg, and Gay Crusader for Mr 'Fairie' Cox and of Gainsborough for Lady James Douglas. He also trained many good racehorses, such as Buchan and Craig-an-Eran, Pogrom and Saucy Sue, Short Story and Book Law, for Lord Astor, who was the chief patron of his stable.

Altogether Alec Taylor turned out over 1,000 winners of races worth nearly £540,000 and was top of the list of winning trainers 12 times.

George Lambton

The Honourable George Lambton was for many years trainer and manager of Lord Derby's thoroughbreds at Stanley House, and Swynford, Tranquil, Sansovino, Colorado, and Hyperion were among the many famous horses which passed through his hands.

Dick Dawson trained for the Aga Khan at Whatcomb, and Diophon, Salmon Trout, and Blenheim were his classic successes for his chief patron. He also trained the Derby and St Leger winner, Trigo and the flying filly Mumtaz Mahal.

Atty Persse of Stockbridge trained The Tetrarch, Tetratema, and Mr Jinks for Major Dermot McCalmont.

Fred Darling

The most successful trainer of the thirties and forties was Fred Darling, the Master of Beckhampton, son of the late Sam Darling, who was responsible for Galtee More and Ard Patrick. Fred Darling trained the horses leased by King George VI from the National Stud; the late Lord Woolavington and the late Lord Dewar were patrons of his stable, and so was the former's daughter, the Honourable Lady Macdonald-Buchanan, and the latter's nephew, Mr J. A. Dewar.

Darling trained the winners of nineteen classic races, including seven winners of the Derby; Captain Cuttle, Manna, Coronach, Cameronian, Bois Roussel, Pont l'Eveque, and Owen Tudor; and three of the St Leger; Hurry On, Coronach, and Sun Chariot. He was always very successful with his two-year-olds like Tiffin and Myrobella, and he also trained Pasch, winner of the 2,000 Guineas and Eclipse Stakes, Big Game, winner of the 2,000 Guineas and Champion Stakes, and Tudor Minstrel, another winner of the 2,000 Guineas.

Frank Butters

Frank Butters of Fitzroy House at one time trained for the late Lord Derby and subsequently the Aga Khan became his chief patron. Among the famous horses which passed through his expert hands were Fairway, Toboggan, and Fair Isle, for the former; and for the latter, Bahram, Mahmoud, Udaipur, Masaka, Firdaussi, Turkhan, Tehran, Migoli, and Felicitation. Sir Alfred Butt, owner of Petition, was another patron of this stable.

Joe Lawson

Joe Lawson succeeded Alec Taylor in charge of the Manton stable and trained Lord Astor's horses for a number of years, as well as those of many other owners. His classic successes were with Never Say Die in the Derby and St Leger; Orwell, Pay Up, Kingsway, and Court Martial in the 2,000 Guineas; Dancing Time in the 1,000 Guineas; Pennycomequick in the Oaks; and Exhibitionist and Galatea II in the 1,000 Guineas and the Oaks. He also prepared Trimdon to win the Gold Vase and two Gold Cups, Tiberius to win the Gold Cup, and Rhodes Scholar to win the Eclipse Stakes. In 1931 Joe Lawson headed the list of winning trainers with the then record total of £93,900 won in stake money by horses in his stable in a single season.

Sir Jack Jarvis

The late Sir Jack Jarvis trained at Park Lodge, Newmarket, and his chief patron was the late Lord Rosebery, for whom he trained the classic winners Blue Peter, Ocean Swell, and

Sandwich. For the late Lord Rosebery's father he produced two classic winners, Ellangowan and Plack, and other good horses which he trained were Golden Myth, Flamingo, Campanula, Miracle, Foxhunter, Flyon, Honeyway and Happy Laughter.

Walter Earl and Marcus Marsh

Earl became the trainer of the late Lord Derby's racehorses and won all the five war-time classics for his principal patron; the 2,000 Guineas with Garden Path; the 1,000 Guineas with Herringbone and Sun Stream, the Derby with Watling Street, the Oaks with Sun Stream and the St Leger with Herringbone. He also saddled Gulf Stream to win the Eclipse Stakes, and Alycidon to win the Ascot, Goodwood and Doncaster Cups.

Marcus Marsh, son of old Richard Marsh, trained Windsor Lad, and was later in charge of the Aga Khan's horses at Fitzroy House, Newmarket. He brought out Palestine to win the 2,000 Guineas in 1950 and Tulyar to win the Derby, St Leger, Eclipse Stakes and King George VI and Queen Elizabeth Stakes in 1952, when he headed the list of winning trainers with £92,093 in stakes won by horses under his care.

Sir Cecil Boyd-Rochfort and Sir Noel Murless

Up until his retirement in 1968, Sir Cecil Boyd-Rochfort trained the racehorses bred by the Queen. Whilst until the time at which the National Stud decided to dispose with the mares and young stock and to concentrate on the purchase of stallions, most of the yearlings bred by the National Stud were leased to the Queen for their racing careers and were trained by Noel Murless. Boyd-Rochfort was responsible for Hypericum, winner of the 1,000 Guineas, Above Board, winner of the Yorkshire Oaks, and Rising Light, winner of the Jockey Club Stakes, for the late King, whilst for the Queen he trained Pall Mall, winner of the 2,000 Guineas, Canisbay, winner of the Eclipse Stakes, Aureole, winner of the King George VI and Queen Elizabeth Stakes, Above Suspicion, winner of the St James's Palace Stakes, Agreement, winner of the Doncaster Cup, twice, and Atlas, also winner of the Doncaster Cup. He also trained four classic winners for the late Mr William Woodward, as well as the Eclipse Stakes winners Royal Minstrel, Loaningdale and Boswell and the Ascot Gold Cup winners Precipitation, Flares and Zarathustra. The first named horse was owned by Lady Zia Wernher, for whom Captain Boyd Rochfort also trained Meld, winner of the 1,000 Guineas, Oaks and St Leger. For the late Sir Humphrey de Trafford he trained Alcide, winner of the St Leger and King George VI and Queen Elizabeth Stakes, and Parthia, winner of the Derby. For Brigadier W. P. Wyatt he trained Premonition, winner of the St Leger and also won a war-time substitute St Leger with Lord Portal's Sun Castle.

Sir Noel Murless, formerly of Warren Place at Newmarket, headed the list of winning trainers six times; in 1948; 1957 with over £116,000 on stakes winnings; 1959 with record winnings of £145,694; in 1960 with over £118,000; in 1970 with £199,524 and in 1973 with £132,984. For the Queen he trained Carrozza, winner of the Oaks, Pindari, winner of the King Edward VII Stakes and Hopeful Venture, winner of the Grand Prix de Saint-Cloud and Hardwicke Stakes. Other famous horses for whom he was responsible included Queenpot, Ridge Wood, Abernant, Arctic Explorer, Crepello, Petite Etoile, St Paddy, Aurelius, Twilight Alley, Royal Palace, Busted, Fleet, Connaught, Caergwrlc, Lupe and Mysterious.

Both Captain Boyd-Rochfort and Noel Murless had knighthoods conferred upon them. In 1966 Boyd Rochfort was created a Knight Commander of the Royal Victorian Order. It was in 1971 that Noel Murless received his knighthood.

W. R. Hern and Ian Balding

All the horses bred by the Queen at the Royal Stud at Sandringham are trained by Dick Hern and Ian Balding. Dick Hern saddled Highclere to win the 1,000 Guineas and French Oaks and Dunfermline to win the Oaks and the St Leger in Her Majesty's colours. He also trained Brigadier Gerard to win the 2,000 Guineas, Eclipse Stakes and King George VI and Queen Elizabeth Stakes for Mrs John Hislop and two further winners of the St Leger in Hethersett and Bustino. He headed the trainers' list in 1972 with a total of £206,767 in stakes money.

Ian Balding trained Example, who won the Park Hill Stakes and Prix de Royallieu for the Queen. However, the best horse to pass through his hands was Mill Reef, winner of the Derby, Eclipse Stakes, King George VI Stakes and Prix de l'Arc de

Triomphe. Balding was the leading trainer in 1971 with £157,488.

Peter Walwyn, Henry Cecil and other trainers.

Peter Walwyn headed the trainers list in 1974 and 1975. The outstanding horse to pass through his hands is Grundy, winner of the Derby, Irish Sweeps Derby and King George VI and Queen Elizabeth Stakes. He also trained Humble Duty to win the 1,000 Guineas, Polygamy to win the Oaks and English Prince to win the Irish Sweeps Derby.

Henry Cecil, a stepson of Sir Cecil Boyd-Rochfort, was the leading trainer in 1976 and in 1978. He has won the Eclipse Stakes with Gunner B and Wolver Hollow, and the 2,000 Guineas twice with Bolkonski and Wollow. Arthur Budgett, the leading trainer of 1969, who has now retired from training, registered a Derby double with the half-brothers Blakeney and Morston, both out of the famous broodmare Windmill Girl. Barry Hills, formerly travelling head-lad to John Oxley (who himself won the Oaks with Homeward Bound) has saddled Rheingold to win the Prix de l'Arc de Triomphe and Enstone Spark to win the 1,000 Guineas. Michael Stoute enjoyed fantastic success in 1978, winning the Oaks with Fair Salinia and the Ascot Gold Cup with Shangamuzo. The late Matthew Peacock of Manor House, Middleham was the leading trainer in the North of England and the best horse he ever turned out was the Derby winner Dante. Charles Elsey of Malton followed him with such classic winners as Musidora, Frieze, Nearula, Honeylight and Cantelo. Bill Elsey, son of Charles Elsey, has won the Oaks with Pia and the St Leger with Peleid.

Dick Perryman, who was once a successful jockey, later became a successful trainer having saddled Chamossaire to win the St Leger and Airborne to win the Derby and St Leger; and the same is true of Harry Wragg, who has prepared Psidium to win the Derby, Darius to win the 2,000 Guineas and Eclipse Stakes, Abermaid and Full Dress II to win the 1,000 Guineas and Intermezzo to win the St Leger. Douglas Smith saddled Sleeping Partner to win the Oaks for the late Lord Rosebery.

Other trainers who must also be mentioned are the late Captain T. Hogg, who prepared Colombo and many others for the late Lord Glanely; the late Captain O. Bell, who prepared

King Salmon and Rockfel; the late Reg Day, who had under his care the St Leger and Ascot Gold Cup winner Solario and the Oaks and 1,000 Guineas winner Sweet Solera; Fred Armstrong, who trained Sayajirao and My Babu for the Maharajah of Baroda; the late Walter Nightingall, trainer of Colonist II for the late Sir Winston Churchill, also of Straight Deal and Niksar; the late G. S. Colling, who turned out Nimbus to win the Derby and 2,000 Guineas for Mrs M. Glenister; Noel Cannon, who trained Scottish Union at Druid's Lodge to win the St Leger for the late Mr J. V. Rank; E. Williams, who was responsible for Supreme Court; N. Bertie, who trained Pinza and Belle of All; G. Brooke with Neasham Belle and Our Babu; R. J. Colling with Ambiguity and Rosalba; Tom Waugh, who trained Privy Councillor; J. Tree, trainer of Only For Life, and Juliette Marny; Jack Watts, who saddled Indiana to win the St Leger; W. Wharton, who trained Night Off to win the 1,000 Guineas for the late Major Lionel Holliday; G. Smyth, trainer of Charlottown; Fulke Johnson-Houghton, who trained the full-brothers Ribocco and Ribero, also Ile de Bourbon; J. Sutcliffe, jnr, trainer of Right Tack; H. Thomson Jones, trainer of Athens Wood; the late Bernard van Cutsem, trainer of High Top and Park Top; W. Watts, the trainer of Waterloo; H. R. Price, who trained Ginevra and Bruni for Mr C. A. B. St. George; John Dunlop, trainer of Shirley Heights and Scottish Rifle; P. Nelson, trainer of Snow Knight; D. Sasse, trainer of Roland Gardens and Coup de Feu; R. Hannon, trainer of Mon Fils; M. H. Easterby, trainer of Mrs McArdy; J. Hindley; W. Hastings-Bass, and Clive Brittain, trainer of Julio Mariner.

Vincent O'Brien, Paddy Prendergast and other Irish trainers

Vincent O'Brien, who trains at Cashel in Co. Tipperary, has enjoyed greater success than any other trainer in the history of the Irish Turf. He has trained the winners of thirteen English classics and has been responsible for such horses as Ballymoss, Gladness, Larkspur, Long Look, Valoris, Glad Rags, Pieces of Eight, Sir Ivor, Nijinsky, Roberto, Boucher, and The Minstrel. In 1977 he headed the trainers' list with a total stake money of £439,124.

The late Paddy Prendergast, the leading trainer in 1963 and 1965, saddled such horses as Ragusa, Noblesse, Khalkis, Pourparler, Martial and Meadow Court. Kevin Prendergast has saddled Nebbiolo to win the 2,000 Guineas; Stuart Murless, brother to Sir Noel Murless, sent out Nocturnal Spree to win the 1,000 Guineas; and Mickey Rogers trained the Derby winners Hard Ridden and Santa Claus.

French Trainers

Francois Mathet trained for the late M. Francois Dupré, saddling Relko to win the Derby and Coronation Cup, Match III to win the King George VI and Queen Elizabeth Stakes and Bella Paola to win the 1,000 Guineas and Oaks. Etienne Pollet prepared Sea-Bird II to win the Derby, Hula Dancer to win the 1,000 Guineas, Thunderhead II to win the 2,000 Guineas, Right Royal V to win the King George VI and Queen Elizabeth Stakes, and Pan II to win the Ascot Gold Cup. Francois Boutin, has trained Nonoalco to win the 2,000 Guineas, La Lagune to win the Oaks, Malacate to win the Irish Sweeps Derby and Sagaro to win the Ascot Gold Cup, three times. Alec Head has prepared Lavandin to win the Derby and Rose Royale II to win the 1,000 Guineas and Champion Stakes; C. Bartholomew has prepared both Kashmir II and Pardallo. But the French trainers who have enjoyed most success in England in recent years are Angel Penna and Maurice Zilber. Angel Penna, who was born in the Argentine, was appointed trainer to Daniel Wildenstein and sent out Flying Water to win the 1,000 Guineas, Pawneese to win the Oaks and King George VI and Queen Elizabeth Stakes and Crow to win the St Leger. Zilber, who was born in Egypt, saddled Empery to win the Derby and Dahlia to win the King George VI and Queen Elizabeth Stakes twice, and Benson and Hedges Gold Cup, twice.

CHAPTER XI

Celebrated Jockeys

No better rider ever crossed a horse;
Honour his guide, he died without remorse.
Jockeys attend—from his example learn
The meed that honest worth is sure to earn.

Epitaph on a celebrated jockey.

John Singleton

OLD John Singleton, who was born in 1715 and died in 1975, was the first jockey to make a name for himself on the English Turf. He had but two masters all his life, Mr Read and the Marquess of Rockingham, for whom he rode many winners.

At the end of the eighteenth and the beginning of the nineteenth century the leading jockeys were Frank Buckle, Sam Chifney, and Jem Robinson, together with William Clift, Thomas Goodison, and the three Arnulls, Sam, John, and William.

Frank Buckle

Frank Buckle, known as 'The Pocket Hercules', who was born in 1766 won the Derby five times, the Oaks nine times, the St Leger twice, and 'all the good things at Newmarket'. He was the leading jockey of his day, and on his death in 1832 the epitaph printed at the head of this chapter was written in his honour.

Sam Chifney

Sam Chifney, senior, born in about 1750, rode the horses of the Prince of Wales, afterwards King George IV, and after the incident of Escape, already referred to, when the Prince withdrew from the Turf, he paid 'his honest and good servant' a pension of 200 guineas a year, being convinced that his jockey had been the victim of a miscarriage of justice. Chifney died in the Fleet Prison in 1807.

Jem Robinson

In 1824 this noted jockey wagered that he would win the Derby and the Oaks and get married all within the week. He duly landed the treble event and won his wager of £1,000. Altogether he won the Derby six times. It is recorded that in 1836 Lord Jersey presented Jem Robinson with £200 for winning him the Derby on Bay Middleton, having already given him a similar sum for winning the 2,000 Guineas on the same horse. This was considered generous remuneration in those days, for only ten years earlier the Duke of Grafton had deemed £20 sufficient reward to old John Day for winning the 2,000 and the 1,000 Guineas for him in the same week.

Other Jockeys of the Early Nineteenth Century

Clift, who was the son of a shepherd, began life as a stable boy to a horse called Bloody Buttocks, later known as Copper Bottom (hardly an improvement in nomenclature). Clift won thirteen classic races and Goodison eight, while the Arnull family between them rode the winners of twenty.

Their chief rivals in the north were John Jackson, who rode the winner of the St Leger eight times, and Will Scott, the younger brother of the trainer John Scott, who rode nine winners of the Doncaster classic as well as four Derby and three Oaks winners.

Other successful jockeys of those days were Sam Chifney, junior, Frank Butler, who rode West Australian to win the Triple Crown for Mr Bowes in 1853, Jim Templeman, Nat Flatman, Job Marson, and Ben Smith, together with old John B. Day, who rode for Lord George Bentinck, young John, Sam, and Alfred Day.

Fred Archer

The most famous jockey in the second half of the nineteenth century was Fred Archer, nicknamed 'The Tinman', who was born in 1857, the son of a steeplechase jockey who won the Grand National. He was apprenticed to Matthew Dawson's stable and soon showed that he was a genius in the saddle. He won the Derby five times, on Lord Falmouth's Silvio in 1877, the Duke of Westminster's Bend Or in 1880, Mr Lorrilard's Iroquois in 1881, Lord Hasting's Melton in 1885, and the Duke

of Westminster's Ormonde in 1886; the Oaks four times, on
Lord Falmouth's Spinaway in 1875, Jannette in 1878, and
Wheel of Fortune in 1879, and on Lord Cadogan's Lonely in
1885; and the St Leger six times, on Silvio in 1877, Jannette in
1878, Iroquois in 1881, Dutch Oven in 1882, Melton in 1885,
and Ormonde in 1886.

Lord Falmouth paid Archer a retainer fee of £100 per
annum to ride his horses in the black jacket, white sleeves, and
red cap, and for thirteen consecutive years this remarkable man
was head of the list of winning jockeys. During his career in the
saddle Archer won 21 classic races, had 8,084 mounts and rode
2,478 winners, his highest number in any one season being 246
winners in 1885.

A year later Archer shot himself while delirious during an
illness, brought on by severe wasting, when trying to reduce his
weight to 8 stone 6 pounds to ride St Mirin in the Cambridgeshire, only to be beaten by a head in the only important race in
the calendar which he had never won. So this celebrated jockey
died before he reached the age of thirty and left a fortune of
£60,000.

Other Jockeys of the Late Nineteenth Century

John Watts rode nineteen classic winners, including such
outstanding horses as Memoir, La Fleche, Ladas, and Persimmon; George Fordham, known as 'The Demon', who was one of
the best jockeys of all time, rode fifteen; Tom Cannon, thirteen,
including Brigantine, Robert the Devil, and Shotover; John
Osborne, twelve, including Lord Clifden, Pretender, and Apology; Tom Chaloner, ten, including The Marquis, Macaroni,
Achievement, and Formosa; Charlie Wood, nine, including St
Gatien and Galtee More; and 'Tiny' Wells, eight, including the
Derby three times for Sir Joseph Hawley on Beadsman, Musjid, and Blue Gown; 'the lucky baronet' presenting his jockey
with the entire Derby stakes of £6,000 after his third victory in
the premier classic race, at that time the handsomest present
ever made to a jockey.

The story goes that Queen Victoria by way of conversation
once asked this diminutive rider what his weight was, to which
Tiny Wells replied, 'Please, Ma'am, master told me never to
say how much I weighed'.

Other good jockeys of the late Victorian age were Harry Custance, who rode Thormanby and Lord Lyon; Maidment, who rode Hannah and Cremorne; Sam Loates, who rode Sir Visto, and Tom Loates, who rose Isinglass and St Frusquin; G. Barrett, who rode Common and other horses trained by John Porter; and F. Barrett, who rode Ayrshire and Donovan for the Duke of Portland.

Jockeys of Edwardian Days

At the turn of the century Tod Sloan and other American jockeys were responsible for introducing into this country 'the monkey-on-a-stick' style, the American seat and riding methods, a forward crouching attitude with short reins and shortened stirrup leathers, said to have been copied from the Red Indians, and designed to save wind pressure and bring forward the centre of gravity.

The leading jockeys of the time were Danny Maher, who rode Rock Sand, Bayardo, and Neil Gow; Frank Wooton, who rode Swynford; Herbert Jones, who rode Diamond Jubilee and Minoru; and Mornington Cannon, who rode Flying Fox.

Steve Donoghue

Steve Donoghue was the best jockey of the nineteen-twenties. He headed the list of winning jockeys ten years in succession and won the Derby six times; two of them war-substitute races on Pommern in 1915 and on Gay Crusader in 1917, then the hat-trick in 1921 on Humorist, 1922 on Captain Cuttle, and 1923 on Papyrus, and finally on Manna in 1925. But Donoghue's favourite mount was the veteran Brown Jack, and his greatest triumph when he rode the faithful old gelding to victory in the longest race in the calendar, the Queen Alexandra Stakes at Ascot, for the sixth consecutive year, to the excited shouts of 'Come on, Steve' and to the accompaniment of loud and prolonged cheers for a gallant racehorse and a splendid jockey.

Joe Childs, Brownie Carslake, and Freddy Fox

Childs was a beautiful rider and won two war-substitute Derbys on Fifinella in 1916 and on Gainsborough in 1918, together with the Epsom Derby on Coronach in 1926. He also scored in the St Leger on Gainsborough, Polemarch, Solario, and Coronach.

Carslake was a very fine long-distance jockey who never managed to win the Derby, but scored three victories in the St Leger on Keysoe, Salmon Trout, and Scottish Union.

Fox, who headed the list of winning jockeys in 1930, won the Derby on Cameronian and Bahram and the St Leger on Firdaussi.

Leading Jockeys of Recent Times

The leading jockeys of recent years have been Gordon Richards, Harry Wragg, Charlie Elliott, Tommy Weston, Michael Beary, Bill Nevett, Rae Johnstone, Charlie Smirke, the two brothers Eph and Doug Smith, Harry Carr, Scobie Breasley, Pat Eddery, Willie Carson, Joe Mercer, Geoff Lewis and Lester Piggott.

Gordon Richards

The champion jockey of recent years was born in Shropshire in 1904 and first learnt the art of riding racehorses from Steve Donoghue. His career in the saddle began in 1920 and ended in 1953, when he became a trainer. He was top of the list of winning jockeys 25 times, but, remarkable to relate, never rode the winner of the Derby until the last year of his jockeyship, when he stormed home on Pinza to defeat Aureole in the premier classic on Epsom Downs, and later won the King George VI and Queen Elizabeth Stakes on the same good horse. Gordon Richards gained thirteen successes in other classics, on Singapore, Chumleigh, Turkhan, Sun Chariot, and Tehran in the St Leger; on Rose of England and Sun Chariot in the Oaks; on Pasch, Big Game, and Tudor Minstrel in the 2,000 Guineas; and on Sun Chariot, Queenpot, and Belle of All in the 1,000 Guineas. The Beckhampton stable for many years had first claim on the services of Gordon Richards, who also held a retainer from Fitzroy House stable.

The proudest moment in the life of this brilliant jockey, who always upheld the finest traditions of his profession, was no doubt the day on which he won his 247th race of the season in 1933 and so beat Fred Archer's previous record of 246 winners set up in 1885, and this by a curious coincidence occurred on the anniversary of the day on which Archer took his own life. Gordon Richards ended up that year with 259 wins, a new record that he himself surpassed in 1947 with the astonishing total of 269 winning mounts in the season. During his career as a jockey he rode a total of 4,870 winners out of 21,828 mounts. A knighthood was conferred on him in the Queen's Coronation Honours list.

Sir Gordon Richards became a trainer at Ogbourne Maisey, near Marlborough. The most successful horse he trained was Reform, winner of the Sussex Stakes and Champion Stakes. He has retired to become racing manager to Lady Beaverbrook.

Other Jockeys

Harry Wragg, nicknamed 'The Head Waiter', because of his masterly skill at riding a waiting race and then coming up with a long and perfectly timed run to snatch victory on the post, was riding as first jockey for the late Lord Derby until the end of the 1946 season, when he retired from the saddle to take up training. He rode the winners of thirteen classic races; Felstead, Blenheim, and Watling Street were his winning Derby mounts, Sandwich and Herringbone his St Leger ones.

Charlie Elliott won the King George VI and Queen Elizabeth Stakes on Supreme Court and had fourteen classic successes to his credit, among them being Call Boy, Bois Roussel, and Nimbus in the Derby, but he never won the St Leger. Elliott had the unique distinction of winning the Ascot Gold Cup on Souepi in 1953, and training the winners of the same important race in 1954 and 1956, viz., Elpenor and Macip. Tommy Weston rode eleven classic winners, including the late Lord Derby's two Derby winners, Sansovino and Hyperion, and the same owner's three St Leger winners, Tranquil, Fairway, and Hyperion. Michael Beary won the Derby on Mid-day Sun, the Oaks on Udaipur, and the St Leger on Trigo, while Billy Nevett rode three Derby winners, Owen Tudor, Ocean Swell, and Dante.

Rae Johnstone had many successes for M. Marcel Boussac, including Galcador in the Derby and Scratch II and Talma II in the St Leger. He also won the Derby on My Love and

Lavandin, and had seven other classic victories to his credit. Charlie Smirke rode for the Aga Khan, and his classic successes include Mahmoud and Tulyar in the Derby, Bahram and Tulyar in the St Leger, and Palestine in the 2,000 Guineas. He also won the Derby and St Leger on Windsor Lad, the Derby on Hard Ridden, the St Leger on Never Say Die, the 1,000 Guineas on Rose Royale II, and the King George VI and Queen Elizabeth Stakes and the Eclipse Stakes on Tulyar.

The two best jockeys to come to the fore in pre-war years were E. Smith who rode for Jack Jarvis's stable, and his brother D. Smith, who rode for Cecil Boyd-Rochfort's stable and subsequently for Walter Earl's stable. The former won the 2,000 Guineas and the Derby for Lord Rosebery on Blue Peter, the King George VI and Queen Elizabeth Stakes and the Coronation Cup for Her Majesty with Aureole, and the St Leger on Premonition; and the latter won the 2,000 Guineas on Our Babu and the Queen's Pall Mall and the 1,000 Guineas for King George VI on Hypericum, and for Prince Aly Khan on Petite Etoile. Douglas Smith, who held a trainer's licence, was champion jockey five times. Scobie Breasley, the brilliant Australian jockey, topped the table in 1957, 1961, 1962 and 1963. His classic successes were the 2,000 Guineas on Ki Ming, the 1,000 Guineas on Festoon and the Derby on Santa Claus and Charlottown; he also rode the famous Ballymoss to victory in the King George VI and Queen Elizabeth Stakes, Eclipse Stakes and Coronation Cup.

Harry Carr rode for the Queen and held a retainer for Boyd-Rochfort's stable. He won the Derby on Parthia, the St Leger on Hethersett, the St Leger and King George VI and Queen Elizabeth Stakes on Alcide; the Oaks, St Leger and 1,000 Guineas on Meld; and many other important events in the calendar.

Garnet Bougoure was the leading jockey of his day in Ireland and won the King George VI and Queen Elizabeth Stakes, St Leger, Eclipse Stakes and Great Voltigeur Stakes as well as the Irish Sweeps Derby on Ragusa; the Oaks on Noblesse, the Eclipse Stakes on Khalkis and the 1,000 Guineas on Pourparler. Bill Williamson won the Prix de l'Arc de Triomphe twice, on Vaguely Noble and Levmoss, and the 1,000 Guineas twice, on Abermaid and Night Off. Jimmy

Lindley, now a racing correspondent for BBC Television, won the 2,000 Guineas on Only For Life and Kashmir II, the St Leger on Indiana and the King George VI and Queen Elizabeth Stakes on Aggressor.

Amongst other good jockeys who are now retired must be mentioned Cliff Richards, Bobby Jones, Tommy Carey, Sammy Wragg, Edgar Britt, Ken Gethin and Tommy Lowrey, who won the St Leger on Chamossaire and the Derby and St Leger on Airborne. The outstanding jockeys of to-day are Lester Piggott, Pat Eddery and Willie Carson.

Lester Piggott and more good Jockeys of to-day

Lester Piggott was leading jockey for the first time in 1960, by which time he had already ridden three winners of the Derby; Never Say Die, Crepello and St Paddy; two winners of the Oaks, Carrozza and Petite Etoile; his first winner of the St Leger, St Paddy; and 2,000 Guineas, Crepello; two winners of the Ascot Gold Cup, Zarathustra and Gladness; and three winners of the Eclipse Stakes, Mystery IX, Darius, and Arctic Explorer. He has since ridden two further winners of the 2,000 Guineas, in Sir Ivor and Nijinsky. Six further winners of the St Leger in Aurelius, Ribocco, Ribero, Nijinsky, Athens Wood and Boucher; five further winners of the Derby, Sir Ivor, Nijinsky, Roberto, Empery and The Minstrel; three further winners of the Oaks, Valoris, Mysterious and Juliette Marny; the 1,000 Guineas on Caergwrle; six winners of the King George VI and Queen Elizabeth Stakes, Meadow Court, Aunt Edith Park Top, Nijinsky, Dahlia and The Minstrel; seven further winners of the Ascot Gold Cup, Pandofell, Twilight Alley, Fighting Charlie, who won the race twice and Sagaro, who won the race three times, and four further winners of the Eclipse Stakes on St Paddy, Pieces of Eight, Wolver Hollow and Artaius, Piggot headed the jockeys' list in 1960 and from 1964 to 1971.

Pat Eddery, who rode his first winner in 1969, has enjoyed a phenomenal rise to fame in the intervening period. He has headed the jockeys' list three times in 1974, 1976 and 1977. His principal successes have been the Irish 2,000 Guineas, Epsom Derby, Irish Sweeps Derby and King George VI and Queen Elizabeth Stakes on Grundy, the Oaks on Polygamy, the

Eclipse Stakes on Coup de Feu and the Ascot Gold Cup on Erimo Hawk.

Willie Carson, who headed the list of winning jockeys in 1972, 1973 and 1978 has won the 2,000 Guineas on High Top and the Oaks and St Leger on the Queen's Dunfermline. Geoff Lewis partnered Mill Reef to success in the Derby, Eclipse Stakes, King George VI and Queen Elizabeth Stakes and Prix de l'Arc de Triomphe. At the Epsom meeting of 1971 he won not only the Derby but also the Oaks on Altesse Royale and the Coronation Cup on Lupe. He also won the 2,000 Guineas on Right Tack.

Joe Mercer was formerly retained by W. R. Hern. He partnered Brigadier Gerard to success in the 2,000 Guineas, Eclipse Stakes, King George VI and Queen Elizabeth Stakes and Champion Stakes, twice. He has also won the Oaks on Ambiguity, the St Leger on Provoke and Bustino, the 1,000 Guineas and the French Oaks on the Queen's Highclere and the Ascot Gold Cup on Parbury. Greville Starkey enjoyed considerable success in 1978, winning the Derby on Shirley Heights and the Oaks on Fair Salinia. He had previously won the Oaks on Homeward Bound and the Eclipse Stakes and Prix de l'Arc de Triomphe on Star Appeal. Edward Hide won the 1,000 Guineas on Waterloo and Mrs McArdy, the Derby on Morston, the Oaks on Pia and the St Leger on Cantelo and Julio Mariner. Ron Hutchinson has won the 2,000 Guineas on Martial, the 1,000 Guineas on Full Dress, the St Leger on Intermezzo, the Eclipse Stakes on Scottish Rifle and the Ascot Gold Cup on Ragstone. George Moore won the 2,000 Guineas on Taboun, the 1,000 Guineas on Fleet and the 2,000 Guineas and Derby on Royal Palace.

Other jockeys who have ridden important winners are Pat Glennon, who won the Derby on Sea Bird II, J. Purtell, Stan Clayton, Frank Durr, Paul Cook, Ernie Johnson, Sandy Barclay, Tony Murray, Bryan Taylor and James Reid and the Irish jockeys Johnny Roe and George Curran. French jockeys who have ridden with success in England since the war include Poincelet, Palmer, Boullenger, Pyers, Garcia, Deforge, Thiboeuf and Paquet, while Dettori is an Italian jockey who has done well here. The outstanding French jockey today is, however, Yves Saint-Martin, He has won the Derby on Relko, the

2,000 Guineas on Nonoalco, the 1,000 Guineas on Flying Water and Altesse Royale, the Oaks on Monade and Pawneese and the St Leger on Crow. He has also won the King George VI and Queen Elizabeth Stakes on Pawneese. Saint-Martin rides principally for Mr Daniel Wildenstein.

G. Bouyouse, the leading jockey in Ireland who rode for Paddy Prendergast's stable, won the King George VI and Queen Elizabeth Stakes, St Leger, Eclipse, the Great Voltigeur Stakes, as well as the Irish Derby on Ragusa; the Oaks on Noblesse; the Eclipse on Khalkis; and the 1000 Guineas on Pourparler.

Jockeys' Fees and Apprentices' Allowances

A jockey may receive a retaining fee from an owner or trainer, who then has first claim on his services. In flat races a jockey is paid a fixed fee of £15.55 (plus VAT where applicable except that in the case of apprentice jockeys the fee shall be inclusive of VAT where applicable).

An apprentice can claim an allowance of 7 lb until he has ridden ten winners, 5 lb until he has ridden 50 winners, and 3 lb until he has ridden 75 winners.

CHAPTER XII

Racing Facts and Figures

*The Dail decided to grant £250,000 to pay for Tulyar,
the Aga Khan's Derby and St Leger winner, which has
been bought by the Irish National Stud.*

Daily Telegraph.

Stake Money

A COMPARISON of the amount in stake money won by different
equine champions is no absolute guide to their relative merits,
any more than the home test is, as the value of sweepstakes
depends on the number of original entries received for a race,
the number of forfeits declared at various times, the number of
actual runners in a race, and the amount of money added to the
stakes by the race-course executive or by sponsors, all of which
are variable factors. Furthermore some racehorses remain in
training longer than others and compete for more of the
valuable prizes.

Since the Horserace Betting Levy Board was formed, the
prize money added to prestige and feature races has now
increased to such an extent that it is difficult to draw a fair
comparison between the total amassed by the champions of the
present decade and those of earlier years.

Winners of over £100,000 in stakes

It is, however, not without interest to study the list of
thoroughbreds who have won the most money in stakes during
their days on the Turf. Rheingold comes first with £361,746,
Alleged second with £338,615, The Minstrel third with
£333,197; Grundy fourth with £326,423 and Mill Reef, whose
winnings of £309,225, included the Prix de l'Arc de Triomphe,
comes fifth.

Dahlia, whose winnings in England and Ireland alone
amounted to £277,739, is the leading filly. Brigadier Gerard

comes next on the list with £243,926, followed by Nijinsky with £246,135; Shirley Heights with £201,580; Wollow with £200,739; Royal Palace with £166,063; Santa Claus with £156,426; Ragusa with £146,588; Ribocco with £140,531; Pawneese, whose earnings in England alone amounted to £131,626, is the highest earning filly after Dahlia. She is followed by Empery with £117,809; Sir Ivor with £116,819; Roberto with £115,564; Dunfermline with £106,977; Ballymoss with the equivalent of £106,490, including the Prix de l'Arc de Triomphe; and Meadow Court with £100,500.

Other important stake money winners

After Meadow Court comes Ribero with £91,690; Sodium with £96,232, Snow Knight with £96,261; Park Top, whose winnings in Great Britain alone amounted to £83,717; Mysterious with £78,887, Bruni with £77,085; Altesse Royale with £76,934; Tulyar with £76,417; Bolkonski with £75,282; Nebbiolo with £74,987; Artaius with £74,902; Juliette Marny with £74,482; Bustino with £74,042; Baldric II with £71,079; Connaught with £69,212; and Blakeney with £68,685.

Petite Etoile was for a long time the leading filly with £67,786; she is followed by Morston with £67,038; Prince Regent with £62,639; Humble Duty with £63,696; Right Tack with £59,880; Scottish Rifle with £59,370; Giacometti with £58,459; Isinglass with £57,455; Mrs McArdy with £56,378; Alcide with £56,041; Rose Bowl with £55,664; Donovan with £55,154; Lupe with £53,764; Indiana with £52,175; Peleid with £52,008; Busted with £51,911; Hula Dancer with £50,548; Athens Wood with £50,155; Tambourine II with £50,027; Boucher with £49,586; Coronach with £48,224; Coup de Feu with £47,924; Pinza with £47,701; Fleet with £47,284; High Top with £46,968; Polygamy with £46,487; Noblesse with £46,444; Intermezzo with £46,159; Provoke with £45,622; Rock Sand with £45,618; Reform with £44,711; Waterloo with £43,822; Parthia with £43,186; Bahram with £43,086, closely followed by the filly Meld with £43,051; Fairway with £42,722; Lemberg with £41,954; Hethersett with £41,927; another filly Cantelo, with £40,265; Flying Fox with £40,096; Aurelius with £40,045, Sleeping Partner with £39,145; and Vitiges with £38,609. Sceptre, who was the highest filly until Meld and subsequently Petite Etoile, Altesse Royale, Mysterious and finally Dahlia passed her comes next with £38,225; Palestine with £38,216; Darius £38,105; Larkspur £38,080; Pourparler with £37,347; Pretty Polly with £37,297; Alycidon, £37,206; Supreme Court £36,950; Pia, £36,797; Psidium, £36,758; Prince Palatine £36,354; Windsor Lad, £36,257; Aureole, £36,225; Aggressor, £36,203; Ayrshire, £35,915; Only For Life, £35,352, Lorenzaccio, £35,328; Bella Paola, £35,004; Privy Councillor, £34,842; and Ginevra £34,923.

After these came Persimmon £34,706; La Fleche £34,703; and Crepello £34,201; followed by St Frusquin, Nimbus, Orme, Blue Peter, Book Law, Cameronian, Never Say Die, Nasram II, Canisbay, Niksar, Kashmir II, Long Look and Wolver Hollow.

Racing Records of Famous Thoroughbreds
Ballymoss won six races and finished second in his other three starts; St Paddy was first past the post nine times in 14 starts; and Tulyar won 9 out of 13 races. Ballymoss and Tulyar only ran for two seasons on the Turf, but St Paddy was three years in training.

Petite Etoile on the other hand, raced for four seasons, winning 14 times and being second in her other five races; Isinglass was also four years in training and won 11 out of his 12 races, including the Triple Crown; Alcide won 8 races, was second three times and only once unplaced, in his first race; Pinza won five races; Parthia 6; Bahram was the unbeaten winner of all his 9 races; including the Triple Crown; Meld won 5 out of 6 starts; Fairway 12 out of 15; Pretty Polly 22 out of 24; and Ormonde all his 16 races, including the Triple Crown and £28,465 in stakes.

Sea-Bird II won 7 of his 8 starts, finishing second his only remaining start.

The rivals Mill Reef and Brigadier Gerard both raced for three seasons; Mill Reef won 12 races and finished second in his other two starts, while Brigadier Gerard ran 18 times, winning 17 races and finishing second in his only other race. Grundy won 8 races, and was second twice and fourth once from 11 starts. The Minstrel won 7 races and was placed twice from nine starts. Nijinsky ran 13 times, winning 11 races and finishing second in both his remaining starts. Sir Ivor won 7 races and was placed in the remaining four. Royal Palace won 9 races and was placed once and unplaced only in his first start. Relko won 9 races. Santa Claus won four races and was placed twice from seven starts.

Bloodstock Prices

Not only has the value of stakes greatly increased, war years excepted, since Victorian times, but the prices paid for the best thoroughbreds have steadily risen.

Dispersal of Famous Studs

When Lord Londesborough's stud, including the stallions Stockwell and West Australian, was disposed of in 1860, it yielded a total of 20,689 guineas; and the Middle Park Stud, which was broken up in 1872, on the death of its founder, Mr William Blenkiron, brought in the sum of 124,620 guineas, Blair Athol being sold for 12,500 guineas, then the record price ever paid for a thoroughbred, and Gladiateur for 7,000 guineas.

The sale of Lord Falmouth's bloodstock in 1884 realized 110,000 guineas; the Sefton Stud realized 70,000 guineas in 1894; the Duke of Westminster's Eaton Stud, including Flying Fox and a yearling filly by Persimmon out of Ornament, full sister to Ormonde, subsequently named Sceptre, fetched 120,290 guineas in 1900; Sir Daniel Cooper's bloodstock was sold in 1909 for 90,310 guineas; and Sir Edward Hulton's bloodstock, including the brood-mare Straitlace, realised 288,380 guineas in 1925.

Flying Fox was sold for 37,500 guineas to Monsieur Edmond Blanc and on the same day Sceptre was bought by Mr R. S. Sievier for 10,000 guineas, at that time the record prices ever paid for a thoroughbred and for a yearling respectively.

On the death of the third Lord Astor in 1966, all the bloodstock at Cliveden were offered under the sealed bid system. They were bought by Mr W. M. Hackman, who owned a stud in Virginia in the United States of America. Mr Hackman resold the mares, foals and yearlings at the Saratoga Springs Summer Sales for £400,000, whilst 20 horses in training were sold to Lord Rotherwick. The Cliveden establishment was bought by Louis Freedman.

On the death in 1974 of the sixth Lord Rosebery, his executors ordered the complete sale of all the bloodstock bred at Mentmore. The young stock was disposed of at the Newmarket October Yearling Sales of 1974 and 1975 respectively. At the last named sale the executors were the leading vendors, the 15 lots sold realising an aggregate of 115,090 guineas. During the previous year they were second on the list of vendors, having sold 16 yearlings for 77,860 guineas.

High Priced Yearlings

The highest price previously paid for a yearling was 5,500 guineas given by Baron de Hirsch for La Fleche in 1890, and after the sale of Sceptre for 10,000 guineas no yearling again sold for five figures until Lord Glanely paid 11,800 guineas for Westward Ho in 1919 and 14,500 guineas for Blue Ensign for the Sledmere Stud in the following year. This sum was not exceeded at public auction until in 1936 the Hon. Dorothy Paget paid Lord Furness 15,000 guineas for a yearling colt, half brother to Orwell; then in 1945 the Gaekwar of Baroda paid 28,000 guineas for a full brother to Dante, by Nearco out of Rosy Legend by Dark Legend, a colt subsequently named Sayajirao, who won the St Leger in 1947.

The first yearling to be sold for a figure in excess of £50,000 was the filly La Hague, an own sister to Fleet, the winner of the 1,000 Guineas, who realised 51,000 guineas at the Newmarket Houghton Sales of 1969. The following year the filly Cambrienne, by Sicambre out of Djebellica, who was submitted at the Newmarket Houghton Sales by Commander P. Fitzgerald, realized 65,000 guineas to the bid of the Irish trainer Vincent O'Brien.

In 1971 the colt Princely Review, by Native Prince out of Review, sent up by Commander Fitzgerald, realised 117,000 guineas to the bid of Sir Douglas Clague. This was the first yearling to realise a six figure sum at a European auction. Four years later the colt Million, by Mill Reef out of Lalibela, was submitted by the Dalham Hall Stud at the Newmarket Houghton Sales and was brought for 202,000 guineas by a group of breeders headed by Lady Beaverbrook. In 1977 the colt Lychnis, by Lyphard out of Chain, was bought by BBA (Ireland) Ltd. for 250,000 guineas from Comte Roland de Chambure.

This figure was equalled at the Goffs September Yearling Sales in Dublin in 1978, when a filly by Mill Reef out of Hardiemina realised 250,000 guineas to the bid of the BBA, acting on behalf of a client of the French trainer Francois Boutin.

This figure was, however, to be surpassed when, at the Newmarket Houghton Sales of 1978 a yearling colt by Grundy out of Parsimony, submitted by the Overbury Stud, realised 264,000 guineas to the bid of Mr Humphrey Cottrill, who was acting on behalf of Mr Khaled Abdullah.

High Priced Foals

When the filly foal Canterbury Tale was sold for 37,000 guineas at the Newmarket December Sales of 1968 she established a record that was to last for nine years. This record was, however, to be broken twice in the space of twenty-four hours in 1977. On the first day of the Foal section of the Newmarket December Sales, Mr Michael Motion, the owner of a bloodstock agency, paid 38,000 guineas for a colt foal by Town Crier out of Strathcona, submitted by Mylerstown Stud. And on the following day, Motion paid 63,000 guineas for a colt by Morston out of Crowdie, the property of Mr C. M. Budgett.

At the Newmarket December Sales of 1978 a filly by Mill Reef out of River Deep, submitted by International Bloodstock, realised 74,000 guineas to the bid of the French bloodstock agent, M. Alain Decrion, who was acting on behalf of an undisclosed client.

Record Priced Horses in Training

The first horse in training to realise a six figure sum at a public auction was Vaguely Noble, who was sold by Mr L. B. Holliday to Mr and Mrs Robert Franklyn for 136,000 guineas. The first filly to top the 100,000 guineas mark was Ginevra, who realised 106,000 guineas at the 1972 Newmarket December Sales, a figure which was passed two years later by Northern Gem at the 1974 Newmarket December Sales. Both these records were broken at the 1977 Newmarket December Sales when Mrs McArdy was sold for 154,000 guineas.

Even this figure was, however, totally eclipsed, when, at the Newmarket December Sales Swiss Maid realised the sum of 325,000 guineas, being 'bought in' by her trainer Paul Keeleway.

Record Sums paid for Brood-Mares

Meanwhile the prices paid for proved performers on the Turf had also reached fantastic figures. The brood-mare Flair had been sold for 15,000 guineas; Lord Furness had bought Salamandra in foal to the Tetrarch for 16,000 guineas, the offspring being the St Leger winner Salmon-Trout, and Strait-lace, winner of the Oaks in 1924, had been sold for 17,000 guineas in 1925, which remained a record for her sex until 1948 when Ferry Pool was bought for 18,000 guineas by the Sezin-cote Stud. In 1954 Messrs Askew paid 36,000 guineas for Refreshed to the executors of the late Mr John Dewar, whose 48 lots at the Newmarket December Sales in 1954 made 395,595 guineas; and in 1964 Chandelier, the dam of Crocket, was knocked down for 37,000 guineas.

At the Newmarket December Sales of 1971 record prices for broodmares were overtaken in quick succession. Romping was sold for 59,000 guineas, Matatina for 60,000 guineas and Vela for 62,000 guineas. Miss Charisma realized 67,000 guineas at the Newmarket July Stakes of 1974. At the Newmarket December Sales of 1976, Chain realised 84,000 guineas to the bid of Heron Bloodstock Services while Istiea, submitted by the Kildangan Stud, was sold to BBA (Ireland) Ltd. for 142,000 guineas.

Record Sums Paid for Stallions

Mr J. B. Joel paid £40,000 for Prince Palatine in 1913; Tracery was sold to an Argentine breeder for 53,000 guineas in 1920; and Captain Cuttle, winner of the Derby in 1922, was sold for £50,000 and went to Italy in 1928.

Four years later Solario was bought by a syndicate of British bloodstock breeders at the Newmarket Sales in July 1932 for the sum of 47,000 guineas. Mr Martin Benson paid the Maharajah of Rajpipla £50,000 for Windsor Lad after he had won the Derby in 1934; and the Aga Khan sold to American breeders three of his Derby winners, Blenheim, for £45,000 in 1936; and in 1940 Bahram for £40,000 and Mahmoud for £20,000. In 1937 Monsieur E. Esmond bought Donatello II for £47,500, but Mr Martin Benson then beat all records by paying £60,000 for Nearco, after he had rounded off an unbeaten career in Italy by winning the Grand Prix de Paris in 1938. Nearco was a brown horse by Pharos out of Nogara by Havresac II (a grandson of St Simon out of a granddaughter of Flying Fox) out of Catnip (a daughter of Spearmint) who was bought by Senator Tesio for £100.

It was also reported at the time that after Dante had won the 1945 Derby Mr Benson offered Sir Eric Ohlson the then huge sum of £125,000 for the son of Nearco and Rosy Legend; an offer which, however was not accepted by the owner of this famous thoroughbred.

In 1953 the Irish National Stud paid HH the Aga Khan £250,000 for his champion racehorse Tulyar; at that time a world record price for a thoroughbred.

These prices, however, seem small in contrast with the £1,000,000 paid by the National Stud in 1975 for a three-parts holding in Grundy, the six million dollars paid for Blushing Groom, and, in 1977, the $4½m for a 50% holding in The Minstrel. In 1978, however, all these figures were surpassed when Acamas was sold for the world record sum of £4,000,000 to a group of breeders, which included the Aga Khan and Captain A. D. D. Rogers.

Record Bloodstock Sales

In 1978, Messrs Tattersalls Newmarket December Sales passed a record eleven million mark when 1,223 lots sold for 11,802,280 guineas, a turnover well in excess of the 1977 record. This sum included the sum of 325,000 guineas paid for the Champion Stakes winner Swiss Maid and the 224,000 guineas paid for the four-year-old filly Royal Hive.

CHAPTER XIII

Betting on Horses

Lord Hippo suffered fearful loss
By putting money on a horse
Which he believed, if it were pressed
Would run far faster than the rest.

Hilaire Belloc, *More Peers*.

The Totalizator and the Bookmakers

In 1928 the House of Commons passed 'A Bill to amend the Betting Act 1853, to legalize the use of totalizators on certain race-courses, and to make further provision with regard to the betting thereon'. This measure was subsequently approved by the House of Lords and received the royal assent. In 1929 the Betting Tax, imposed in 1926 by Mr Winston Churchill as Chancellor of the Exchequer, was abolished; nominations of horses to future events, including the classics, ceased to become void on the death of the nominator, as had happened, for instance, in the case of St Simon on the death of Prince Batthyany; an improved type of starting gate was introduced; and a form of totalizator made its appearance on the July course at Newmarket. In 1930 the Jockey Club decided that in future in the event of a dead-heat the stakes would be divided and the race would not be run off as was the previous practice; and the totalizator was installed on the Rowley Mile course at Newmarket.

These were momentous years for the Turf, and the introduction of the 'tote' was perhaps the most significant event of all. It has meant that some part at least of the vast sums which annually passed through the betting 'ring' are now available for the well-being of the sport; for increasing the stakes out of the race-fund; reducing entrance fees and forfeits; assisting owners to defray the cost of transporting horses to race-meetings; for improving the accommodation provided for the public on race-courses and reducing the charges for admission to the several enclosures; and for Turf charities and other worthy objects connected with horse-racing, thoroughbred breeding, veterinary science, and research. (See also page 38 under Horserace Betting Levy Board).

Many gloomy prophets shook their heads at the time and foretold that the new machine would put an end to the book-makers; that no longer would the 'roar of the ring' reverberate across the stands and enclosures, lawns and paddocks of our racecourses; that half the fascination to the Turf would be lost when the doomed 'pencillers' and 'tic-tac' men, with all the paraphernalia of their trade, were forced out of business. But nothing of the kind occurred and obviously there is room on the Turf, both for the 'bookie' and the 'tote'.

A great many people who have played a prominent part in the conduct of racing, have advocated that all betting trans-actions on horse-racing in Great Britain should be conducted through the 'tote'. Prominent amongst them was Woodrow Wyatt, M.P., who was elected Chairman of the Horserace Totalisator Board in 1976. Presumably those who favour a 'Tote monopoly' base their arguments on the fact that in France, where all betting is conducted through the Pari-Mutuel (France's equivalent of the tote), and consequently all money spent on betting is utilised in the interests of racing, the sport is in a more healthy financial state; for example there are more funds available for prize money.

There is no doubt that the Pari-Mutuel has done great service to the French racing industry. But it is by no means certain that, even if a 'Tote Monopoly were to come about, it would be of comparable benefit to racing in England. Many punters prefer to bet with the bookmakers, since they know in advance the odds that they are likely to receive for their money. Furthermore bookmaking has grown into a major industry, and to render it obsolete would be unlikely to benefit racing. The leading bookmakers, notably Hills, Ladbrokes and Corals have put a great deal into racing, through the sponsorship of races, while Ladbrokes now own Lingfield racecourse.

The biggest dividend ever paid out on by the tote was the 'daily double' was the sum of £5062 13 0 in old money on March 25th, 1938, which represented odds of 10,124 to 1. However, this divident appears small beside those paid out on the Tote Jackpot, which was introduced at the Royal Ascot meeting in 1966. In this bet, the punter must name the winners of all the races at a specified meeting. The punter who succeeds in naming all the winners, can win a stupendous dividend. The biggest individual dividend paid out for a tote jackpot two days later on June 18th. For the sum of five shillings in old money, the return was £63,114 5 0.

On an average, the bookmakers' starting prices for odds on favourites have been more favourable to the backer than the 'tote' returns. And although no bookmaker would ever quote the odds of 10,124 to 1 for a 'double', many leading bookmakers have introduced attractive multiple bets which can produce very good odds indeed. Such bets have largely come about through the increased coverage of racing by television companies that has been so marked a feature of post-war racing, see page 000.

TOTALISATOR DIVIDENDS

Tote dividend	Equivalent odds	Tote dividend	Equivalent odds
11.25p	1 to 8	27.5p	7 to 4
12.5p	1 to 4	30p	2 to 1
13.75p	3 to 8	32.5p	9 to 4
15p	1 to 2	35p	5 to 2
16.25p	5 to 8	37.5p	11 to 4
17.50p	3 to 4	40p	3 to 1
18.75p	7 to 8	45p	7 to 2
20p	Evens	50p	4 to 1
21.25p	9 to 8	60p	5 to1
22.50p	5 to 4	65p	11 to 2
23.75p	11 to 8	70p	6 to 1
25p	6 to 4		

Note: The basic tote unit of 10p is always included in the dividend declared by the Tote.

STARTING PRICES

Odds on	Amount won	Odds against	Amount won	Odds against	Amount won
1 to 4	25p	21 to 20	£1.5p	9 to 2	£4.50p
2 to 7	28.75p	11 to 10	£1.10p	5 to 1	£5
30 to 100	30p	6 to 5	£1.20p	11 to 2	£5.50p
1 to 3	33.3p	5 to 4	£1.25p	6 to 1	£6
4 to 11	36.25p	11 to 8	£1.37.5p	13 to 2	£6.50
2 to 5	40p	6 to 4	£1.50p	100 to 15	£6.66
4 to 9	44.6p	13 to 8	£1.62.5p	7 to 1	£7
1 to 2	50p	100 to 60	£1.66.6p	15 to 2	£7.50p
8 to 15	53.33p	7 to 4	£1.75p	8 to 1	£8
4 to 7	57.1p	15 to 8	£1.77.5p	100 to 12	£8.333
60 to 100	60p	2 to 1	£2	9 to 1	£9
8 to 13	61.77p	9 to 4	£2.25p	100 to 11	£9.807
4 to 6	66.7p	5 to 2	£2.50p	10 to 1	£10
8 to 11	72.9p	11 to 4	£2.75p	100 to 9	£11.13
4 to 5	80p	3 to 1	£3	100 to 8	£12.50p
5 to 6	83.33p	100 to 30	£3.33.33p	100 to 7	£14.28
10 to 11	90.08p	7 to 2	£3.50p	100 to 6	£16.66
20 to 21	95p	4 to 1	£4	20 to 1	£20
Evens	£1				

Note. The above amounts do not include the stakes of £1

HORSERACE TOTALISATOR BOARD AND COMMITTEE OF TATTERSALLS
The Horserace Totalisator Board is responsible to Parliament for the operation of the totalisator and a committee of Tattersalls is recognised by the Jockey Club as the responsible authority for settling disputes between backers and bookmakers

Betting Taxes

As has been stated, the Betting Tax imposed by Mr Winston Churchill as Chancellor of the Exchequer, was abolished in 1928. However a new Betting Tax was re-introduced in the Budget of April 1967 when the rate was fixed at 2½% on all bets. In March 1968 the rate was increased to 6%, but in order that people should be encouraged to come racing all on-course bets remained taxable at the old rate. In 1972 all tax was reduced to 4%, and this had remained the rate for bets laid on the racecourse, although the tax on off-course betting was raised to 7.5% in 1974. It was later raised to 8% and then increased once more to its present figure of 9%.

Effect of Television on Racing

In recent years there has been a marked increase in the coverage of racing both by BBC Television and by many of Independent television companies licensed by the Independent Broadcasting Authority. Many people found that although television could never convey the atmosphere of a racecourse, they obtained a better view than they would have done if they had been on the racecourse, and also expert advice. They also appreciated not having to pay entry charges and travelling costs and not having to endure poor facilities.

The result was that the attendance figures at race-meetings have begun to show a sharp decline.

The increase in coverage of racing by television has however been of benefit to racing in that many firms have come forward to sponsor racing, knowing well that they will benefit from the accruing publicity, that they would not receive if the races were broadcast only in sound. Also the introduction of televised racing has led to the introduction by many leading bookmakers of multiple bets that have been attractive to backers in view of the large odds at which they stand to win. The two principal bets that have come into being are the ITV 7 and the BBC Triella. In the first, the backer has to name the winners of all the races due to be televised by ITV on a specific day. In the second, the backer must name the first and second horses in correct order in the three races televised by BBC.

Heavy Wagers, Big Wins, and Bigger Losses

This book is not written for, and is unlikely to be read by, those moralists who believe that it is a mortal sin to have a shilling on a horse, nor has it been compiled to encourage fools to part with their money even quicker than they otherwise might do. But it would be manifestly absurd to ignore the fact that betting is an integral part of horse-racing, and to omit any reference to the subject of wagering in a volume devoted to the Turf would be merely ridiculous.

The gambling instinct is one that has been present in

human nature from the earliest days of mankind, and if reasonably controlled and moderately exercised it can provide amusement and excitement in a manner that does no harm to anyone. Suffice it to say that one should never put more money on a horse than one can afford to pay out if one loses one's wager.

Vast sums have of course been won and lost on the Turf. In 1832 John Gully and Robert Ridsdale between them won £100,000 when the latter's horse St Giles won the Derby and the former's horse Margrave won the St Leger. In 1843 Mr Bowes won £50,000 and Lord George Bentinck £30,000 when the former's horse Cotherstone landed them the odds in the Derby, and Lord George cleared £100,000 by betting alone in 1845. In 1858 Sir Joseph Hawley won £80,000 when Beadsman won him his second Derby; in 1860 Mr Merry won £500,000 when his horse Thormanby won the Derby; in 1878 Mr Gretton cleared £40,000 when Isonomy passed the post first in the Cambridgeshire; and in 1884 John Hammond landed the autumn double and £104,000 over Florence in the Cambridgeshire and St Gatien in the Cesarewitch.

Coming to more recent times, the biggest recorded wager which was successful was the huge sum of £250,000 which was taken out of the 'ring' by the Druid's Lodge Stable syndicate when Hackler's Pride (ridden by the now well-known trainer Jack Jarvis) won the Cambridgeshire in 1903, after they had backed their horse down from 33 to 1 to start favourite for the race at 9 to 2. The same syndicate also landed enormous coups when Ypsilanti won the Jubilee in 1903 and again in 1904; when Hackler's Pride won the Cambridgeshire again in 1904; and when Christmas Daisy won the Cambridgeshire in 1909 and for the second time in 1910. Both James White, in spite of winning £100,000 on Irish Elegance in the Royal Hunt Cup, and Horatio Bottomley were heavy and unsuccessful gamblers on the Turf; but Mr Charles Beattie was a very successful professional backer, who won £30,000 when Verdict defeated Epinard by a neck in the Cambridgeshire in 1933, and who subsequently left a fortune of £200,000 when he died, while Mr William Chandler, bookmaker turned backer, is reputed to have lifted £120,000 from the 'ring' when Ocean Swell won the war-substitute Derby at Newmarket in 1944.

A large bet which just failed to come off was one placed by

Mr H. F. Clayton, who wagered £100 to £100,000 that his own horses would win the Cesarewitch and the Cambridgeshire in 1931. Six Wheeler only lost the Cesarewitch by 1½ lengths to Noble Star, and Disarmament duly won the Cambridgeshire by 3 lengths.

In contrast to some of the large amounts which have been won on rare occasions, it must be remembered that in the aggregate much larger sums have been lost much more frequently, and mention was made in an earlier chapter that the Marquis of Hastings lost £120,000 when Hermit won the Derby. The celebrated 'penciller' known as 'Leviathan' Davis was £50,000 out of pocket when Voltigeur finished first in the Derby of 1850, and £100,000 in the following year when Teddington won the Blue Riband of the Turf; but far more money has gone into the 'ring' than ever came out of it, otherwise old-established firms like William Hill, and Ladbrokes, to say nothing of the smaller turf accountants, would long ago have closed their offices.

Betting Systems

There are of course many touts and tipsters, who are prepared to sell to the budding punter 'inside information straight from the horse's mouth', from the picturesque and familiar race-course character Ras 'Prince' Monolulu, with his hoarse cry of 'I gotta horse', to the many relatives of 'Gipsy' Lee on Epsom Downs and the advertisers in the sporting Press, each with his own 'infallible' system.

However, although many people sneer at systems, there can be little doubt that some method of selecting horses to back and some mathematical scheme of staking are in the long run more likely to yield satisfactory results than haphazard plunging, or at any rate to limit losses to what is reasonable.

Portman's Golden Rule for Backers

The late Mr Arthur B. Portman, proprietor and editor of *Horse and Hound*, who wrote under the pen-name of 'Audax', and who was probably in his day the greatest expert on horse-racing in this country, once told the author that in his opinion the golden rule for the backers of horses was never to wager on the result of a handicap. He was obviously right, because a handicap is expressly framed to give every horse in the race an equal chance of winning. There can, therefore, be little doubt that a punter, to be successful over a period of time, must restrict his wagering to weight-for-age races, in which, more often than not, in spite of the 100 to 1 outsiders who have even won the Derby, that horse will win which has the best form and the best breeding for the particular distance over which the race is run.

Conclusion

That is why a sound knowledge of the breeding and past racing of thoroughbreds is essential for a full enjoyment of the pleasures of the Turf and for a profitable outcome to the hazards of wagering on animals who are not machines. Such knowledge it has been the endeavour of the author to impart to his readers in this book on Horce-racing.

Selected Bibliography

The Bloodstock Breeders' Review – The British Bloodstock Agency Ltd. (Annual Volumes).

A History of the English Turf – Sir Theodore Cook, Editor-in-Chief of *The Field*. Virtue and Company. (3 Volumes) 1904.

A History of the English Turf, 1904–30 – Captain T. H. Browne, Turf Editor of *The Field*. Virtue and Company. (2 Volumes) 1931.

The History of the Racing Calendar and Stud Book – C. M. Prior. The Sporting Life. 1926.

Memoirs of a Racing Journalist – Sidney Galtrey, 'Hotspur' of the *Daily Telegraph*. Hutchinson & Co, Ltd. 1934.

Memories of Racing and Hunting – The Duke of Portland. Faber & Faber Ltd. 1935.

The Breed of the Racehorse – Freidrich Becker. The British Bloodstock Agency Ltd. 1936.

Thoroughbred Racing Stock – Lady Wentworth. George Allen & Unwin Ltd. 1938.

Racing England – Patrick R. Chalmers. B. T. Batsford Ltd. 1939.

Flat Racing – The Lonsdale Library. Various Authors. Seeley Service & Co, Ltd. 1940.

Royal Newmarket – R. C. Lyle. Racing Correspondent of *The Times*. Putnam & Co, Ltd. 1945.

The Book of the Horse – Various Authors. Nicholson & Watson, Ltd. 1946.

The Derby Stakes, 1900–1953 – Vincent Orchard. Hutchinson & Co, Ltd. 1954.

British Blood Lines – Chas. Jerdein & F. R. Kay. J. A. Allen & Co. 1955.

My Story – Gordon Richards. Hodder & Stoughton. 1955.

Bloodstock Breeding – Sir Charles Leicester. Odhams Press. 1957.

The Jockey Club – Roger Mortimer. Cassell. 1958.

Breeding the Racehorse – Federico Tesio. J. A. Allen & Co. 1958.

The British Racehorse – Turf Newspapers Ltd. 1949–1963.

The Derby Stakes – Roger Mortimer. Cassell & Co. Ltd.

Introduction to the Thoroughbred – Peter Willett. Stanley Paul.

The Thoroughbred – Peter Willett. Weidenfield & Nicolson. 1970.

Breeding for Racing – John Hislop. Secker and Warburg.

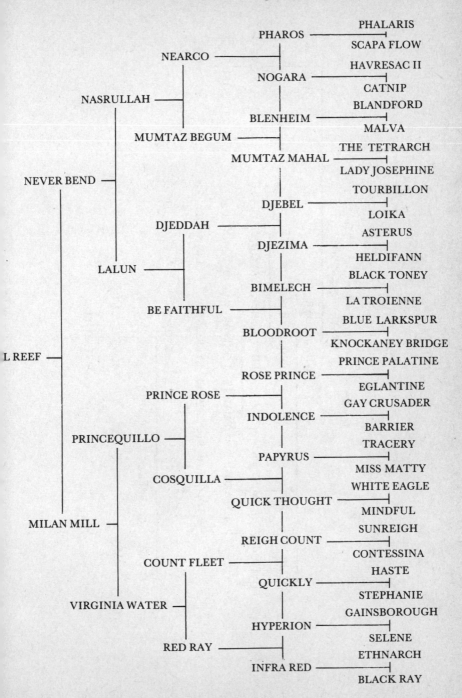

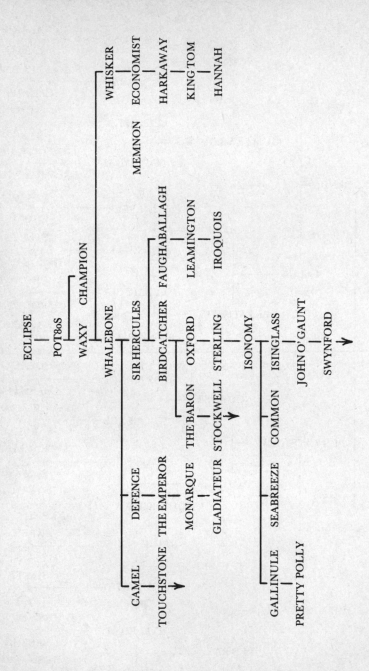

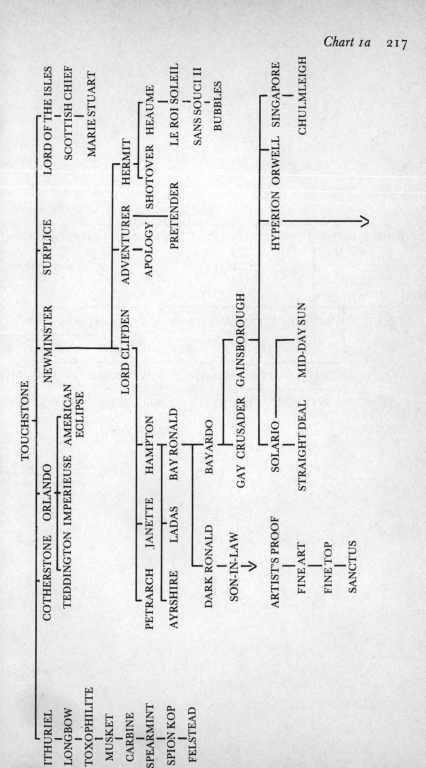

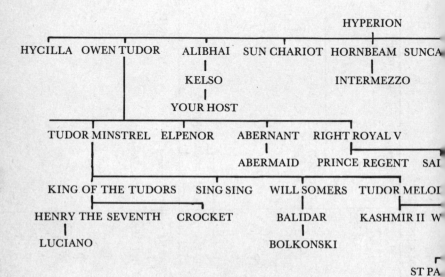

HYPERION

HYCILLA   OWEN TUDOR   ALIBHAI   SUN CHARIOT   HORNBEAM   SUNCA

KELSO   INTERMEZZO

YOUR HOST

TUDOR MINSTREL   ELPENOR   ABERNANT   RIGHT ROYAL V

ABERMAID   PRINCE REGENT   SAI

KING OF THE TUDORS   SING SING   WILL SOMERS   TUDOR MELOI

HENRY THE SEVENTH   CROCKET   BALIDAR   KASHMIR II W

LUCIANO   BOLKONSKI

ST PA

CONNAUGHT

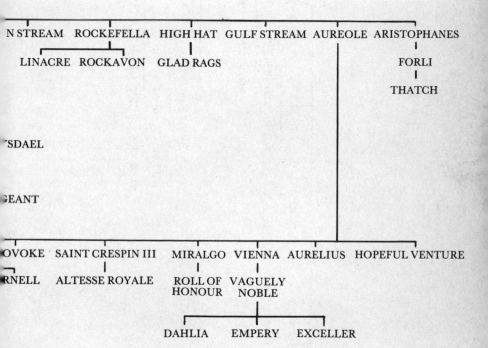

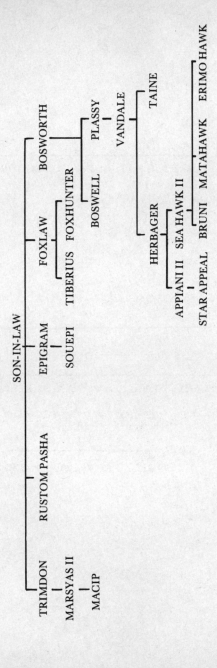

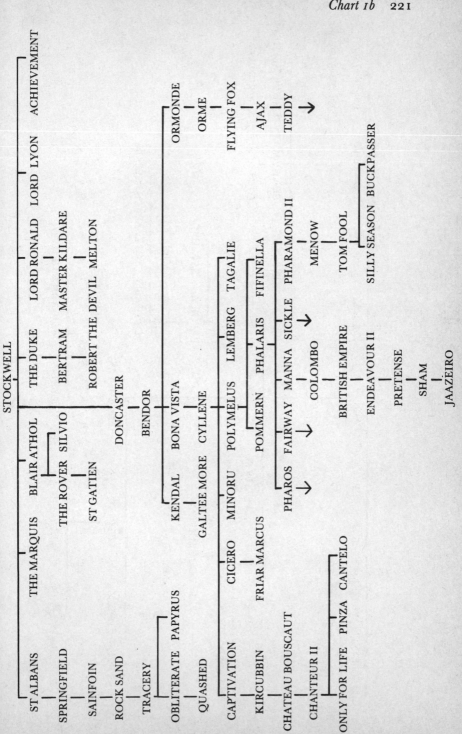

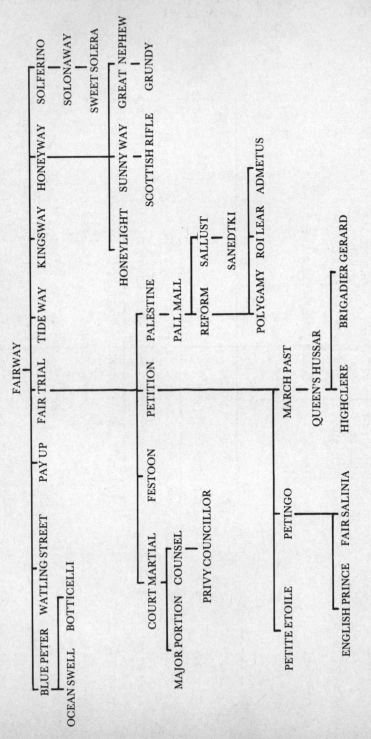

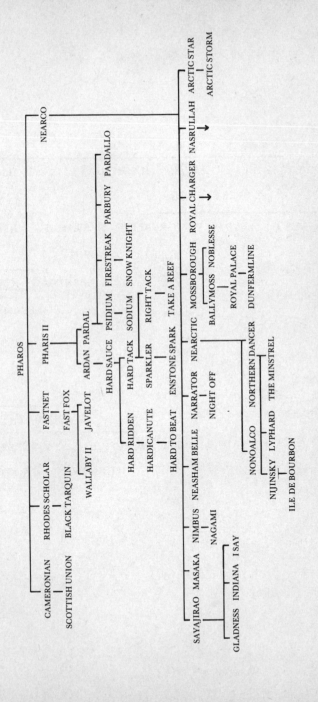

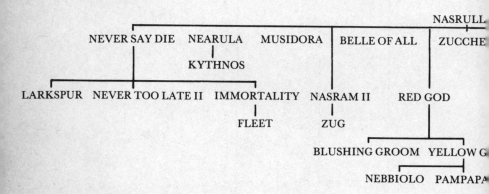

NASRULL

NEVER SAY DIE   NEARULA   MUSIDORA   BELLE OF ALL   ZUCCHE

KYTHNOS

LARKSPUR   NEVER TOO LATE II   IMMORTALITY   NASRAM II   RED GOD

FLEET   ZUG

BLUSHING GROOM   YELLOW G

NEBBIOLO   PAMPAPA

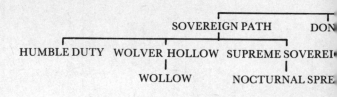

SOVEREIGN PATH   DON

HUMBLE DUTY   WOLVER HOLLOW   SUPREME SOVEREI

WOLLOW   NOCTURNAL SPRE

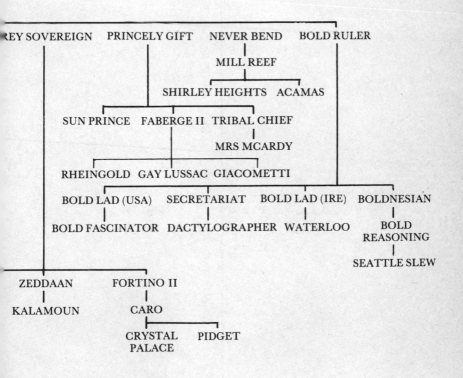

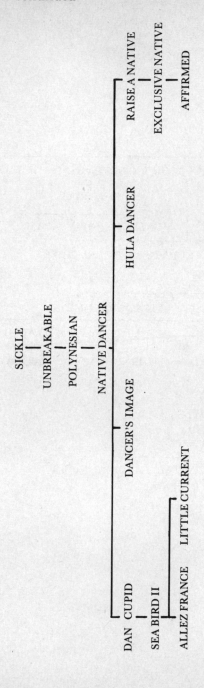

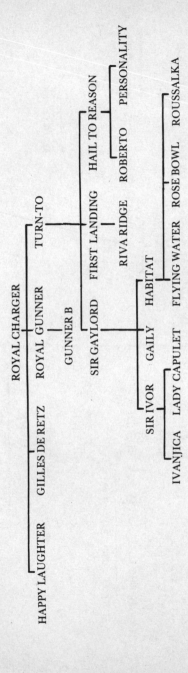

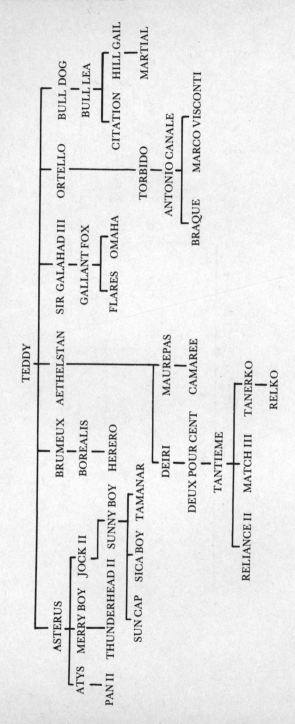

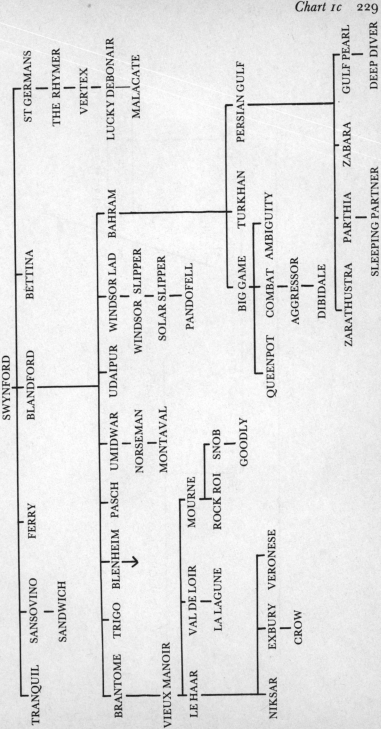

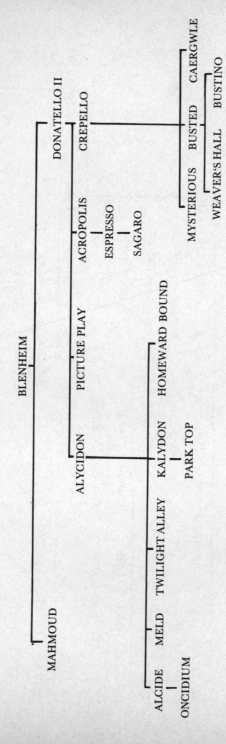

Chart 2 231

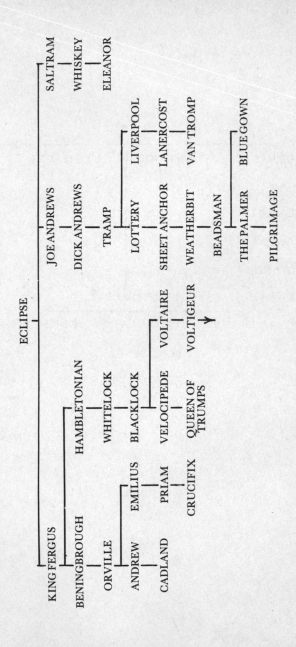

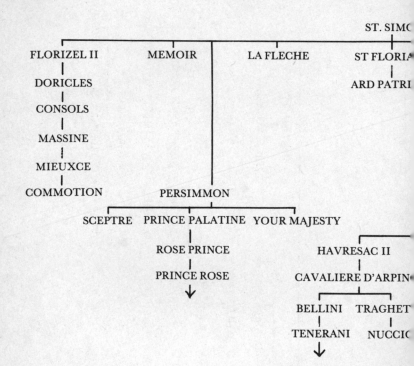

Chart 2—continued   233

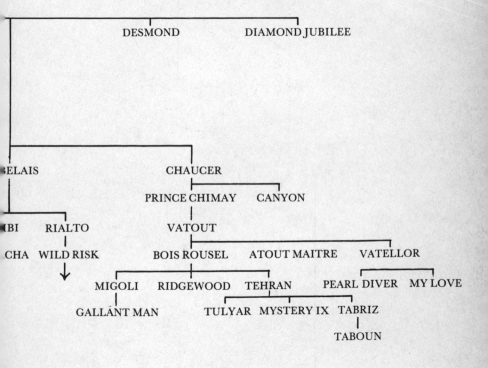

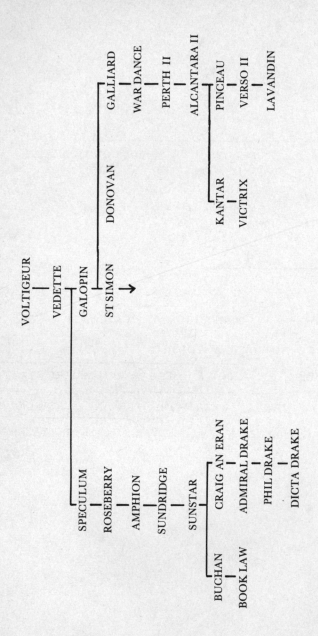

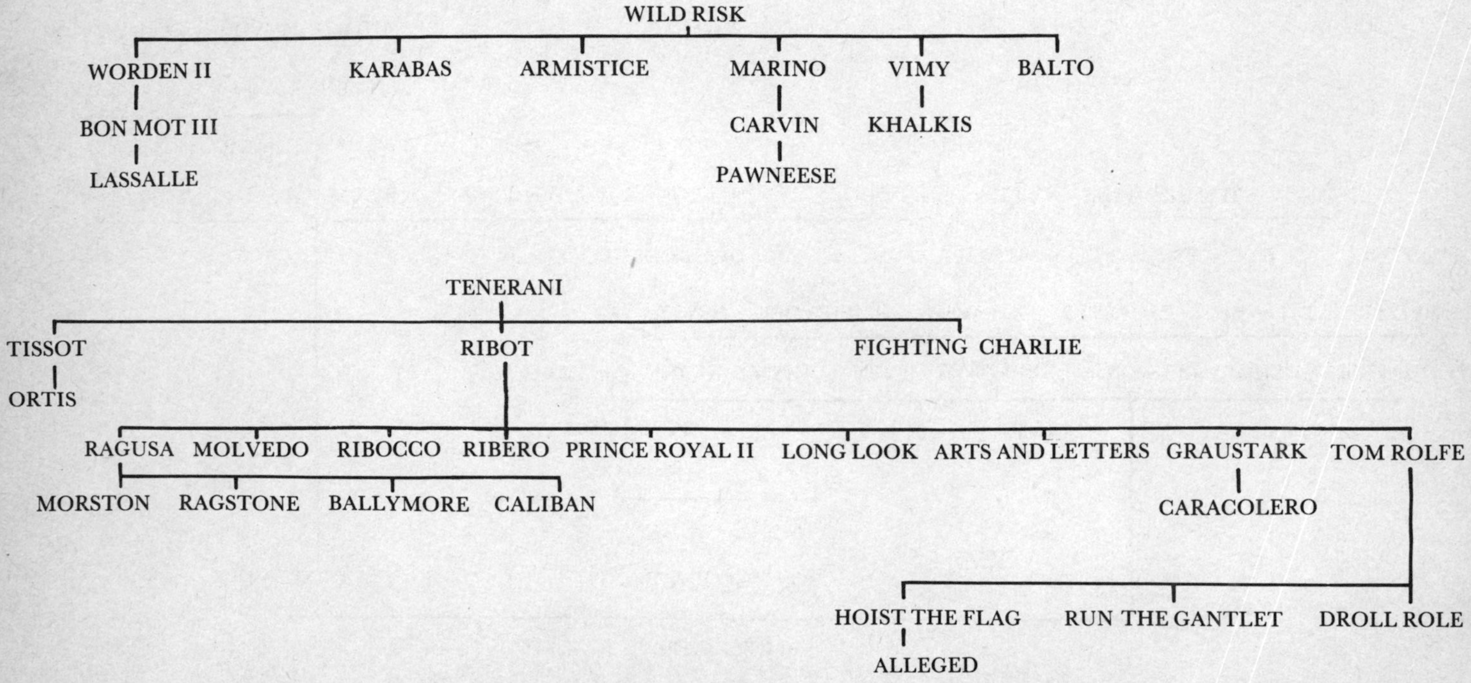

Chart 2—continued   235

WILD RISK

WORDEN II
BON MOT III
LASSALLE

KARABAS

ARMISTICE

MARINO
CARVIN
PAWNEESE

VIMY
KHALKIS

BALTO

TENERANI

RIBOT

FIGHTING CHARLIE

TISSOT
ORTIS

RAGUSA
MORSTON

MOLVEDO
RAGSTONE

RIBOCCO
BALLYMORE

RIBERO
CALIBAN

PRINCE ROYAL II

LONG LOOK

ARTS AND LETTERS

GRAUSTARK
CARACOLERO

TOM ROLFE

HOIST THE FLAG
ALLEGED

RUN THE GANTLET

DROLL ROLE

PRINCE CHEVALIER

PRINCE ROSE

PRINCE BIO

PRINCEQUILLO

ROUND TABLE

BALDRIC II

ARTAIUS

IRISH BALL

TAMBOURNE II

ROSE ROYALE II

SICAMBRE

NORTHERN LIGHT II

PRINCE TAJ

CELTIC ASH

SICARELLE

PHAETON

DíATOME

SHANTUNG

TIZIANO

ATHENS WOOD

VITIGES

STELL PULSE

VALORIS

COURT HARWELL

SOLTIKOFF

CHARLOTTESVILLE

FULL DRESS II

GINEVRA

MEADOW COURT

CHARLOTTOWN

ARCTIC PRINCE

ARCTIC EXPLORER

DOUTELLE

PRETENDRE II

CANONERO , II

CANISBAY

ORANGE BAY

Chart 3   237

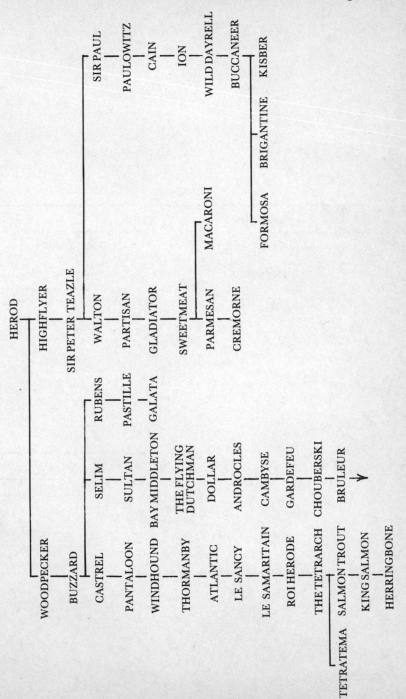

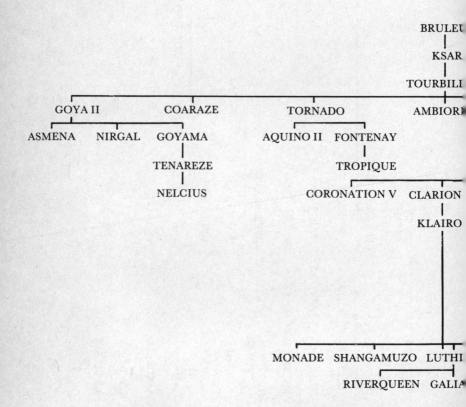

Chart 3—continued   239

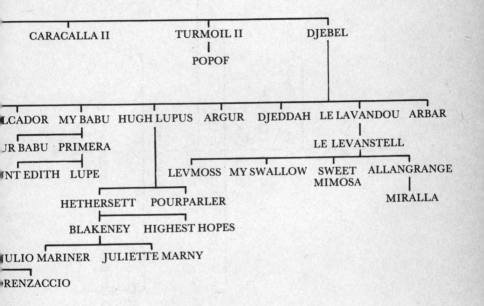

CARACALLA II   TURMOIL II   DJEBEL
                     |
                  POPOF

LCADOR MY BABU HUGH LUPUS ARGUR DJEDDAH LE LAVANDOU ARBAR

JR BABU PRIMERA   LE LEVANSTELL

NT EDITH LUPE   LEVMOSS MY SWALLOW SWEET ALLANGRANGE
                                          MIMOSA
                                                      MIRALLA
         HETHERSETT POURPARLER

      BLAKENEY HIGHEST HOPES

ULIO MARINER JULIETTE MARNY

RENZACCIO

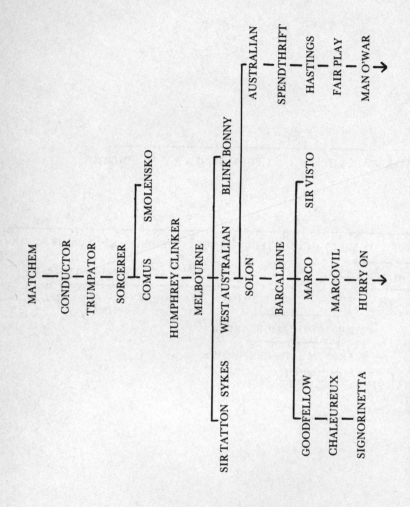

Chart 4—continued   241

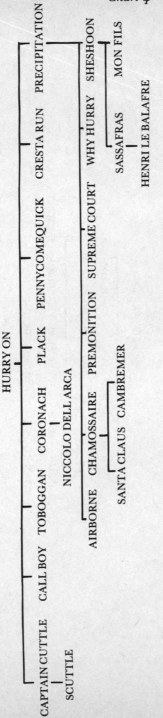

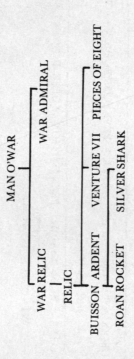

MAN O'WAR
WAR ADMIRAL
WAR RELIC
RELIC
BUISSON ARDENT
VENTURE VII
PIECES OF EIGHT
SILVER SHARK
ROAN ROCKET

Chart 5 243

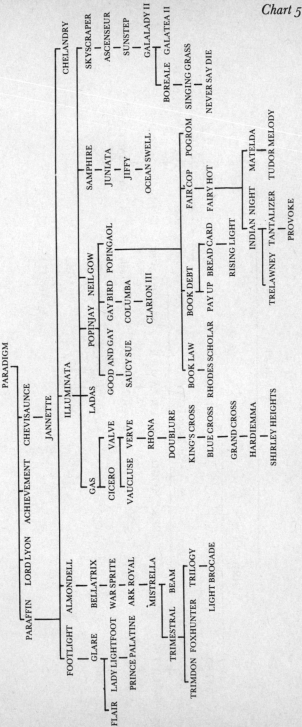

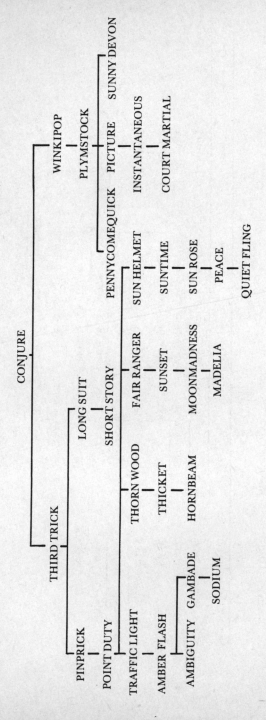

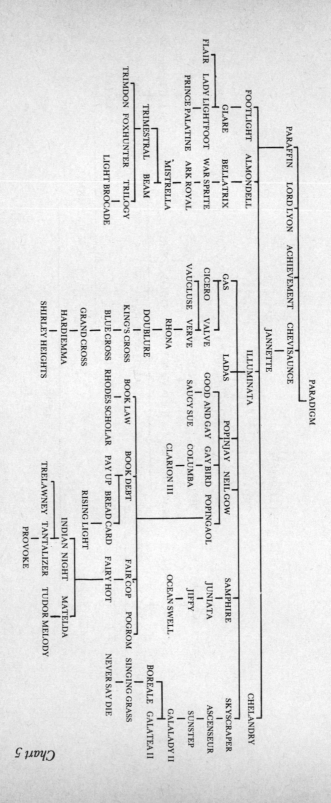

Chart 5   243

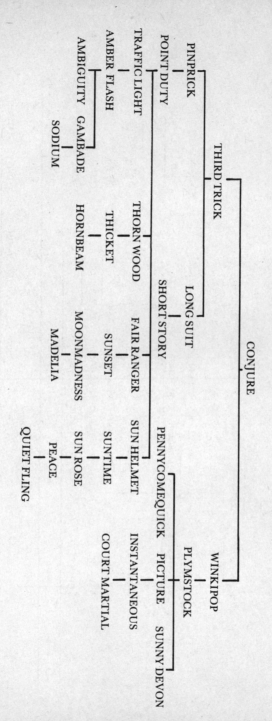

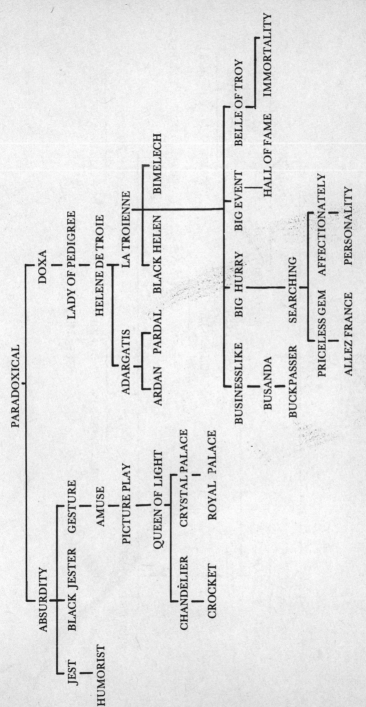

Chart 7 245

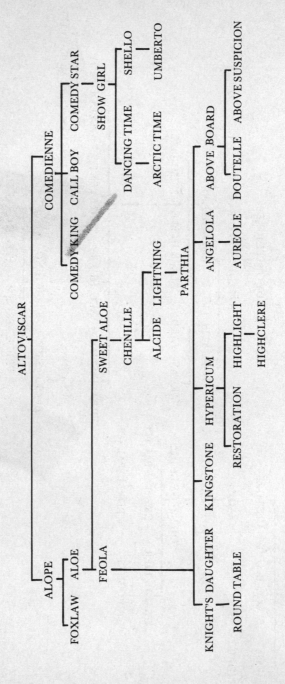

Chart 9 247

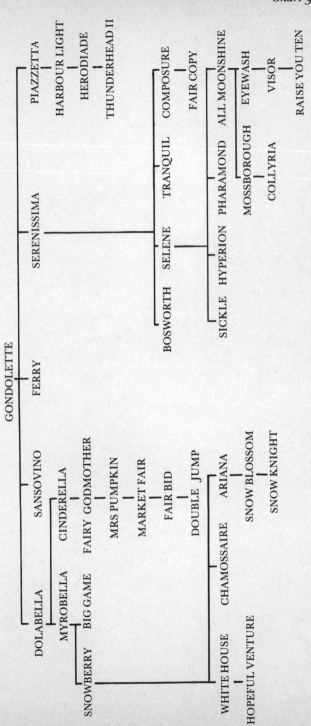

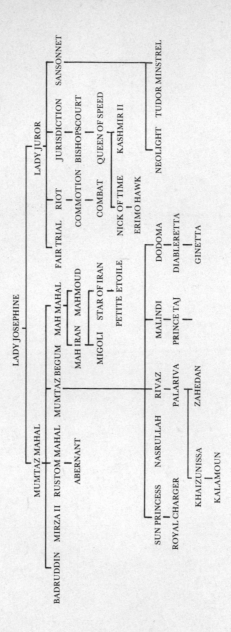

Chart 11   249

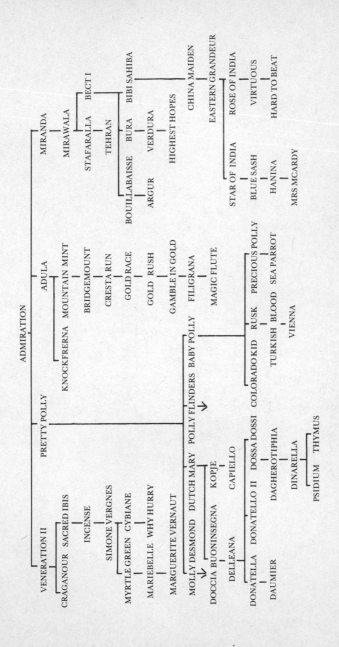

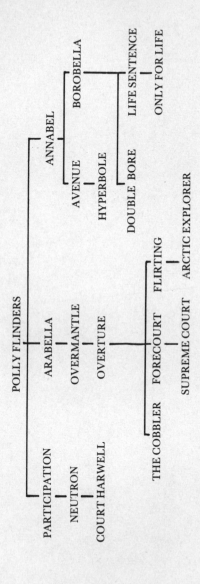

Chart 11—continued 251

MOLLY DESMOND

MOLLY ADARE

LADY MAUREEN
— MAURETANIA
— MONTAGNANA
— FLUTE ENCHANTEE GUERSANT
— LUTHIER

BRAVE EMPRESS
— EASTERN EMPEROR ACE OF SPADES
— SUNSET GUN
— STYLIST PATTERN
— ARTAIUS

BRAZEN MOLLY
— LA PAIVA
— BRIGADIER GERARD

SARITA
— SISTER SARAH
— BLACK PETER LADY ANGELA LADY SYBIL CAERLISSA
— NEARCTIC ESQUIRE GIRL
— LUCYROWE

EDIE KELLY
— FIGHTING EDIE
— FORMENTERA
— FLYING WATER

CHALLENGE
— ST PADDY

GOLDEN SILENCE
TIP THE WINK
TRIAL GROUND
PREMONITION

FEARLESS FOX QUEEN CHRISTINA
— ORTHODOX ELEANOR CROSS
— THREE WEEKS LADY CROSS
— PARDAO VICTORIA CROSS
— CRIMEA II

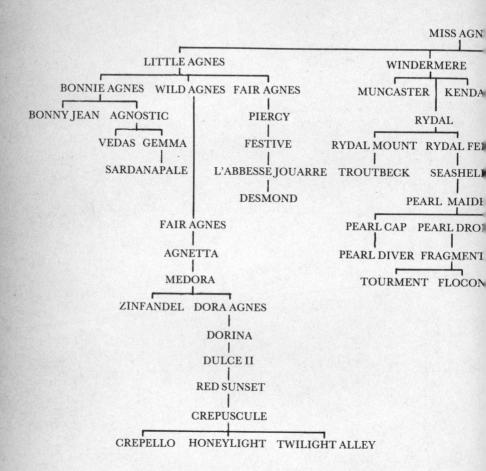

Chart 12—continued   253

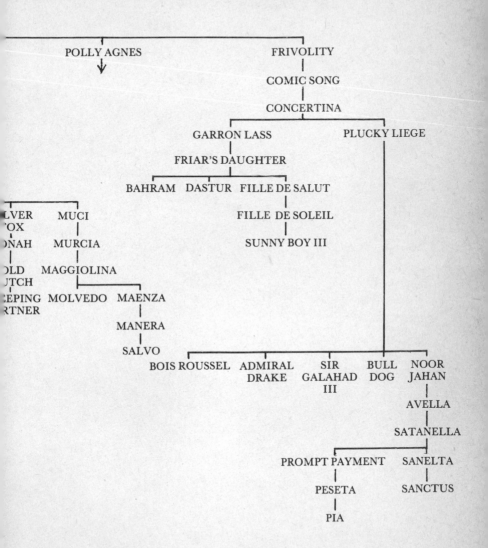

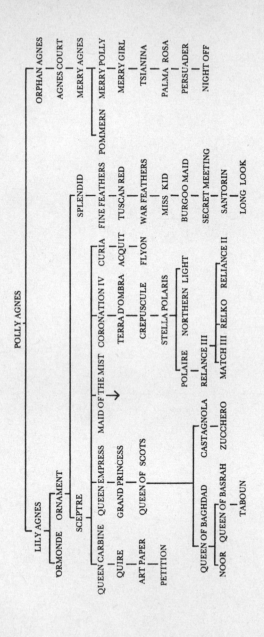

Chart 12—continued   255

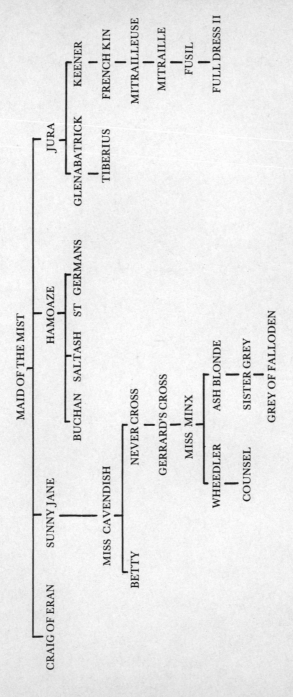

Index

Addenda

Page 11 Storm Bird (1980) is another famous two-year-old to be rated at the top of the Two-Year-Old Free Handicap.

Page 15 Troy (1979) is another famous three-year-old to be placed at the top of the Three-Year-Old Free Handicap.

Page 16 Le Moss is added to the list of horses who have won the Ascot Gold Cup twice.

Page 18 Troy, Ela-Mana-Mou and Shergar have also won the King George VI and Queen Elizabeth Stakes.

Page 20 Since the Champion Stakes was scheduled to receive additional prize money, eleven fillies have been successful, the latest of whom was Cairn Rouge.

Page 22 To the famous sprinters of recent years add Moorestyle and Marwell.

Page 27 Sea Pigeon won the Ebor Handicap in 1979 carrying 10 stone.

Page 28 Baronet won the Cambridgeshire in 1978 as a six year old with 9.0 and again in 1980 as an eight year old with 9.3.

Page 65 Star Appeal is the sire of Madam Gay, winner of the French Oaks.

Page 69 High Line is the sire of Master Willie the winner of the Eclipse Stakes, the Coronation Cup, the Benson and Hedges Gold Cup and the Jockey Club Stakes; and of Shoot a Line, the winner of the Irish Guineas Oaks, the Yorkshire Oaks and the Park Hill Stakes.

Page 70 Tudor Music, a son of Tudor Melody, won the 2,000 Guineas, the St James' Palace Stakes, the Queen Elizabeth II Stakes and the Waterford Crystal Mile in the colours of Grecian born Mrs. Andry Muinos, the owner of a London restaurant.

Page 73 Vaguely Noble is also the sire of Gay Mecene, winner of the Grand Prix de Saint-Cloud.

Page 81 Sparkler is also the sire of the Oaks winner Scintillate, who was out of the famous broodmare Set Free, dam of Juliette Marny and Julio Mariner. Hard to Beat sired Dunette, who won the French Oaks and dead-heated for the Grand Prix de Saint-Cloud.

Page 82 Hawaii, the sire of Hawaiian Sound, is also sire of the Derby winner Henbit. High Top is the sire of Cut Above (St Leger) and of Top Ville (French Derby).

Page 84 Northern Dancer is also the sire of Northern Baby (Champion Stakes); Nureyev, who was disqualified after finishing first in the 2,000 Guineas; and Storm Bird, the champion two-year-old of 1980. Lyphard is also the sire of Three Troikas, who won the French 1,000 Guineas, and the Prix de L'Arc de Triomphe.

Northfields is the sire of Northjet, winner of the Prix Jacques Le Marois.

Page 87 Ile de Bourbon was also the winner of the Coronation Cup. Green Dancer is the sire of Aryenne (French 1,000 Guineas).

Nijinsky is the sire of King's Lake, the controversial winner of the Irish 2,000 Guineas. Having finished first, beating To-Agori-Mou by a short head, he was then disqualified by the Stewards at the Curragh on the grounds of interference. He was subsequently reinstated as the winner following an appeal to the Stewards of the Irish Turf Club. King's Lake was also the winner of the Sussex Stakes and the Joe McGrath Memorial Stakes.

Niniski, a further son of Nijinsky, won both the French and Irish St Leger, as well as the John Porter Stakes.

Page 89 Kalamoun became the sire of Bikala (French Derby) and of Shaka-pour, who dead-heated in the Grand Prix de Saint-Cloud.

Page 91 Riverman is the sire of Detroit (Prix de l'Arc de Triomphe); Gold River (Prix de l'Arc de Triomphe and French St Leger); Policeman (French Derby); and Irish River (French 2,000 Guineas)

Page 92 Mount Hagen is the sire of Dickens Hill, the winner of the Irish 2,000 Guineas and Eclipse Stakes and second to Troy in both the Derby and Irish Sweeps Derby. Secretariat is the sire of General Assembly, who won the Travers Stakes in the United States and was imported to stand as a stallion in Ireland.

Page 93 Mill Reef is also the sire of Fairy Footsteps who won the 1,000 Guineas and of Glint of Gold, winner of the Italian Derby, Grand Prix de Paris and Preis von Europa and second in the Derby and the St Leger.

Page 94 Great Nephew headed the sires list again in 1981, the principal contribution to his success being Shergar, perhaps the most brilliant horse he ever sired. Bred by the Aga Khan, Shergar was a bay colt by Great Nephew out of Sharmeen by Val de Loir out of Nasreen, by Charlottesville out of Ginetta, the winner of the French 1,000 Guineas, who herself traced at four removes to the brilliant Mumtaz Mahal. Shergar was the winner of six races to the value of £391,874. His victories included the Derby, which he won by ten lengths from Glint of Gold; the Irish Sweeps Derby, which he won by four lengths from Cut Above; and the King Edward VI and Queen Elizabeth Stakes, which he won by four lengths. Shergar was owned by the Aga Khan, trained by Michael Stoute and ridden by Walter Swinburn and Lester Piggott. He was syndicated for £10,000,000 to stand at his owner's Ballymany Stud in Co. Kildare.

In addition Great Nephew has sired Mrs Penny, winner of the French Oaks; and Nikoli, winner of the Irish 2,000 Guineas.

Page 95 Para 4. Sanedtki was the winner of the Prix de la Foret, twice.

Sallust is also the sire of Tap on Wood, who won the 2,000 Guineas, providing the brilliant young American rider Steve Cauthen, then sixteen years of age, with his first success in an English classic.

Page 96 Petingo was also the sire of Troy whose winnings of £415,735 constitute a record for a horse trained in Europe. Bred by Sir Michael Sobell, he is a bay colt by Pentingo out of La Milo by Hornbeam out of

Pinprick by Pinza out of Miss Winston by Royal Charger. He was the winner of eight races including the Derby, the Irish Sweeps Derby and the King George VI and Queen Elizabeth Stakes, and the Benson and Hedges Gold Cup. He was owned by Sir Michael Sobell, trained by W. R. Hern and ridden in all his races by Willie Carson. He was syndicated for £7.2 million to stand at the Highclere Stud, near Newbury.

Petingo headed the list of winning sires in 1979. Pitcairn, a further son of Petingo, was the sire of Ela-Mana-Mou, whose winnings of £286,582 included the King George VI and Queen Elizabeth Stakes and Eclipse Stakes; and of Cairn Rouge who won the Champion Stakes, the Irish 1,000 Guineas and the Coronation Stakes, at the Royal Ascot meeting. Pitcairn was the leading sire in 1980.

Page 97 Grundy was the sire in his first crop of the Oaks winner Bireme. He has also sired Kirtling, winner of the Milan Grand Prix.

Page 98 Brigadier Gerard is the sire of Vayrann, winner of the Champion Stakes, and of Light Cavalry the winner of the St Leger, the Princess of Wales's Stakes and the King Edward VII Stakes.

Page 98 Buckpasser is the sire of Quick as Lightning, the winner of the 1,000 Guineas.

Page 99 Affirmed now holds the world record for stakes money won, his earnings amounting to $2,398,818.

Page 104 Val de Loir is the maternal grandsire of Shergar and of Vayrann.

Page 108 Labus, a son of Busted, is the sire of Akarad, winner of the Grand Prix de Saint-Cloud.

Page 110 Gallant Man is the great grandsire, through Gallant Romeo and the Preakness Stakes winner Elocutionist of Recitation, winner of the French 2,000 Guineas.

Page 116 Run the Gantlet is the sire of that very game horse Ardross, the winner of the French St Leger (which is now open to horses above three years of age), the Ascot Gold Cup, the Goodwood Cup, the Jockey Club Cup and the Geoffrey Freer Stakes. April Run, the winner of the Prix Vermeille and the Turf Classic at Aqueduct Park in the U.S.A. is a daughter of Run the Gantlet, who is also the sire of Providential, winner of the Washington International Stakes.

Page 120 Blakeney is the sire of Tyrnavos, winner of the Irish Sweeps Derby. Rarity a further son of Hethersett, is the sire of One In A Million, winner of the 1,000 Guineas.

Ashmore is the sire of Val d'Erica, winner of the Italian 1,000 Guineas and Italian Oaks.

Page 125 The year 1980 saw the first occasion on which an English classic race was won by a male line descendant of Man O'War. Mr Khaled Abdullah's Known Fact, who had finished second to Nureyev, was awarded the race following the disqualification of the last named horse for interference. The male line of Known Fact comes down through War Relic, Intent, Intentionally and In Reality.

Page 128 Troy is a member of No.1 family. Ela-Mana-Mou belongs to No. 3 family. Shergar belongs to No. 9 family.

Page 133 Crystal Palace is also the mother of Glass Slipper, the dam of Light

Cavalry (St Leger) and Fairy Footsteps (1,000 Guineas).

Page 134 Aroma, a daughter of Aloe, is the fourth dam of Known Fact (2,000 Guineas)

Page 135 Myrobella is also fifth dam of Policeman, winner of the French Derby.

Lady Josephine Ginetta is the third dam of Shergar, winner of the Derby, Irish Sweeps Derby, and King George VI and Queen Elizabeth Stakes.

Page 137 Descendants of Pretty Polly are To-Agori-Mou (2,000 Guineas, St James' Palace Stakes, Waterford Cystal Mile and Queen Elizabeth II Stakes) and Marwell (King's Stand Stakes, July Cup and Cheveley Park Stakes).

Miss Agnes Keener is also fifth dam of One In A Million (1,000 Guineas).

Page 139 Set Free is the dam of Scintillate, in addition to Juliette Marny and Julio Mariner. Glass Slipper the dam of Light Cavalry and Fairy Footsteps, should be added to the list of famous Brood Mares.

Page 165 Major General Sir Randle Feilden, C.B. C.B.E. K.C.V.O. died on October 28th, 1981.

Page 172 The Queen has also won the Princess of Wales's Stakes with Milford, the Queen's Vase with Buttress, the Ribblesdale Stakes with Expansive and the Hoover Fillies Stakes with Height of Fashion.

Page 173 Mr H. J. Joel also owned Light Cavalry (St Leger) and Fairy Footsteps (1,000 Guineas).

Sir Michael Sobell is the owner of Troy, who won the Derby, Irish Sweeps Derby, King George VI and Queen Elizabeth Stakes and Benson and Hedges Gold Cup.

Page 174 Colonel J. J. Astor owned the St Leger winners Provoke and Cut Above. Mrs Arpad Plesch won the Derby twice, with Psidium and Henbit. The Hon James Morrison was also the owner of Scintillate, winner of the Oaks. Mr. R. D. Hollingsworth won the Oaks with Bireme. The present Aga Khan owned the brilliant Shergar, who won the Derby, the Irish Sweeps Derby and the King George VI and Queen Elizabeth Stakes, as well as Vayrann, who won the Champion Stakes. Mr A. R. Shead, won the 2,000 Guineas with Tap On Wood. Mr William Barnett won the Eclipse Stakes with Master Willie.

AMERICAN OWNERS

Page 175 Mr Ogden Phipps was the owner of Quick as Lightning winner of the 1,000 Guineas. Mrs Bertram Firestone won the Oaks with Blue Wind.

FRENCH OWNERS

Page 176 Madame R. Binet was the owner of Dickens Hill, winner of the Eclipse Stakes. Monsieur A. Rolland won the St Leger with Son of Love.

Page 177 The Conte d'Alessio was also the owner of Le Moss, twice winner of the Ascot Gold Cup.

Grecian born Mrs Andy Muinos, won the 2,000 Guineas with To-Agori-Mou and the King George VI and Queen Elizabeth Stakes and Eclipse Stakes with Ela-Mana-Mou. Mr Khaled Abdullah won the 2,000 Guineas with Known Fact.

Page 178 The stallions standing at the National Stud in 1981 were Mill Reef, Grundy, Blakeney and Star Appeal. Other stallions under the management of the National Stud were Final Straw, who stood at the Egerton Stud; Homing who stood at the Highclere Stud in Berkshire; Sagaro, who stood at the Limestone Stud in Lincolnshire; and Royal Palace, who stood at the Chesters Stud in Northumberland.

IRISH TRAINERS

Page 187 Dermot Weld has saddled Blue Wind to win the Oaks. Mick O'Toole prepared Dickens Hill to win the Eclipse Stakes.

FRENCH TRAINERS

R. Collet has saddled Son of Love to win the St Leger.

Page 194 Douglas Smith no longer holds a trainer's licence.

Page 195 Lester Piggott has since won the 1,000 Guineas on Fairy Footsteps; the Oaks on Blue Wind; the Ascot Gold Cup twice, on Le Moss and Ardross; and the Irish Sweeps Derby on Shergar. He was leading jockey in 1981.

Pat Eddery has scored a further victory in the Oaks on Scintillate.

Page 196 Willie Carson headed the list of winning jockeys again in 1980. He has won the Derby twice, on Troy and Henbit, the Irish Sweeps Derby on Troy; the King George VI and Queen Elizabeth Stakes, twice, on Troy and Ela-Mana-Mou; the Oaks on Bireme; the 2,000 Guineas on Known Fact; and the Eclipse Stakes on Ela-Mana-Mou.

Page 196 Joe Mercer headed the list of winning jockeys in 1979. He has scored a further victory in the 1,000 Guineas on One In A Million, two further successes in the St Leger on Light Cavalry and Cut Above, and a further success in the Ascot Gold Cup on Le Moss.

Greville Starkey has won the 2,000 Guineas on To-Agori-Mou. Other jockeys who have ridden important winners include the brilliant young American rider Steve Cauthen, who won the 2,000 Guineas on Tap On Wood; the very promising young rider Walter Swinburn, who won the Derby and King George VI and Queen Elizabeth Stakes on Shergar; Brian Rouse and Philip Waldron. A. Lequex is a further French jockey to ride an important winner in this country.

Page 199 The horse who has now won most in stakes money is Troy, who amassed a total of £415,735. He is followed by Shergar with £391,874. Rheingold is now in third position.

HIGH PRICED YEARLINGS

Page 203 At the Newmarket Houghton Sales of 1979, a bay colt by Lyphard out of Swanilda, submitted by Count Roland de Chambure realised 625,000 guineas to the bid of Mr H. Thomson Jones. This figure was, however, exceeded at the Newmarket Houghton Sales of 1981, when a bay colt by Mill Reef out of Arkadina, who had been offered by the Loughmore Stud, was secured by the B.B.A. (Ireland) Ltd for 640,000 guineas.

HIGH PRICED FOALS

At the Newmarket December Sales of 1979, a colt by Mill Reef out of Anadyomene, submitted by Burningfold Farm, was purchased by Mr W. McDonald for 108,000 guineas. This was the first occasion on which a foal had realised a six figure sum at a European auction.

Page 204 Record sums paid for Brood Mares. At the Newmarket December Sales of 1979 the six year old mare Val's Girl, submitted by the executors of the late Sir Charles Clore in foal to Artaius, was purchased by Mr Ted Curtin for 205,000 guineas.

Page 205 Record sums paid for Stallions.

Troy was syndicated for £7.2 million in 1979. Shergar was the subject of a record £10 million syndication.

RECORD BLOODSTOCK SALES

At the Newmarket December Sales of 1979 1,266 lots sold for an aggregate of 14,245,347 guineas, a turnover more than three million in excess of the 1978 total. This included the 205,000 guineas paid for Val's Girl and the 290,000 guineas paid for Swiss Maid, who was submitted for sale for the second time, and was purchased by Mr Michael Motion, a bloodstock agent.